591.59
Lew

179291

Lewis, D. Brian

Biology of commu-
nication

# Biology of Communication

# TERTIARY LEVEL BIOLOGY

A series covering selected areas of biology at advanced undergraduate level. While designed specifically for course options at this level within Universities and Polytechnics, the series will be of great value to specialists and research workers in other fields who require a knowledge of the essentials of a subject.

Titles in the series:

| | |
|---|---|
| *Experimentation in Biology* | Ridgman |
| *Methods in Experimental Biology* | Ralph |
| *Visceral Muscle* | Huddart and Hunt |
| *Biological Membranes* | Harrison and Lunt |
| *Comparative Immunobiology* | Manning and Turner |
| *Water and Plants* | Meidner and Sheriff |
| *Biology of Nematodes* | Croll and Matthews |
| *An Introduction to Biological Rhythms* | Saunders |
| *Biology of Ageing* | Lamb |
| *Biology of Reproduction* | Hogarth |
| *An Introduction to Marine Science* | Meadows and Campbell |
| *Biology of Fresh Waters* | Maitland |
| *An Introduction to Developmental Biology* | Ede |
| *Physiology of Parasites* | Chappell |
| *Neurosecretion* | Maddrell and Nordmann |

# Biology of Communication

### D. BRIAN LEWIS, M.Sc., Ph.D.

Principal Lecturer in Neurobiology
City of London Polytechnic

and

### D. MICHAEL GOWER, M.Sc.

Senior Lecturer in Animal Behaviour
City of London Polytechnic

A HALSTED PRESS BOOK

## John Wiley and Sons

New York—Toronto

Blackie & Son Limited
Bishopbriggs
Glasgow G64 2NZ

Furnival House
14–18 High Holborn
London

Published in the U.S.A. and Canada by
Halsted Press,
a Division of John Wiley and Sons Inc.,
New York

**Library of Congress Cataloging in Publication Data**

Lewis, D. B.
The biology of communication.
(Tertiary level biology series)
"A Halsted Press book."
Includes bibliographical references.
1. Animal communication. 2. Neurophysiology.
I. Gower, D. M., joint author. II. Title.
QL776.L49 1980    591.5′9    79-20920
ISBN 0-470-26859-X

*179291*

Printed in Great Britain by
Thomson Litho Ltd., East Kilbride, Scotland

# Preface

THE STUDY OF ANIMAL COMMUNICATION HAS TRADITIONALLY FORMED AN important part of the study of animal behaviour. In recent years it has tended to become a sub-field in its own right, attracting workers of varied interests; it is also receiving increasing attention at the undergraduate level. Another recent development is an area which has come to be known as *neuroethology*. The problem for the neuroethologist is that much of behaviour is not reliable or "reflex-like" in its expression. Communicative behaviour, on the other hand, often is, and here neurophysiology can make a significant contribution to our understanding of the underlying mechanisms.

Some excellent texts on animal communication are available, as are collected essays on the neural substrates of specific behaviour patterns, but none of these provides a broad synthesis of concepts in neurophysiology and behaviour. The aim of this book is to draw attention to those areas where neurophysiology is relevant to the behaviourist. The book is not an introduction to animal behaviour or neurophysiology; some prior knowledge of these fields is assumed. It is the integration of these fields that we have attempted.

The aspects upon which we have concentrated are simpler systems which are largely under genetic control. After considering the circumstances in which we find communication occurring between animals, we discuss their sensory capabilities and the ways in which sensory input is integrated. Classical ethological models are then discussed in the light of these findings. The origins and subsequent "shaping" of signals by natural selection is the result of specific constraints imposed upon each of the sensory modalities. To simplify comparisons, we have concentrated on the distance modalities of olfaction, audition and vision. Finally, we consider communication not as isolated units of stimulus and response, but as lengthy sequences of interaction between individuals. Some of the examples have been chosen to provide material for introducing statistical techniques of analysis, which are covered in the last chapter. This area is of interest because many of the problems in behavioural work are not immediately apparent. Examination of the methods used to collect and analyse data helps to highlight some of these.

Our thanks are due, of course, to our past students, for whom much of the material was originally gathered together in the form of lectures. We should also particularly like to thank Henry C. Bennet-Clark for reading early drafts of the manuscript and for his constructive criticism at all stages; Anthony Stevens and Wendy Fox for help with the mathematics of chapter seven; Mary Hutchings for her untiring chasing of references; and Judy Whittick for the typing of early drafts. Our colleagues have helped with critical discussion, but misunderstandings are our own. Finally, we thank those whose social lives have been interrupted for their extreme forbearance.

D.B.L.
D.M.G.

# Contents

# CHAPTER ONE

# WHAT IS COMMUNICATION?

## Problems of definition

In order to delimit the area under consideration, it is important at the outset to agree on a definition of the word *communication*. Many authors have found the phenomenon of communication very difficult to define, and most of the definitions are unsatisfactory because they have been either too restrictive or have allowed the inclusion of interactions which are not accepted as "proper" communication. For example, Wilson (1975) defines communication in terms of the altering, by one organism, of the probability pattern of behaviour in another organism, in a fashion adaptive to either one, or both, of the participants. His approach is essentially quantitative, and originates from the application of information theory to behavioural interactions. As a result, it allows us to investigate the communication process from an objective basis. Unfortunately, however, the definition also allows the inclusion of a diverse array of interactions (predator-prey, for example) that on other grounds are considered non-communicative. Certainly the predator receives information about the presence of the prey, but the prey can in no way be considered to communicate its existence and availability to the predator.

Klopfer and Hatch (1968) defined communication as a process in which information is exchanged between animals to the mutual adaptive advantage of both. Wilson, and a number of other authors, did not adopt the "mutual adaptive advantage" idea—probably because, in certain communication sequences, no adaptive advantage accrues to one of the parties at that particular time, e.g. many female insects mate only once; further male attention becomes undesirable and interferes with other important behaviour patterns such as egg-laying. Yet the interaction between a courting male and an unresponsive female is still communication: the very fact that the female does not respond eventually communicates something to the male, who will then direct his efforts elsewhere. This example also highlights the weakness in defining communication in terms of a change in probability patterns: there are many instances in which the ongoing behaviour of the female is not changed by the male's signalling. Yet this absence of change can be communicative, as Halliday (1975) showed in his study of newt courtship.

Other authors confine communication to intraspecific interactions. Certainly the most impressive examples are to be found in this context, but many interspecific interactions have been described that on all other grounds must be termed communicative. Preston (1978), for example, in a detailed study of two goby-shrimp symbioses, showed conclusively that the behaviour of one partner was likely to change the on-going behaviour of the other, to the mutual advantage of both. Preston applied information theory to her data and showed that between 0·31 and 0·35 bits per act were transmitted. Clearly, this kind of interaction cannot be excluded from the study of communication.

All these problems can be overcome to some extent by referring to the evolution of the signalling systems alone. Even so, it is impossible to achieve a definition, at once comprehensive and specific, of a term so widely used (and misused). Yet some formal working definition is necessary for the development of the thesis of this book. Accordingly, we define *communication* as *the transmission of a signal or signals between two or more organisms where selection has favoured both the production and the reception of the signal(s)*.

Even with this definition, further problems arise when communicative behaviour is studied in detail.

*The interval between emission and response*

There are well-documented cases where considerable delay occurs between the emission of the signal and the recipient's response. The best examples come from studies of social insects—in particular, the honeybee *Apis mellifera*. The queen substance, secreted by her mandibular gland, must be passed to each worker at a rate of about 0·1 $\mu$g per day. The active molecule is trans-9-keto-2-decenoic acid and it has at least 3 separate effects:

  (i) It prevents the workers from rearing the larvae as queens.
  (ii) It prevents the workers' ovaries from developing.
  (iii) It acts as a sexual attractant to the drone during her nuptial flight.

Quantification of the information transferred in the first two of these effects, and even recognizing it as communication *per se*, is highly problematical.

Chemical signals operating between conspecifics are termed *phero-mones*. These are subdivided into *releasing pheromones*, where the effect is relatively rapid (e.g. in the gypsy moth, p. 14), and *priming pheromones*, where the effect is delayed and is primarily physiological. The existence of priming pheromones is now suspected in mammals, including man. Relatively few examples of priming signals are known for other sensory modalities, but Lehrman (1965) showed that final maturation of the follicles prior to mating and egg-laying in female doves depended on the female having visual contact with the male of her species for several days.

The application of conventional methods of analysis to the effects of priming signals has yet to be attempted—an indication of the difficulties involved.

*Variability in communication behaviour*

The experimental analysis of communication depends upon the repeated observation of a particular sequence. The signal is assumed to be identical from test to test, and the change in the recipient's behaviour to this "unit" is monitored. Lumping of behaviour in this way is typical of many ethological studies but, whereas it facilitates analysis, there can be no doubt that the amount of information being passed is always under-estimated. The study of such rigid "invariable" behaviour patterns dates back to Lorenz (1950) and his concept of instinct. His main argument is that each example of true instinctive behaviour shows a core of absolutely fixed, and more or less complex activity—the *Fixed Action Pattern* (FAP). Such patterns are items of behaviour which are as constant as anatomical features. Since they are innate, in the sense of being inherited, they are species-specific and may be used for systematic phylogenetic studies. Such FAPs are characteristically evoked, or released, by complex environ-mental situations such as elaborate visual or auditory stimuli to which the senses appear to be inherently tuned. These releasers (and they include the displays of other individuals) trigger FAPs through the inter-mediation of *Innate Releasing Mechanisms* (IRMs) located "somewhere" in the central nervous system. This understanding of the FAP and the IRM will be challenged in the remainder of the book. In practice, no two performances of what most ethologists are prepared to call fixed action patterns (and often, without further ado, "signals" or "displays") are the same, and we must rely on the skills of the observer to pick out those features of the behaviour that may be "meaningful" to a recipient animal. Inevitably, small variations in display tend to be missed or ignored by the observer, which means that estimates of information flow may be far too low.


### Contextual information

Conversely, there are many sources of information available to the recipient over and above that originating in the display itself. Such information has been termed *contextual information* (e.g. Smith, 1977). Contextual sources of information have only been formally recognized as a separate category relatively recently, and there are as yet few rigorous studies on the subject.

The importance of context will vary from situation to situation, and we should expect it to play a larger part in the interactions of primates, as compared with insects, for example. Even in the latter, however, it cannot be disregarded.

Possible sources of contextual information include the following.

*Bonding.* Ransom and Ransom (1971) report that they could detect at least nine kinds of bonds among the individuals of a wild baboon troop. These included troop bonds, sibling bonds, peer bonds, etc. Jehl (1973) reports that stilt sandpipers *Micropalma himantopus*, that are pairing for the first time, display far longer and far more conspicuously than individuals that are rejoining mates of the previous year. Indeed, such experienced pairs may show little or no formal courtship, and hence make an earlier start at nesting. This is an important advantage because of the shortness of the Arctic summer. Similar effects of partner familiarity on courtship have been reported for a variety of birds.

*Status.* Social animals tend to form dominance hierarchies and, although initial establishment of the hierarchy may involve much displaying, once established, the hierarchy is maintained by relatively little display. Altmann (1965, 1967) found that dominant rhesus monkeys or baboons communicated with greater efficiency than subordinates, using less intense or entirely different signals involving a smaller expenditure of energy. The effects of past experience are clear here.

*Location.* The location of displays, both in time and space, can be important. For example, in stickleback territorial disputes, the location of the contest usually determines which fish attacks and which flees. The fish that is in its own territory is more likely to attack. The order in a sequence in which a display occurs and the number of times it is repeated can also be informative. Hence Beer (1973) reports that captive laughing gull chicks only flee and hide if they hear a recording of numerous alarm calls by many gulls. Isolated alarm calls, even by their own parents are ignored.

*Metacommunication.* This is commonly referred to as "communication about communication"—or, more precisely, the providing of information about the frame of reference within which another message is to be viewed. The most frequently quoted example is the play behaviour of animals such as chimpanzees, which is distinguishable from true fighting because of differences in facial expression and other differences in behaviour. Hence a unit X may be shown during play and during fighting. During play it may be accompanied by unit Y and during fighting by unit Z. The usual ideas on metacommunication are that Y and Z are modifying the effects of X. An alternative viewpoint is that we have two distinct signals, XY and XZ, in which case the category of metacommunication becomes superfluous to some extent.

Ideally, contextual effects in communicative interactions should be investigated by quantifying responses to a display which does not itself vary but whose context does. In fact, present accounts of contextual information (e.g. W. John Smith, 1977) usually point out that the behaviour shown by communicators in general (i.e. by both signallers and recipients) varies in different contexts. This is a weakness and, until more rigorous analyses of the effects of context are undertaken, we are only making educated guesses about the phenomenon. Nevertheless, because of the undoubted use of contextual information by communicating animals, the informative value of particular signals is likely to be over-estimated unless this is taken into account.

Thus, for different reasons, estimates of information flow are likely to err on both the high and the low side. It would be over-optimistic of us to expect these errors to cancel each other out.

## The functions of communication

Almost all the million or so species of animals have communication systems of one kind or another which are tailored to the particular needs of that species and which organize interactions between individuals. Furthermore, a large variety of interspecific communicative interactions exists. The resultant diversity defies simple classification, and so the following review is by no means exhaustive. It is merely illustrative.

It should be added that the use of the term *function* here is rather broad and roughly equates with "beneficial consequences" of the behaviour in question.

*Interspecific interactions*

*Signals emitted by flowers.* The scent and coloration of insect-pollinated flowers is undoubtedly the result of special selection. Not only are insects attracted from a distance by the scent but, on alighting, they are guided to the nectaries by specialized colour-patterns known as honey-guides. Daumer (1958) pointed out that hardly any bee-pollinated flowers are purely red, an observation correlated with the fact that bees are red-blind. Further, many flowers possess ultraviolet honey-guides which are invisible to us. The petals of the evening primrose *Oenothera biennis* (figure 1.1) are rich in ultraviolet information, except for the central regions which are ultraviolet-free. Daumer showed that inexperienced bees performed 164 central probing reactions out of 200 presentations of the normal petal arrangement of *O. biennis*, whereas when the petals were separated and arranged "inside-out", only 72 of 200 inexperienced bees probed at the centre of the arrangement, the remainder probing at the corners. The

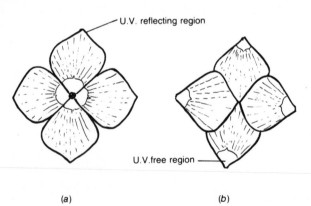

U.V. reflecting region

U.V. free region

(a)                                                        (b)

**Figure 1.1** *Oenothera biennis*, the evening primrose. (*a*) Normal petal arrangement, (*b*) petals reversed (modified from Daumer, 1958).

ultraviolet-free areas thus act as a guidance signal, promoting pollination by the bee which, in turn, obtains nectar and pollen.

*Signals emitted by cleaners.* Certain marine fish are habitually cleaned of ectoparasites by small "cleaner fish" of several unrelated families. All are characterized by black longitudinal stripes on either a yellow or a blue background. Eibl-Eibsfeldt (1959) suggests that this may be a "guild sign" advertising the "cleaning occupation". One of the most common and best-known cleaners is *Labroides dimidiatus*. The ethology of this species was investigated by Potts (1973) in the shallow-reef environment of the island of Aldabra. Adults usually lived in pairs and were highly territorial although, since intraspecific aggression declined with increasing distance from central landmarks, the extent of the territories was difficult to estimate.

Clear-cut signals are given by both cleaners and their customers. *Labroides* typically initiates a cleaning encounter with an undulating dance, which displays the black stripe and blue coloration to the customer. Frequently the cleaners would then approach and "stabilize" the customer. Stabilization served to quieten the host and was most commonly seen with species which normally move a great deal. The usual form of stabilization employed by *Labroides* was to approach rapidly and lie parallel to the host, making contact only with the extended pelvic fins. On some host species, cleaners were seen to wriggle over the flank of the host, giving a more intense tactile signal. Frequently, cleaners would stabilize a number of hosts in quick succession before cleaning them. A wide variety of host species was described, ranging from small reef species to open-water predators, including some sharks. The type of invitation posture adopted by prospective hosts varied according to species. "Head-up" and "head-down" postures were the common forms of invitation. There was also some patterning of the order in which *Labroides* cleaned the various customer species. Apparently this was a learned effect, because young *Labroides* showed little difference in the way in which they approached and cleaned hosts.

Many species of hosts allowed cleaners into the gills and mouth, but whether hosts *learn* to trust the cleaners in this way is not known. The ectoparasites of the hosts form the bulk of *Labroides* food, but Potts did record apparent independent feeding by some cleaners.

Cleaning symbiosis has also been reported for a freshwater species, the bluegill sunfish *Lepomis macrochinis* (Sulak, 1975). Juvenile *Lepomis* confine their cleaning activities to conspecifics, but adults habitually clean another centrarchid, the largemouth bass *Micropterus salmoides*. Cleaning takes place most frequently in particular fixed areas of the Florida Everglades. Sulak proposes that these are cleaning posts, equatable with those of *Labroides*. The invitation posture adopted by *Micropterus* is a head-down display, similar to its feeding posture.

The undulating dance of *Labroides*, used before final approach to a customer, is, in fact, very similar to a display employed in intraspecific agonistic encounters. The cleaning display may have been derived from this display. Certainly the "motivational" background underlying the two situations is likely to be a similar conflict of approach and withdrawal tendencies.

Several species of gaudily-coloured shrimps such as the banded shrimp *Stenopus hispidus* (Decapoda, Stenopodidae) also clean fish. The shrimps employ tactile signals and wave their red and white banded body and appendages. The shrimps are, apparently, quite palatable to several of the species they serve, and are readily accepted in crushed form. Nevertheless, they are rarely molested, and are allowed to walk over the body surface and even into the mouths of their clients. Clearly these interactions are of mutual advantage: food for the cleaners and freeing of ectoparasites for the fish.

Interspecific signalling also occurs in a wide variety of more permanent relationships. Gobies use the holes dug by shrimps of the genus *Alpheus* as shelter. The gobies sit at the burrow entrance and, in return, warn the shrimps of danger by a flick of the tail. Gobies never give warning signals in the absence of the shrimps, which communicate their presence outside the burrow by antennal contact with the fish. Other examples can be drawn from hermit crabs' (*Eupagurus* spp.) relationships with various sea anemones (e.g. *Calliactis*, *Adamsia*) and from ant-aphid relationships.

### Intraspecific interactions

(a) *Aggregational signals*. Slime-mould amoebae provide a well-documented example of an aggregational signal. Several species of the genus *Dictyostelium* have been studied, but *D. discoideum* is perhaps the most thoroughly analysed (Robertson, 1974). Aggregation seems to commence as a result of the exhaustion of their food supply, and individual amoebae move towards aggregation centres. The aggregated amoebae migrate for a short distance as a single unit, and then form a fruiting body containing differentiated stalk cells and spore cells.

The signal causing aggregation has been shown to be cyclic adenosine monophosphate (cAMP), which is released by individual amoebae in pulses at 5-minute intervals. Low concentrations of cAMP cause chemotaxis alone, while high concentrations produce both chemotaxis and the relaying of the signal by the recipient, i.e. the recipient releases its own pulse of cAMP. Following this release there is a refractory period of at least 2 minutes, during which an amoeba is not sensitive to further pulses. The signal pulse is relatively short-lived (less than 2 seconds) because the cAMP is deactivated by an extracellular phosphodiesterase. These factors guarantee that an amoeba cannot be stimulated by its own signal reflected from its neighbours.

(b) *Alarm signals.* The alarm chattering of blackbirds, the ground thumping of rabbits, the display of the white rear and undertail of fleeing antelopes, are examples of alarm phenomena that occur in all social, and many non-social, species.

Highly developed alarm systems are found among the social aculeates. Many species of ants and termites possess stridulatory ridges on the abdomen which, when rubbed by the metapostnotum, produce air-borne high-pitched squeaks and ground vibration. Air-borne sound receptors do not occur in ants, which detect the stridulation by means of highly sensitive vibration receptors in the legs (Markl, 1970).

Both bees and ants can also spread alarm by agitated running, the signal probably being transmitted as vibration in the hive or colony.

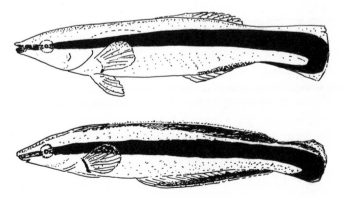

**Figure 1.2**    The cleaner *Labroides dimidiatus* and, below, its mimic *Aspidontus taeniatus* (after Eibl-Eibsfeldt (1970) *Ethology*, Holt, Reinhart and Winston).

Mandibular and anal gland secretions also transmit alarm, and in the ant *Tapinoma nigerrimum* the alarm chemicals are known to be methyl heptenone and propyl-isobutyl-ketone. Similarly, bee-sting odour alarms honeybees. One of the components, banana oil or iso-amyl-acetate, has been isolated and succeeds in exciting bees. However, it fails to induce stinging, although a used bee-sting does. This suggests that not all the effective chemicals have been identified.

Von Frisch (1941) suggested that "Schreckstoff" given off from injured minnow skin (*Phoxinus phoxinus* L.) is an alarm signal. It is highly effective in producing alarm and retreat, as little as 0·002 mg of fish skin (about 0·01 mm$^2$) in a 14-litre aquarium being sufficient. It would appear to be a specially-evolved signal, because the alarm substance is produced in specialized epidermal cells (club cells) which do not open onto the surface, but only release their contents when the skin is injured. These cells are found in all species that produce the "schreck-reaktion" (Pfeiffer, 1974). "Schreckstoff" may also alarm heterospecifics, but far greater concentrations are required.

Birds spread alarm mostly by vocalization, and an interesting dichotomy occurs between "hawk calls" and "ground predator calls". "Hawk calls" are given while stationary and hidden, are of a high-frequency pure tone, and begin and end softly—all factors which make the localization of the emitter difficult (see chapter 2). "Ground predator calls" (such as the blackbird chatter) are often given in flight, are louder, and are sharp and staccato.

Alarm vocalizations may carry additional information which is determined by the signal intensity. The staccato call of the herring gull may be of low intensity if the signaller is relatively safe on the water, when nearby gulls simply become attentive and look around. Alternatively, it may be loud and piercing when danger is imminent on land, and conspecifics immediately take flight.

Vocal alarm signals also abound among the mammals, e.g. moose, elk and deer bark, European chamois whistle, and primates shriek.

Visual alarm signals are also widespread. Many flock birds, such as doves, quail and mynahs, employ flashing displays of the tail or wing feathers. Among the social herbivorous mammals, the bobbing of the ano-genital region of a fleeing animal is an obvious signal.

A variant of the alarm signal is the departing signal. Before jumping, many grasshoppers (Acrididae) emit a short series of sound pulses. A startled animal that jumps without singing alarms adjacent individuals. Similarly, if the wood mouse *Apodemus sylvaticus* is startled, it runs noisily, but without the ultrasonic squeaks emitted during normal movement.

An even more specialized signal is the true distress signal emitted upon capture. It is usually sudden and dramatic (loud noises, exposure of eye spots, release of repellents); undoubtedly the function is not one of communication but is aimed at startling the predator. However, communication of alarm with distress vocalizations could be said to be a concomitant. In jackdaws and starlings, distress calls can bring about mobbing of the predator, but in most species they cause immediate flight of conspecifics.

(c) *Food signals*. Food guidance systems are most elaborate among the social insects. In ants, a successful forager signals her find by agitated running and antennal waving. The nest mates congregate around her, often stroking her with their antennae to discover details of the type of food. In primitive species, the scout then leads nest mates to the food, but in more-advanced species, an odour trail, deposited by the returning foragers, is followed.

Certain stingless bees of Brazil behave much as ants do: unorientated running excites other workers in the hive, and these then leave the nest and seek food, apparently at random. In one group of stingless bees (*Melliponini*) an odour trail from food to hive is laid by returning workers who descend to the ground at intervals. After agitated running in the hive, they lead other workers to the food source.

From simple systems of this type far more efficient methods have evolved, culminating in the honeybee (*Apis mellifera*) "dance". Here, the returning forager transmits information about four parameters. The type of food is indicated by means of the odour adhering to the body hairs, and by the regurgitation of small droplets of nectar and pollen. The amount and quality of the food is indicated by the duration and "vivacity" of the bees' dancing. The more vivid dances are characterized by additional relatively-high-frequency vibrations of the abdomen. The distance of the food source is indicated firstly by the type of dance, and secondly by the length of the waggle run in the figure-of-eight dance. If the food is close to the hive, the returning forager executes a "round dance" (figure 1.3), which is simply dancing in a circle. In *Apis mellifera carnica*, the Austrian subspecies, the round dance is produced when the food source is at or below 85 m distance; in *A.m. ligustica* (Italian subspecies) at or below 35 m, and in *A.m. fasciata* at or below 12 m. In these species the round dance is simply an indication that food is close to

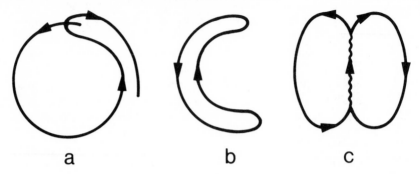

**Figure 1.3** The main dances of the honey bee. (*a*) Round dance, (*b*) a transitional form known as the sickle dance, and (*c*) the tailwagging dance.

the hive. In the closely-related *Apis indica*, on the other hand, a food source as close as 2 m is indicated by a figure-of-eight dance. With the exception of *A.m. carnica* (von Frisch's subject), the races or subspecies of *A. mellifera* show a sickle dance that is intermediate between the round and the figure-of-eight dance (figure 1.3). At increasing distances the figure-of-eight dance takes over, and distance is now correlated with the length of the central waggle run, the length of the run increasing with increasing distance. But this correlation is not linear, the increase in run length being less steep at longer distances. The frequency of the tail-wag remains constant at about 13 wags per second.

The direction of the food source is indicated by the direction of the waggle run. Bees dancing on a horizontal surface outside the hive will perform the waggle run at an angle to the sun which is indicative of the angle of the food source from the hive entrance. For bees dancing in darkness on the vertical faces of the hive combs, such direct cues are not available. The angle that a direct line to the food source makes with the sun becomes transposed to the angle of the waggle run to the vertical. Some directional information also exists in the sickle dance, the line dividing the sickle figure through the middle of its open side corresponding to the direction of the waggle run.

(*d*) *Signals employed in agonistic situations.* Agonistic behaviour is shown by fighting conspecifics, and includes attack, retreat, and threat behaviours. The most highly-developed signals are shown, not during overt attack or retreat, but during the intermediate stages. Except for appeasement signals, no fundamental differences occur in the types of signals employed, even between the extremes of territorial and within-group conflicts. The associated contextual information may differ: location becomes more important in territorial disputes, while status is important in hierarchical disputes.

The main question to be answered in this section is why animals employ threat displays at all. Why not use the advantage of surprise, and attack at the earliest opportunity, inflicting as much damage as possible on the opponent? The present consensus of opinion is that individuals benefit from avoiding overt damaging fighting, and that threat displays and relatively harmless contests of strength have evolved as a substitute method of resolving disputes. Threat displays may serve to decide contests without the combatants ever making contact. Numerous (anecdotal) reports in the ornithological literature suggest the effectiveness of bird song in this respect, territorial disputes often being settled without the individuals making visual contact. Siamese fighting fish will often flee from an opponent after a relatively brief series of "broadside" and "frontal" displays. The assumption here is that the animals are unevenly matched and that a few threat displays are sufficient to indicate this.

Threat signals may also serve to orientate the combatants so that, when fighting does occur, as for example in the pushing contests of stags, the stereotyped attacks are not directed at vulnerable spots. It may well be that the fighting routines that are most exhausting have been selected for, as another method of minimizing injury. Hence the development of mouth fighting in *Tilapia* spp., and horn locking and pushing in many ungulates.

However, a number of intraspecific agonistic encounters have been recorded where severe damage or death occurs. In the Lacertidae, e.g. *Lacerta muralis*, the participants grasp each other on the back or neck with the jaws, presumably as a means of indicating their strength to each other. While being grasped each lizard remains quite passive. In *Lacerta melliselensis* however, the grasp may be accompanied by strong shaking movements which have been seen to break the opponent's spine. Indian elephants occasionally mortally wound opponents with their tusks, and lions occasionally kill in pride disputes.

(*e*) *Appeasement signals.* Appeasement displays develop in species possessing some degree of social organization. The loser, if he is to stay in the social group, cannot simply run away but must come to terms with his conqueror. To this end, appeasement signals may serve to terminate a contest or to prevent one occurring. Examples of appeasement signals are the adoption of the female sexual presentation posture in many pri-

**Figure 1.4**   Appeasing female chacma baboon (redrawn from Bolwig, N. (1959) *Behav.* **14**, 136–163).

mates, and ano-genital presentation in Canidae and Muridae, where the appeasing animal rolls onto its back and spreads its hind legs to expose the abdomen and ano-genital area (figure 1.4).

(*f*)  *Courtship and mating signals*. The signals employed in courtship have two main functions: they facilitate mutual awareness and recognition of opposite-sexed conspecifics, and they enable the paired individuals to cooperate to fertilize the female's eggs. The second stage does not always terminate the interaction. If the pair cooperate in raising the offspring, "courtship" signals will continue after mating in order to maintain the pair bond.

To attract mates from a distance, numerous conspicuous signals have evolved in all three of the distance modalities: visual, acoustic and chemical. In most cases these signals are emitted by the males, but there are exceptions: the female silk worm moth *Bombyx mori* attracts males by releasing the pheromone bombykol, a complex alcohol, trans-10-cis-12-hexadecadienol. It is secreted in glands at the tip of the abdomen. The threshold of male response is extremely low, less than 14 000 molecules of bombykol per ml of air; the chemoreceptors are the large feathery antennae. The male, performing as little more than a sexual guided missile, flies upwind and, under good conditions can home-in on a female from several kilometres distance. In this case the signal's conspicuousness is the result of copious production by the emitter and extreme sensitivity in the receiver.

In the auditory modality, perhaps the most dramatic example of signal intensity is in the cicadas. The Australian cicada *Cystosoma saundersii* produces a low-frequency (800 Hz) sound which reaches a sound intensity level greater than 80 dB at source (Young & Hill, 1977). Signal intensity is further increased because of the aggregation behaviour of the males, which then sing in concert. By this means the intensity is increased to over 100 dB, and the sound radiates over a great area. The female is guided to the centre of the singing population because the receptor organ is maximally sensitive to, and achieves greatest directionality at, 800 Hz. Once inside the population, however, female directional sensitivity is lost because the high sound intensity saturates both ears. The final approach is made by the male in response to what may be a pheromone released by the female during the emission of short "tick"-like sounds (Hill, personal communication). The existence of a pheromone, however, has not yet been established.

The Orthoptera have also evolved acoustic signals, using the heavily sclerotized forewings (tegmina). The sounds are produced either by rubbing the forewings together (Grylloidea, Tettigonioidea) or by rubbing the hind femora against them (Acridoidea). These signals are also of high intensity (120 dB at source in *Homorocoryphus nitidulus vicinus*, Lewis, 1974). In the Grylloidea and Tettigonioidea, sound is usually produced only during the closure of the tegmina, while in the Acridoidea sound is produced, in some species only on the downstroke of the leg, and in other species during both movements. The sounds are therefore pulsed in a temporally species-specific manner which is determined by the rate of closure of the tegmina or the sweep of the leg (figure 1.5). The frequencies emitted are determined by specialised regions of the tegmina and may be pure tones (Grylloidea) or broad-banded (Tettigonioidea and Acridoidea). A single pure tone has an advantage over a broad-band sound in that all the energy of the movement producing the sound is channelled into this single frequency. The intensity of this frequency is therefore greater than the intensity of any one frequency component in the broad-band sound. Thus, assuming equal sensitivity in the receptors, the more-intense single frequency will allow of a greater separation distance between individuals. The disadvantage of a pure tone is that it is far more difficult to localize. To achieve directional sensitivity, animals must compare the input from both ears. Pure tones can be placed only in a broad segment of the environment, and often only left or right; to

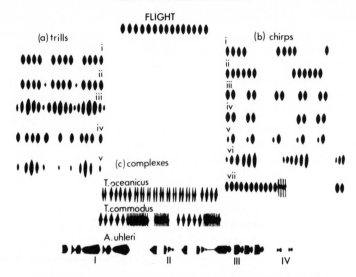

**Figure 1.5** The song patterns of Orthoptera. Based on the wing-beat frequency of flight, the songs have been divided into trills which are more or less continuous, and chirps where the pattern is further broken up. Three complex patterns are also shown. The most complex of known orthopteran songs is that of the bush cricket *Ambycorypha uhleri*, which shows amplitude, rate and frequency modulation.

achieve greater accuracy, either the receptors must be moved to scan the environment, or the animal must move to a new position and triangulate the source. Such strategies are not required for locating broad-band sounds, because each component frequency provides slightly different directional information, and the higher the frequency, the narrower the segment containing the emitter. Comparison of the different frequency components can provide accurate localization of the sound, without movement.

Signalling at a distance in the visual modality has resulted in the evolution of bioluminescence, or movement, or bright colours, or combinations of these. The fireflies, genus *Photinus* (Lampyridae, Coleoptera), produce bioluminescent signals which vary between species in their spatial patterns. Temporal patterning also occurs in a manner analogous to the acoustic signals of Orthoptera (figure 1.5). In contrast to the majority of Orthoptera, however, the initial signal of the male firefly induces temporally species-specific emission responses in the female, and the male then flies to the female.

The fireflies of the genus *Photinus* have developed one of the most effective and dramatic of distance visual signals. A wide variety of species are of the "roving" kind, where males fly about singly, emitting flashes in a species-specific temporal pattern. The responsive females respond to the flashing of conspecific males by giving a single flash. The period of the display or latency of the female's emission is species-specific, and thus provides the male with information concerning species, sex and location. The pair exchanges flashes until the male makes contact with the female (figure 1.6).

Rather than moving singly in search of females, males of certain species of fireflies, ranging from India eastwards to New Guinea and parts of N. Australia, perch in vegetation and attract the females to them. Most of them belong to the genus *Pteroptyx*, and one of the most characteristic features of this type of firefly is that the males synchronize their flashing. Whole trees or groups of trees, completely covered with synchronously-flashing fireflies, have been observed. Buck and Buck (1976) report that congregations of Thai fireflies flashed in unison every 500 milliseconds or so, with no member out of phase by more than 20 ms. Apparently the same aggregation sites were used year after year. Since adult fireflies survive for only about a month, the display sites must recruit continuously. This would only be possible in species which breed all the year round, and hence may explain why this phenomenon is confined to the Tropics. Group displays of fireflies also occur in the West Indies, but in these species the displays are not synchronized. Synchronization is perhaps a further step in the development of this phenomenon, serving further to enhance the effectiveness of bioluminescence as a long-distance signal.

When observed in detail, males displaying in unison are seen to be over-dispersed. This is probably the result of intermale aggression. The communal display is thus equateable with the group displays of birds such as blackcocks, sage-grouse and ruffs, where each bird maintains a small territory in the traditional mating ground or lek. Each male benefits from the mutual display in that many females are attracted, but then is able to court the female without too much interference from neighbouring males.

The bioluminescent signals of fireflies can be switched on and off as required, but most visual signals are permanent adornments which tend to decrease crypticity to friend and foe alike. Bright plumage has probably evolved in birds because of their visual acuity and their ability to escape from predators by flight. But even here, compromises have been made, e.g. many birds confine their epigamic coloration to the breast, which is hidden when on the nest. The dorsal surface is cryptic in coloration, and

**Figure 1.6** Pulse (flash) patterns and flight during flashing in male fireflies of the genus *Photinus* as they would appear in a time-lapse photograph. The species illustrated are not all sympatric. Small triangles near numbers designating species indicate direction of flight. (1) *consimilis* (slow pulse), (2) *brimleyi*, (3) *consimilis* (fast pulse) and *carolinus*, (4) *collustrans*, (5) *marginellus*, (6) *consanguineus*, (7) *ignitus*, (8) *pyralis*, and (9) *granulatus* (from Lloyd, in Sebeok, 1967).

"freezing" behaviour occurs in order not to reveal the location of the nest to potential predators.

Once an interaction has been initiated, the courtship sequence that follows may be extremely brief, the pair copulating almost immediately as in the bush cricket *H.n. vicinus* (Gower and Lewis, unpublished) or, prolonged reaction chains may precede actual fertilization, as in the three-spined stickleback *Gasterosteus aculeatus* (figure 1.7). The courtship of *Gasterosteus* functions mainly as a signalling system to orientate the two

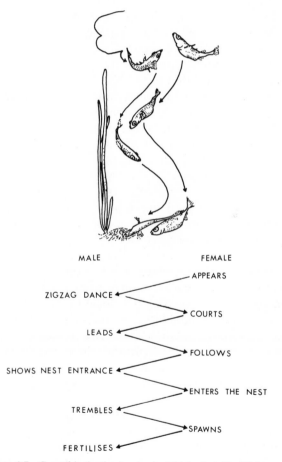

**Figure 1.7** Courtship in the 3-spined stickleback (after Tinbergen, 1951).

partners to each other and to the nest. In fact, the reaction chain described in figure 1.7 is an oversimplification; acts are frequently interpolated between the early steps. The male may engage in "dorsal pricking": he positions himself beneath the female and pricks her with his erect dorsal spines. He may then force himself through the tunnel of weed glued to the river bottom that is his nest. Clearly, all that each signal does is to increase the probability that the partner will respond with the next element in the chain.

(*g*) *Signals of parents and offspring*. One of the best studied interactions between parents and offspring is the begging response of the herring-gull chick. The chicks elicit food from their parents by pecking at a red spot on the tip of the mandibles. The parents then regurgitate food which the chicks consume. As the chicks mature, the pecks become aimed at the bases rather than the tips of the parents' bills. Tinbergen's original studies indicated that the red spot on the long yellow bill of the adult was a very specific signal for releasing and directing the pecking of the chick. In fact, Hailman's (1967) later work, on this and other species, revealed that the release of the response depended on less-specific stimuli, namely movement and redness. The change in orientation of the begging response to the base of the parent's mandibles is of interest because it indicates the superimposition of learning on the basic, very general, inherited response.

In nidicolous species of bird, the food is deposited by the parents directly into the gaping mouths of the nestlings. These respond to quite general configurations landing on the edge of the nest, by gaping. Tinbergen showed that the nestling thrush responds to ⭕ configurations irrespective (within wide limits) of actual size. In turn, the parents respond to the bright red or orange mouths of their young.

In gallinaceous species, such as the domestic fowl, the young are directed to food by the tidbiting and food-calling of the hen. The phenomenon of social facilitation of feeding in chicks described by Tolman (1964) may well be linked with an early food-learning system. Feeding is promoted in the presence of another feeding chick or adult, so that rapid learning of possible new food types and sources may be achieved.

The function of these systems is, of course, to bring about feeding of the young. Communication systems have also developed for retrieving young. In the domestic fowl, "fret" calling by the chick elicits approach by the mother hen. The young of two rodent families, the Muridae and the Cricetidae, emit ultrasonic calls when removed from the nest. In the laboratory mouse *Mus musculus*, the calls are of 10–140 ms in duration and at frequencies between 45 kHz and 88 kHz, far beyond the 18 kHz upper frequency limit of hearing in man. This calling serves to attract the mother to the pup. It initiates retrieval if the pup is outside the nest, when the mother grasps it at the back of the neck. During this "handling", the actual intensity of the ultrasonic cry increases, and may serve to inhibit aggression by the handler. In most of the murid and cricetid rodents that have been studied, the ultrasonic calling of the pups appears to serve these two functions: retrieval by the mother and the inhibition of aggression (Sales and Pye, 1974).

## Exploitation of existing communication systems

Certain displays have evolved because of their effectiveness in misleading the recipients. Moynihan (1975) has proposed the term *antidisplay* for this kind of interaction. Antidisplays are not, of course, communicative under the terms of any of the definitions used earlier. Often-quoted examples, such as the broken-wing display of many ground-nesting birds, or the use of lures by angler fish, cannot be considered to exploit existing communication systems. However, some antidisplays have precisely this function, e.g. the blenny *Aspidontus taeniatus* mimics both the coloration and the undulating dance of the cleaning wrasse *Labroides dimidiatus* (figure 1.2). This enables it to approach prey more closely, bite a chunk out of the animal and flee. This kind of mimicry is known as *Peckham's* or *aggressive mimicry*, and the best example is probably shown by the Florida population of the firefly *Photinus versicolor*. Here, the females mimic the flashes of two or three other species of *Photinus* in order to attract heterospecific males which are then killed and eaten. The flower-mimicking mantids also fall into this category.

There is probably no innate recognition of warning coloration (such as black and yellow stripes) in vertebrates. Naive domestic chicks, for example, showed no tendency to avoid wheat grains painted black and yellow as compared with wheat painted in other colour stripes or other patterns (Gower, unpublished). The typical warning coloration of vespids and distasteful species, such as the Cabbage White caterpillar, are likely to have evolved because they are conspicuous and easily remembered. The phenomenon of convergence of aposematic coloration is termed *Mullerian mimicry* and its development can be explained equally well by this thesis. Aposematism is often accompanied by slow movement and toughness of body surface. Exploitation of this type of communication (if such it be) is seen in the numerous mimics of aposematic species. It is termed *Batesian mimicry* and differs from ordinary "camouflage" in that the prey is easily detected by the predator, but is then avoided. There is no doubt that Batesian mimicry is an effective strategy for its exponents, but it suffers from two severe limitations:

(i) The mimic must restrict its distribution to that of the model.
(ii) The mimic cannot become too abundant relative to the model, because the first sampling is likely to shape the predator's future responses.

Several ploys have been used to moderate the effect of this second problem. The buff ermine *Spilosoma lutea* emerges later in the season than its model, the white ermine *Spilosoma lubricipeda*. Potential predators are therefore more likely to sample the model first. The hoverfly (Syrphidae) mimics of wasps and bees have been shown to limit their adult population numbers at the time when fledglings first start to feed themselves. In a number of species of butterflies (e.g. *Papilio glaucus* of N. America which mimics *Battus philenor*), the mimicry is sex-linked: only some females of *P. glaucus* are mimics, other females and all males are non-mimics. The mimicking morphs have a greater chance of survival but are mated less frequently than the non-mimetic morphs, an interesting example of balanced polymorphism. In all the known cases of sex-linked mimicry, the mimic is always the female; male survival is less important, because one male can fertilize many females. Furthermore, male mating success will probably depend more on species-specific coloration than will female mating success (see chapter 5).

Very few examples of mimicry occur in birds and mammals. The only certain case is that of the flycatcher *Stizorhina frasei* and its model the ant thrush *Neocossyphus rufus*, whose flesh is unpalatable, probably because of the formic acid it ingests with its ant prey (Edmunds, 1976).

Cases of intraspecific exploitation or deceit, where there is a lowering of fitness of the receiver, are rarely reported in the literature, but one clear-cut example has been described in the 10-spined stickleback *Pygosteus pungitius* by Morris (1952). Certain non-territory-holding males lose their black coloration and revert to the cryptic coloration of the females. Normal territorial males allow these pseudofemales into their territories and near their nests. The pseudofemales have been seen to follow real females through the nest before the black male can fertilize the eggs and hence, perhaps, "steal" fertilization. An alternative explanation, however, is that the pseudofemales eat the eggs. Supportive evidence is lacking for both explanations.

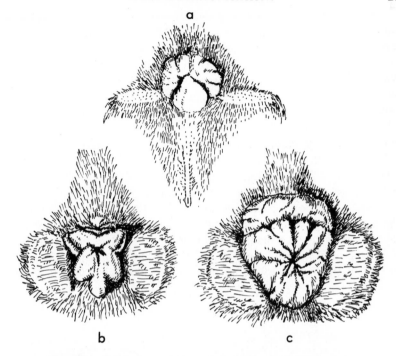

**Figure 1.8** *Colobus verus.* (*a*) juvenile male from below to show the site of the penis; (*b*) and (*c*) early and full oestrus in the female (after Hill (1958) in *Primatologia*, Eds. Hofer, Schultz and Starck, Basel and New York, Bd. III).

The female spotted hyena *Crocuta crocuta* has evolved a pseudopenis which is used in the greeting display when the genitals are exposed and sniffed by conspecifics. Similarly, the male genitalia of the juveniles of the Colobus monkeys *Colobus verus* and *C. badius* do not develop as in other species of colobines, apparently in order to avoid aggression by dominant males, so allowing the juveniles to stay in the troop until they mature. Indeed, the juvenile male genital region is made to resemble that of the female by the production of a pseudovulvar mass around the anus (figure 1.8).

The ano-genital region of the adult male hamadryas baboon *Papio hamadryas* is red and swollen, and strongly resembles that of an oestrous female. This mimicry is employed in a behaviour where the male turns away from his females and "leads". It is probably part of the behavioural repertoire of herding which enables the male to keep a tight rein on his harem. It has been suggested that somehow the male hamadryas is made less fear-provoking by the rear display. However, a simpler explanation is that large red areas make an effective signal, irrespective of the sex of the signaller. The mimicry is by no means perfect for both the large mane and pendulous penis are clearly visible from the rear: there can be no real confusion on the part of his females as to his sex (figure 1.9). It might therefore be argued, on this interpretation, that this is not deceit in the strict sense.

Exploitation of communication systems is often referred to as misinformation. Otte (1974) has argued that the alleles promoting a particular kind of deceitfulness will only spread in the population to any extent, if the misinformation is directed at unrelated individuals. His suggestion that, because an allele confers deceitfulness, it will also confer "understanding" of the deceitful ploy, is not tenable, however. In the case of the 10-spined stickleback, for example, alleles promoting normal male behaviour must be maintained in the population, despite the occurrence of pseudofemales, otherwise no true females would be courted and in-

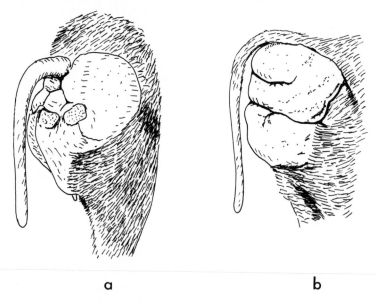

a                                              b

**Figure 1.9**    Male (*a*) and oestrus female (*b*) hamadryas baboon from the rear (after Wickler (1967) in *Primate Ethology*, Ed. Morris, Weidenfeld and Nicolson, London).

duced to spawn, and no nests would be built. An understanding of the deceitful ploy of the pseudofemale will reduce the fitness of the courting male; he may spend so much time distinguishing and chasing away pseudofemales that much less time is available for courtship. A low percentage of pseudofemales must therefore be tolerated in the population. Conversely, there is clear advantage for the pseudofemales in looking as much like true females as possible: they may fertilize the eggs without the effort of courtship. A certain low proportion of these alleles will therefore be maintained in the population (see Dawkins, 1976, for a discussion of the Evolutionary Stable Strategy (ESS) and further references).

Discussions of the genetics of misinformation do not, of course, apply so readily to humans, where deceitful behaviours are probably largely learned. It has been suggested however (Otte, 1974), that the ability to misinform and to detect deception constitutes a potent directional selective force leading to the development of higher mental capacities in man. But the whole argument is really rather tenuous. Humans do appear to employ a great deal of deceit in communication, but this is correlated with numerous other aspects of human ability, and there is no evidence to suggest the existence of a special set of genes controlling deceitfulness.

CHAPTER TWO

# SENSORY SYSTEMS

## The nature of the stimulus and the receptor

In a book on animal communication, the important features of sense organs are those which determine the kinds and accuracy of the information which they transmit to the C.N.S.; i.e. in terms of information theory, the information which is not lost by the receptors. It is obvious that not all the stimuli to which an animal is exposed will influence its behaviour. The animal responds selectively to relatively few changes in its environment and, in the first instance, this "selectivity of response" is the result of the types and capabilities of the receptors. Receptors can thus be thought of as "extracting features" from the environment. The remaining information is lost or rejected by the receptor. Such "feature extraction" may be for the purpose of monitoring general changes that occur in the environment, or may be more specifically related to communication. For whatever purpose, it is clear that sense organs are basically designed to respond to non-random environmental change. During communication, the extraction of a message from the high-level random background noise is, of course, made much easier if that message is structured, patterned and repeated. On this basis, it is not surprising that the capabilities of a given receptor (be it the pheromone receptor of the Gypsy Moth, or the vertebrate ear) are closely correlated with the effective parameters of the conspecific message. Indeed, knowing one (the message or the receptor characteristic), the other can often be predicted and in many instances receptors have evolved in parallel with the signals they are required to detect. But signals from conspecifics are not the only changes in the environment that are of relevance to an animal. In this context we must remember that predator/prey interactions are especially important.

### The complement of receptors

"Feature extraction" from the environment depends, in the first instance, on the animal's complement of receptors, and this may be very different from one animal to another. This point cannot be overstressed. Since the various sensory modalities differ in the kinds of information that they provide the C.N.S., one animal's perceived world may be very different from that with which we are subjectively familiar. Our world is dominated by sight, but a dog probably receives much more useful information from its sense of smell. A clear example of such differences is shown by the occurrence of electroreceptors in some fish, which are absent in others and all other vertebrates. The detection of changes in the electric field probably depends upon the modified neuromast organs found in the Ampullae of Lorenzini in elasmobranchs, the pit-organs of silurids and the mormyromasts of the mormyrids (Lissmann and Machin, 1958).

On the basis of the stimulus to which they are maximally sensitive, receptors can be conveniently classified into:

mechanoreceptors responding to mechanical deformation (airborne, substrate-borne or by contact)

chemoreceptors responding to changes in the chemical composition of the environment (airborne, substrate-borne or by contact)

electromagnetic receptors responding to quanta of light (airborne, water-borne, or by reflection), heat (airborne, substrate-borne or by contact), and electrical or magnetic radiation (airborne or substrate-borne).

The determination and characterization of the modalities used during behavioural interactions is of vital importance for the full understanding of animal communication. There are two approaches to this problem: that of the behaviourist and that of the physiologist. While these are complementary, it is often difficult to compare the results obtained from the two approaches. The reason for this lies principally in the terms *perception* and *reception*.

## *Perception and reception*

Receptor mechanisms are only the first stage of "feature detection" and stimulus analysis; the responses of the sense organs, and the further processing of this information in the C.N.S., contribute equally to the overall *perceptual* process. Each receptor is designed to be maximally sensitive to a particular energy state, but it may be induced to give a response to a change in other energy states, providing the intensity is sufficiently high. But the sensation produced by the non-preferred stimulus is always the same as that produced by the preferred stimulus, e.g. a blow on the eye will produce a sensation of light, a blow on the ear, a sensation of sound.

The interpretation of the responses of the peripherally-placed receptors is a function of specialized, and often localized, regions of the C.N.S. Afferent input passes to these regions along specific pathways associated with specific receptors. Thus an animal's perceptual world is the result of its complement of receptors *and* the analytical capabilities of its nervous system. In a behavioural investigation of the whole animal's response, the two parts cannot be separated.

*Perceptual capability, behavioural approach*

As a first step in analysing a communication system, the perceptual capabilities of the participants may be delimited. Two principal methods have been used.

(i). The animal is placed in a controlled environment and exposed to a naturally-occurring stimulus. Responses are scored according to the latency, intensity or duration of the animal's response, or some other measure of behaviour. Responses of the animal are then measured to a series of test stimuli, each of which differs from the natural stimulus in only one parameter. Tinbergen's analysis of the begging response of the herring gull chick (p. 63) is one example of this kind of analysis; the head of the parent gull was the naturally-occurring stimulus, the models were the series of test stimuli. However, since an animal may perceive a stimulus without producing an overt response, this method has its limitations.

(ii). In conditioning experiments, the animal is trained to respond to one stimulus while ignoring others of similar characteristics. If an animal can learn to respond differently to two stimulus situations, it must be able to distinguish them. An interesting example of this method is provided by the experiments of Lissmann (1958) on the electric fish *Gymnarchus* sp. These fish respond by jerking or avoidance to changes in the electric field around them. In the definitive experiments, fish were trained to respond to the presence of a magnet placed behind a screen and outside the tank. One fish was trained to accept food when the magnet was present and to refuse it for 30 seconds when it was not. Another fish was trained in the opposite way. In this way, the *minimum detectable strength* of magnetic field was investigated. Further, once an animal has been taught to discriminate between two stimuli, it is possible to determine the *minimum discriminable ability* of the system under investigation. Thus, von Frisch (1938) was able to show that minnows could discriminate between tones of different frequencies. In experiments of this kind, stimuli can be presented simultaneously (2-choice situations) or sequentially. The results obtained may sometimes reflect the method of presentation, as in the investigation of the phonotactic behaviour of the cricket (Elsner and Popov, 1978).

Cardiac conditioning is a modern variation of this approach. It has the advantage of speed but is, at present, restricted to vertebrates. Heart rate is monitored by recording its gross electrical activity, either directly or by radiotelemetry. The stimulus to be tested is given before an electric shock or other negative reinforcement. In the first few trials, heart rate changes in response to shock alone, but if the animal can detect the test (conditional) stimulus, heart rate then changes before the onset of the negative reinforcement (unconditional stimulus), concomitant with the presentation of the test stimulus.

While these methods provide empirical information, they say little about the underlying mechanisms by which such stimuli are detected, the information coded and the response analysed.

## Receptor capability, physiological approach

(a) *Ionic mechanisms.* Considering the diversity of receptors in animals, the underlying mechanisms for the reception of a stimulus are remarkably constant from one sense organ to another. Indeed, the underlying principle is common to all living cells.

The reception of environmental changes must have existed from the very beginning of life, and probably depended in the first instance upon the disturbance by the environment of some fundamental property of cellular organization. This property is to be found in the structure of the cell membrane. The membranes of all cells, from *Amoeba* to liver cells, are polarized. A potential difference exists across the membrane, the protoplasm being negative to the value of about 70 mV. This potential difference occurs because of the unequal distribution of ions inside and outside the cell (figure 2.1). The important ions are potassium ($K^+$), sodium ($Na^+$), chloride ($Cl^-$) and the large organic ions which, in the conditions existing in the cell, are negatively charged. We may represent them as $A^-$. The selective permeability of the membrane allows the movement of $K^+$ outwards to a far greater extent than it allows the movement inwards of $Na^+$; the membrane is totally impermeable to $A^-$. The Donnan equilibrium set up as a result of the preferential diffusion of $K^+$

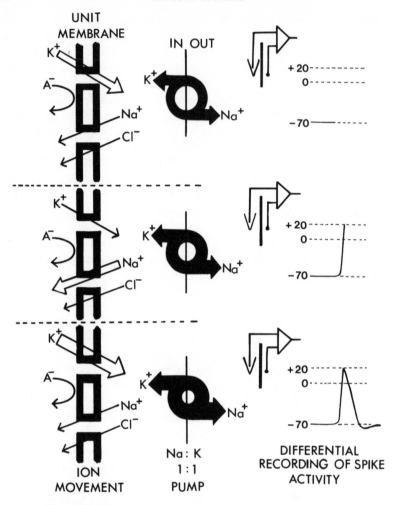

**Figure 2.1** The sequence of events occurring across the nerve axon membrane during the production of an action potential.

The left column presents the sequence of ionic movements in a simplified form—only the major ions are considered.

The middle column represents the 1:1 $Na^+/K^+$ pump mechanism situated in the membrane. The rate of active transport increases to a maximum after the action potential has been produced, and this is represented by the thickness of the arrows.

The right column represents the concomitant change in trans-membrane potential recorded intracellularly with a microelectrode.

The sequence in time is read vertically; the three parameters at any instant are read horizontally.

establishes the potential difference, which is termed the *resting potential*. Thus, the primary effect of environmental disturbance must have been to create localized states of instability of the surface membranes, resulting in a change of ionic permeability. Ionic movements then brought about a measure of depolarization which was conducted decrementally over the surface of the cell. With increasing morphological complexity, certain cells became particularly sensitive to such environmental changes. Stimuli of low intensity produced a *receptor potential*, whose amplitude and duration was correlated with the incident stimulus.

However, such a method can only be used for transmission of information over short distances, since propagation is decremental. Propagation over greater distances became the role of other specialized cells, the neurones. By transiently changing the permeability of the membrane specifically to $Na^+$, the initial decremental potential change of the receptor cells could be translated into one or more *action potentials* in the nerve fibre which became associated with the receptor cell. This action potential is propagated without decrement into the C.N.S.

The responses of even the most complex of sense organs are based initially on such ionic mechanisms; but the degree of receptor complexity determines the degree to which stimulus *analysis* occurs at the periphery rather than in the C.N.S., e.g. touch receptors of mammals are the terminal endings of primary sensory fibres which have their cell bodies in the dorsal root ganglion of the spinal cord. They respond to mechanical deformation of the body surface, and the information is passed directly along the axon to the C.N.S. for evaluation. The vertebrate ear responds to mechanical deformation of the tympanic membrane; but because of the complex arrangement of accessory structures, such as the basilar membrane of the inner ear, and the accessory receptor cells which pass their information to the primary neurones, considerable analysis of the stimulus occurs peripherally. Even more peripheral analysis occurs in the highly complex vertebrate eye. It follows, therefore, that receptor characteristics other than those of ionic movement must be known before their role in communication is fully understood.

(*b*) *Receptor bandwidth.* This represents the limits of the preferred physical stimulus within which the receptor responds when stimulated with moderate intensities. Within particular modalities, receptors tend to respond preferentially to only a small proportion of the total energy state, e.g. (figure 2.2) hearing in man extends over the frequency range 20 Hz to about 18 kHz, the upper limit decreasing with age. The description of

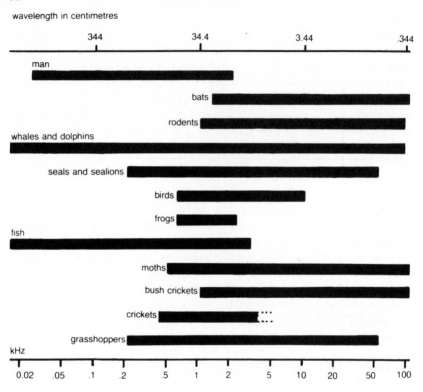

**Figure 2.2** The approximate limits of hearing in various animals, including man. Frequencies are given in kilohertz (kHz, kilocycles per second) and wavelengths ($\lambda$) in centimetres. Sounds above the human maximum are said to be *ultrasonic*.

sound above this frequency as *ultrasonic* is entirely arbitrary and based on the upper human limit. Ultrasonic communication occurs in rodents and bats, and has been used for all the functions of communication discussed in chapter 1 (Sales and Pye, 1974). Many orthopteran songs may extend to 100 kHz, and Sales and Pye describe a new species of bush cricket *Anapictata egestoides*, whose song is an almost pure tone of 50–55 kHz. It was detected whilst using a bat detector to monitor the acoustic environment. The hearing range of this insect has not been investigated, but it will certainly peak at the frequencies of the species song. Fish that rely upon direct stimulation of receptors by means of calcareous otoliths can detect sounds within a limited frequency range, between about 100 Hz and 2 kHz, depending on the species. In those species which have a connection between the swimbladder and the inner ear, the upper frequency limit is raised twofold or more (Tavolga and Wodinsky, 1963). Frogs and reptiles hear various ranges, with an upper limit that is generally lower than in birds, which have about the same frequency range as man.

As in audition, so too in other modalities. Two characteristics of light can be regarded as qualitative properties: plane of polarization, and the wavelength. The use of the polarization plane of light from blue sky in honeybee orientation was discovered by von Frisch (1950), and the cue is now known to be used by many other arthropods as a means of orientation in space (Waterman, 1961). Attempts to demonstrate the same ability in vertebrates and other invertebrates have failed, except in *Octopus* (Moody, 1962) where experiments based on training have demonstrated polarized light perception. Similarly, animals perceive a limited range of wavelengths. For man, most vertebrates and some insects, the range extends from 390 nm in the violet to 760 nm in the red. In most insects, e.g. the honeybee, visible light extends from 300 nm to 650 nm. Within these ranges wide variation occurs in the region of maximum sensitivity.

This variation in receptor bandwidth between animals is also illustrated by comparing the olfactory receptors of a dog and a male silkworm moth. A dog can smell a great array of chemical stimuli, identifying many different compounds and distinguishing between mixtures of the same substances in slightly different proportions. By contrast, the male silkworm moth responds little, or not at all, to compounds other than the pheromonal secretions of the female. Similarly, Mustaparta (1975) showed that olfactory cells innervating the sensilla trichoidea of the pine weevil responded to one, or only a few, substances which were thought to have pheromonal function.

Receptors can therefore be considered as band-pass filters, effectively eliminating stimuli outside the limits of their particular bandwidth. These limits may be imposed on the receptor by structures associated with the cells themselves (such as the membrane receptors of olfactory cells and the photochemical pigments of retinal cells), or by structures accessory to the cells (such as the basilar membrane and other associated structures of the ear).

(*c*) *Receptor sensitivity.* This is a measure of the lowest stimulus intensity which produces a just detectable response. It may be inaccurate, or even dangerous, to base an interpretation of behaviour on the basis of threshold activity of sense organs for two reasons: the response characteristics of sense organs may be quite different at suprathreshold intensities (Kuhne et al., 1979), and animals do not normally communicate at threshold intensities. Nevertheless, a measure of receptor sensitivity is an important factor, since it often suggests the maximum separation distance in the environment of two interacting individuals.

An increase in the sensitivity of the cell membrane will allow appropriate responses to be performed earlier in time. Chemoreceptors are notoriously sensitive to stimulation. A synthesized geometric isomer of bombykol, the female sex attractant of the silkworm moth, is still effective when diluted to $10^{-12}$ $\mu g/cm^3$ of petroleum ether and presented 1 cm from the antennae of males. Using only $0.004$ $\mu g$ of purified sex pheromone from females of the sawfly *Diprion similis*, Casida *et al.* (1963) were able to attract 500 to 1000 males from over 100 to 200 feet within 5 minutes in the field. Even in humans (and many authors have termed man microsmatic), the evil-smelling substance skatol can be detected when its concentration is so low that there may be little more than one molecule of it for each olfactory cell of the nasal epithelium.

To achieve such a high degree of sensitivity in chemoreceptors we must suppose that the receptor includes some amplifying device, though in this case we can only speculate as to what this may be. In the visual system, amplification is brought about by the opening of $Ca^{++}$ channels in the membrane as a result of the change in isomer state of the visual pigment. In the auditory system of mammals, the threshold at the characteristic frequency depends on displacements of the basilar membrane that are of the order of $0.1$ to $1.0$ nm. This minimal amount of energy is amplified because the potential outside the receptor cells in the scala media of the cochlea (figure 2.3) is not zero as for most cells, but $+80$ mV (Davis, 1959).

(*d*) *Stimulus localization.* During communication it is clearly important that the receiving animal recognizes the signal as being that emitted by a conspecific or a predator. Equally important is the necessity to locate the source of this signal in 3-dimensional space.

The means by which touch stimuli are located on the body surface are fairly clear in mammals. The touch receptors in the skin are spatially represented in the sensory cortex of the brain, in a manner which is weighted towards the number of receptors per unit area of the body surface. In other words, those areas such as the lips and fingertips, which have a higher density of receptors, occupy more space than would be expected from their absolute area. That similar "body pictures" occur

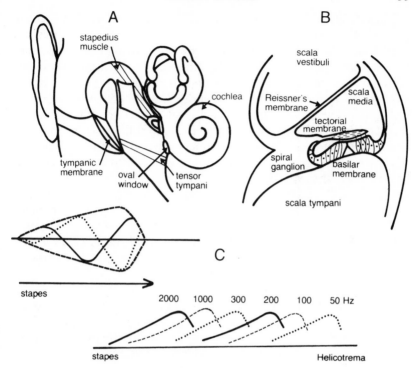

**Figure 2.3** The mammalian ear.

A. The relationships of the outer, middle and inner ear.

B. Transverse section of the cochlea to show the position of the basilar membrane and inner and outer hair cells.

C. The travelling wave theory of hearing. The position of maximum displacement of the basilar membrane varies with frequency; tones of the highest frequency produce maximum displacement near the oval window. Frequency analysis therefore occurs on the basis of the "place principle": the sound frequency is represented within the C.N.S. according to the position of the receptor cells on the basilar membrane (C redrawn after von Bekesy, 1960).

in other animals is largely speculative, particularly for invertebrates, e.g. stimulation of hair receptors on the body surface of insects may result in orientation or cleaning behaviour directed at the source of the stimulus; but how the body surface is represented in the C.N.S. of insects is not known.

Location of a distant stimulus is a problem of a higher order. Accurate localization of the stimulus depends initially on the receptor's ability to produce a differential response which is correlated with the spatial position. Comparison of the inputs of two such receptors will result in a spatial map within the C.N.S., i.e. a given comparator cell within the C.N.S. will respond only when the difference between the two inputs corresponds to a given spatial position. A different position excites a different cell (Knudsen and Konishi, 1978; Coles et al., 1979).

Associated with this problem is that of spatial *acuity*, or the degree of accuracy of localization. Essentially this depends upon the complex organization of the accessory structures, and the number and density of the receptor cells, together with the complexity of the central nervous projections of the axons (p. 100).

## PRINCIPLES AND CONSTRAINTS IN SENSE ORGAN DESIGN

The specialization necessary to achieve maximum sensitivity in each modality is far too great to be encompassed by a single cell. Furthermore, even if "generalist" receptors, responsive to several modes of stimuli such as light, sound and chemicals, were possible, the information as to what kind of stimulus was being received would be lost. Receptor specialization can therefore be regarded as the first step in the coding of the stimulus input.

An increase in specialization and a lowering of threshold results in selection pressure for the adjacent structures to provide protection for the receptor cells. This may be the reason why sense organs become buried below the surface of the body. These accessory structures may themselves become specialized, and so further define the receptor bandwidth or increase its sensitivity, e.g. the enclosure of the vertebrate cochlea in the skull is clearly a protective mechanism. In frogs, reptiles and birds, however, an interaural connection has been retained (or established) which now confers excellent directional properties on the ear (p. 49).

A high degree of bandwidth selectivity in a receptor cell loses information concerning other, potentially meaningful, stimuli in adjacent bandwidths. A broad overall bandwidth can be achieved (while retaining spectral information) by increasing the number of receptor cells, each cell being centred on a slightly different spectral component (figure 2.4, 2.5).

The evolution of complex sense organs with their battery of receptors of high sensitivity and their specialized accessory structures brings a further

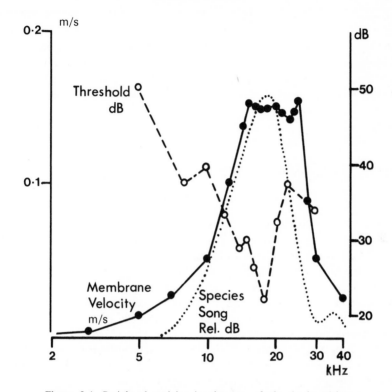

**Figure 2.4** Peripheral activity in the ear of the bush cricket *Homorocoryphus nitidulus vicinus*. The velocity of the tympanic membrane movement was measured using laser vibrometry; it rapidly increases to reach a maximum at around 10 kHz. The threshold responses of the receptor cells appear as almost the reciprocal of the membrane movement because, in this case, the vertical axis is inverted; the best response of the ear as a whole occurs around 18 kHz (but cf. figure 2.5) and corresponds to the peak frequency of the species song (membrane data after Seymour *et al.*, 1978).

reward—the ability to receive and code complex stimulus parameters. Movement may be perceived as a result of the sequential stimulation of a linearly-arranged series of cells, as in the retina; sound frequency analysis is achieved by the linear arrangement of cochlea cells on an accessory structure, the basilar membrane.

From our consideration so far, we may conclude that the responses of sense organs are determined in part by the characteristics of the sensory cells, and in part by the characteristics of the accessory structures associated with them. Further, the only way of determining the contribution of the sense organs to the overall perceptual process is by the physiological recording of their activity. That further information processing occurs centrally, there is no doubt, and this problem of the variation in the responsiveness of the animal is considered in chapters 3 and 4. For the remainder of this chapter we must consider the coding abilities of the sense organs.

## THE CODING OF BASIC STIMULUS PARAMETERS

A general consideration of sense organs shows that, whatever their capabilities for more complex stimulus analysis, receptor cells respond more or less adequately to four basic stimulus parameters: duration, repetition rate, intensity change, and intensity level.

The duration of the receptor potential (p. 31) produced as a result of environmental change follows that of the stimulus and results in a temporally-correlated volley of action potentials in the neurone, e.g. the stretch receptors in lobster muscles are the dendritic zones of neurones that send their dendrites into a strand of muscle, and give off axons that run into the C.N.S. (figure 2.6). The dendrites are excited when the muscle is stretched or contracted. The change in potential is a graded one and lasts for the duration of the stimulus. As a result of this potential change, action potentials are generated in the axons throughout the contraction period (Eyzaguirre and Kuffler, 1955).

However, no neurone can continue its activity at a high rate indefinitely; the action potential (or spike) rate gradually decreases, a phenomenon known as *adaptation* or *habituation*. Those receptors whose adaptation rate is high, produce only one or two spikes at the onset of the stimulus (or its termination in some cases). They are known as *phasic receptors* and are clearly suited for coding temporal information such as the repetition rate of very short stimuli. The ommatidia in the compound eye of fast-flying insects adapt and recover rapidly, and are capable of resolving a flicker rate as high as 300 per second (Autrum, 1958 for references). Etienne (1968) found that the predatory strike of larvae of the dragonfly *Aeschna cyanea* could be elicited by a flickering spot of light. Response probability increased as flicker rate increased towards 40 per second, but then dropped sharply. This upper limit is set by the flicker

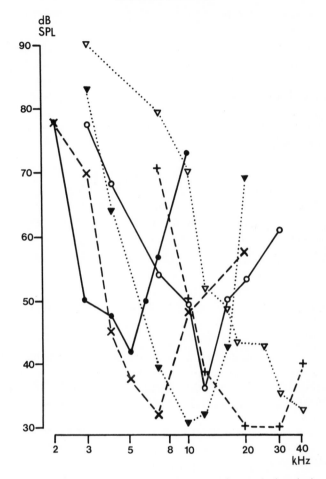

**Figure 2.5** Examples of the threshold curves of some single units in the auditory (tympanal) nerve of the bush cricket *D. verrucivorus*. The threshold curve of the ear as a whole is similar to that of *H. n. vicinus* (figure 2.4) but with a best frequency centred around 10 kHz. The best (or characteristic) frequencies of the single units, however, extend from about 3 kHz to beyond 40 kHz (the upper limit tested). The shape of the threshold curve of the whole organ is the result of a greater number of fibres with best frequencies around 10 kHz, and the fact that the low-frequency fibres have rather higher thresholds. Such an arrangement of frequency-dependent units suggests complex frequency analysis at the periphery. The song of *D. verrucivorus* (figure 4.6) is broad-banded with a dominant frequency around 10 kHz (composite figure after Kalmring, Lewis and Eichendorf, 1978). SPL = sound pressure level.

fusion frequency, determined from the electroretinogram for this species to be 40 per second (Autrum and Gallwitz, 1951).

Phasic receptors are also specialized to provide information about a change in stimulus intensity, e.g. the initial frequency of discharge of some tactile receptors is independent of stimulus intensity, and the adaptation rate is rapid. They are therefore activated only during a change in stimulus level.

Such phasic receptors are poorly adapted for coding absolute intensity level. Proprioceptors, such as the mammalian muscle spindles, adapt slowly and are thus not suited to registering a sudden stimulus change. However, they are able to give an accurate measure of stimulus intensity, which is reflected in the rate of spike production. This is consistent with the function they perform of transmitting information about the state of the muscles, which may be contracted for long periods. Single receptor cells in the insect and vertebrate ear code for airborne sound intensity in the same way, i.e. by *tonic* activity.


## THE CODING OF COMPLEX STIMULUS PARAMETERS


Not all the sensory modalities, as far as we know, are capable of coding for all the complex stimulus parameters that will be dealt with below. For this reason the following account cannot be consistent for all modalities: a modality is mentioned only when its complex coding ability is established.


### Form and pattern

The discrimination of form and spatial patterns is the result of several stimuli impinging simultaneously on the body surface. The *acuity* of such discrimination is a function of the size of the receptor, the density of the cells, and the degree of interaction between cells (figure 2.7).


### (a) Touch

Tactile receptors are most densely distributed over those parts of the body where patterned stimulation is most significant for the animal's survival

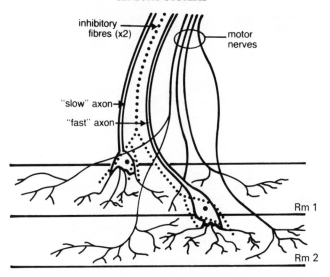

**Figure 2.6** The abdominal muscle stretch receptors of the lobster. Rm1, Rm2, receptor muscles 1 and 2; these are innervated by motor nerves and inhibitory fibres. The activity of the muscle is monitored by the "fast" and "slow" receptors whose responses can be modulated by other branches of the inhibitory fibres. During escape reactions, when Rm1 and Rm2 are stretched, the responses of the receptor cells are inhibited at the periphery.

—on the hands and feet of the primate, and on the snout of the pig. In mammals, the significance of the tactile sense in different parts of the body is reflected in the relative amounts of the sensory cortex devoted to them (p. 34) (Rose and Mountcastle, 1959). Lateral inhibition occurs in the somatosensory system to increase spatial contrast (Gordon and Manson, 1967).

*(b) Vision*

The perception of spatial patterns of light rays constitutes form vision. In the rod-rich retinas of nocturnal vertebrates, finer patterns are sacrificed for increased sensitivity; many receptor cells converge onto the same ganglion cell (figure 2.7). In a cone-rich retina there is much less convergence and, accordingly, form vision is better. The great density of cones in the foveal region of man guarantees maximal efficiency in resolution of the spatial properties of light rays in the direct line of vision. In the peripheral field there is poorer acuity and greater sensitivity.

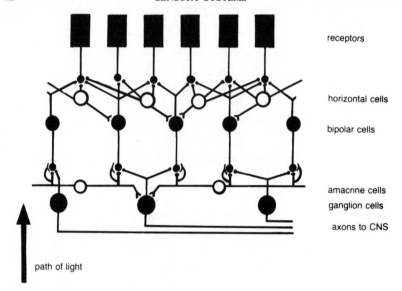

receptors

horizontal cells

bipolar cells

amacrine cells
ganglion cells
axons to CNS

path of light

**Figure 2.7**  The arrangement of cells in the mammalian retina. Black cells, direct pathways; white cells, horizontal pathways. ●, excitatory synapses; ⋏, inhibitory synapses. The ganglion cells receive inputs directly from bipolar cells in the centre of the field and indirectly from more peripheral bipolar cells via the amacrine cells. The amacrine cell input to ganglion cells is inhibitory and is the basis of the centre/surround organization of the retina. The pathway from bipolar—amacrine—bipolar is a local negative feedback loop, making both amacrines and bipolars respond only to transient stimuli. The horizontal cells receive inputs from receptors and provide a sustained inhibition on bipolar cells. The frog retina is similar in organization, except that bipolar input is mainly to amacrine cells and not directly to ganglion cells.

Although the receptive fields of ganglion cells near the fovea tend to be smaller than those in the more peripheral regions, in both cases, the neighbouring receptive fields overlap extensively, so that even a small spot of light affects many axons in the optic nerve. In the frog, some of the ganglion cells in the retina are phasic, and they give a short discharge of impulses if the illumination either increases or decreases, but no discharge under conditions of constant illumination. If the whole retinal field of a ganglion cell is illuminated, the resultant discharge is smaller than with illumination of the centre of the field alone (figure 2.8). Further, stimulation of the peripheral part of the field inhibits the discharge of the ganglion cell evoked by a stimulus delivered to the centre of the field (Barlow,

Responses

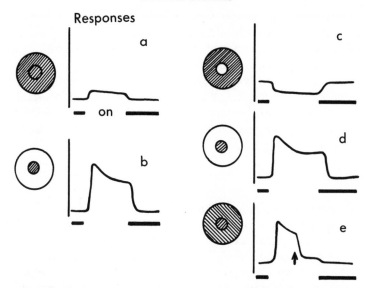

**Figure 2.8** The responses of a single frog retinal ganglion cell to illumination of the centre and peripheral portions of its receptive field.

In (a), illumination of the whole of the receptive field produces much less neural activity than the illumination of the centre only (b, d).

In (c), illumination of the periphery produces inhibition of background activity.

In (e), illumination of the centre alone produces a high response level which is inhibited when the periphery is also illuminated (↑).

1953). Comparable results have been obtained in cats (e.g. Wiesel, 1960), where some retinal ganglion cells respond with increased firing to illumination of the centre of the receptive field and with decreased firing on illumination of the periphery.

This lateral inhibition between the peripheral and central regions of the receptive field of the ganglion cell further accentuates the boundaries between differently-illuminated parts of the field. The underlying mechanism can be outlined as follows (figure 2.7). The ganglion cells connect directly with the bipolar cells, which in turn receive their input from the receptor cells. The ganglion cells receive two inputs: directly from the bipolar cells in the centre of the field, and indirectly from the more peripheral bipolar cells, *via* the amacrine cells. The bipolar cells are excitatory on the ganglion cells, whereas the amacrines are inhibitory. Thus, for an "on-centre" ganglion cell, stimulation of the centre of the field, but not of the periphery, causes direct excitation of the ganglion cell; stimulation of the periphery causes inhibition of the ganglion cell *via* the amacrine cells. Simultaneous stimulation of the centre and of the periphery results in summation of excitation and inhibition, with a weaker ganglion cell response. In animals with colour vision, the antagonistic zones may be colour-coded, the centre responding maximally to light of one wavelength, and the periphery to another (Hubel and Wiesel, 1964). Similar lateral inhibitory processes have been demonstrated in the eye of the horseshoe crab *Limulus* (Hartline, Wagner and Ratliff, 1956).

### (c) *Hearing*

Lateral inhibition also occurs in the auditory pathways and preserves the identity of discrete frequencies sounded simultaneously (Whitfield, 1967). However, form discrimination, as understood for the visual system, cannot occur in the auditory system for the simple reason that stimuli, from whatever source, are conveyed to the receptor cells of the cochlea *via* the same route: tympanic membrane, middle ear ossicles, oval window to the basilar membrane (figure 2.3). However, representation of acoustic space does occur and depends upon a comparison of the neural activity

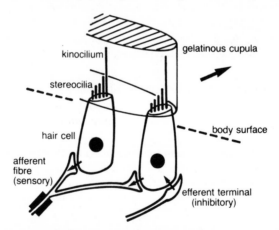

**Figure 2.9** Two hair cells of the lateral line neuromast organ of *Xenopus*. Although each neuromast contains 40 or so hair cells, for clarity only two are shown. Each hair cell receives one sensory ending and some (but not all) also receive a centrifugal inhibitory fibre. The gelatinous cupula envelops all the hair cell cilia which project above the body surface. The direction of water flow for maximum stimulation is shown by the large arrow (redrawn and modified from Flock, 1971).

of the two ears by the central nervous system (p. 49). The interaural difference is correlated with the direction of the sound source.


## Directional sensitivity

### (a) Electric field reception

Elasmobranchs, catfish, electric eels and electric fish are known to be capable of orienting to voltage gradients (Bullock, 1973), which are used as a prey-seeking device (Lissmann, 1958). The electric fish also use their fields for communication (Valone, 1970). Electric fields are strongly directional but can be employed only in quiet water and over a short range. As yet, little is known concerning the actual directional capabilities of the electric fish.


### (b) Olfaction

The source of an olfactory stimulus some distance from the receiver is difficult to find when the only clue is the diffusion gradient from the source, because the molecule diffuses in all directions and the gradient is therefore difficult to monitor. To establish the gradient, the stimulus concentration must be sampled at different spatial positions. This sampling can be made simultaneously by receptors on different parts of the body as in eels, when the receptors are widely separated or, as in flatworms when they are some distance from the source, successively by the same receptors. More efficient localization is possible if the diffusion gradient is aided by movement of the medium. A male silkworm moth may be separated by several kilometres from the female if a wind is blowing in his direction, but in still air he must be within one metre to find her (Wilson and Bossert, 1963). Chemoreceptors are highly responsive, as they must be, to variations in the concentration of the effective chemicals (Hodgson and Roeder, 1956).


### (c) Vision

Directional sensitivity in the visual modality is readily achieved, because light travels in straight lines and can be absorbed or reflected by relatively simple structures. The development of a "choroidal" pigment behind the light-sensitive receptors is initially all that is required. Further directional sensitivity can be achieved by focusing the light and completely enclosing the sensory cells. This has come about independently in the animal kingdom many times. Hence, light can be received only by an eye that is oriented to the source. The acceptance angle of the eye depends upon the curvature of its surface. In vertebrates, the field of each eye averages about 170°. The main difference within vertebrates is in the separation of the two eyes. A large binocular field facilitates depth perception but reduces the overall visual field. Hence in animals that hunt moving prey, overall visual field size has been sacrificed for greater binocular overlap. The compound eye of arthropods may be almost spherical, with a total acceptance angle of about 300°; a large binocular field is achieved without reducing the total field of view. This is because of faceting and the raising of the eye above the head surface.

In invertebrates, the capacity to distinguish the direction of the light stimulus depends ultimately on the acceptance angle of the ommatidia. This phenomenon has been clearly demonstrated for various arthropods by von Buddenbrock and Schultz (von Buddenbrock, 1952). If a single narrow beam of light is made visible to the arthropod, it sets a temporary course subtending a certain angle to the light. If the light is moved, the animal's course shifts appropriately. By this means, the minimum angular displacement of light eliciting a course change was determined. This angle is directly related to the acceptance angle of the individual ommatidia of the species concerned.

In the vertebrates, the position is more complex. In small-aperture eyes, the limit of resolution is set by the diffraction image disc produced at the aperture; at high apertures, resolution and acuity are determined by the receptor grain. However, there is a lower size limit, beyond which the individual receptors, rods or cones, cannot proceed. This limit occurs when the receptors are about 2 $\mu$m in diameter. Above this size light can get into, but not out of, the receptor; below this value light cannot get in. Within these limits, however, excellent directional information can be obtained from regions of high acuity such as the fovea. In man, on the foveal axis, acuity is estimated at 0·5 minute of arc. This compares with 2 to 15 degrees in a range of invertebrate genera and with 1·5 minutes in small passerine birds. Some of the large predatory birds, on the other hand, probably have a visual acuity over the whole retina equal to that of man at the fovea (Pumphrey, 1961).

In cases where a distinct fovea occurs, either the head or the eye must be moved to fixate points of interest in the visual field. Scanning movements thus typify animals with this type of vision.

## (d) Hearing

Directional sensitivity in the acoustic channel is almost exclusively the result of the elaboration of sophisticated accessory structures. Probably the only truly directional mechano-receptor cell is the hair cell found in the neuromast organs of the lateral line system of fish and amphibia. In *Xenopus* the sensory transducers of the neuromast organ are 40 or so hair cells (figure 2.9), all of which connect via sensory hairs to the gelatinous cupula. Because of the close coupling of the water to the cupula, displacement of the water molecules is transferred to the structure with minimum energy loss; displacement of the cupula bends the hair and excites the receptor. Each hair cell is excited optimally by movement in one direction, and this preferred direction is correlated with the spatial distribution of the stereocilia relative to the kinocilium of the hair cell (Flock, 1971). Within a single neuromast, the hair cells respond to displacement in one or other direction along the longitudinal axis of the cupula. Each neuromast receives two afferent nerve fibres; one afferent fibre collects from all hair cells of the same polarity, the other from all hair cells of the opposite polarity (Russell, 1968).

Utilization of the particle movement of the medium is an excellent means of achieving directional information, because medium displacement is a vector quantity, whereas pressure is scalar. However, for maximum efficiency, the mass of the displaced structure must be similar to that of the medium. This problem is an order of magnitude greater for those animals communicating by means of airborne sound. In air, a comparatively large light structure is necessary to monitor medium displacement, and this is liable to damage. This is probably why it is the pressure function of the sound wave that has been exploited for communication over long distances. However, near to the sound source (i.e. in the near field), a displacement receptor is greatly advantaged: as a pressure receiver (such as the human ear) approaches a sound source, the intensity of the sound increases by +6 dB for each halving of the distance; for a displacement receiver (such as the *Drosophila* antenna) on the other hand, particle velocity increases by as much as 12 dB for each halving of the distance. Thus, with quiet sources and small distances, displacement receivers are to be preferred to pressure receivers. Medium displacement is used for communication in *Drosophila* (Bennet-Clark, 1971). During courtship, male *Drosophila* extend one wing towards the female and vibrate it, producing a series of sound pulses. The flies stand on flat surfaces to court, and the male faces the female at a distance of about 5 mm (1/400 of the wavelength at 166 Hz). The antennal arista of the female (figure 2.10) can be set in vibration by sounds of 160–200 Hz, and the amplitude of vibration is greatest when sounds arrive from 90° to the plane of the arista.

The receptor cells of more complex auditory organs are enclosed within the body and have access to the environment only *via* a thin tympanic membrane. The amplitude of the response of the tympanic membrane is dependent upon the intensity of the incident sound. Directional information transmitted by the receptors is dependent upon the variation in the amplitude of the response of the tympanic membrane which, in turn, is dependent upon the angle of incidence of the sound. To achieve a change

**Figure 2.10**   The arista of *Drosophila*. The facets of part of a compound eye can be seen in the background (redrawn from Burnet *et al.*, 1971, *Anim. Behav.* **19**, 409–415).

in sound intensity at the tympanic membrane, two strategies are available, depending on the wavelength of the sound and the dimensions of the body.

(i) *Pressure receivers*. In mammals, since sound has access to only one surface of the tympanic membrane, the inner surface being enclosed by the bony wall of the middle ear, the ear is a pressure receiver.

In man, the wavelength of the sound used in communication is of the same order of magnitude as the dimensions of the head, which acts as a substantial obstacle to the propagation of the sound wave. At the right ear, therefore, the head will create a sound shadow to sound propagating from a source to the left. The left ear, on the other hand, will experience a slight build-up of sound, due to the interaction of the direct wave and its reflection and diffraction from the head. This difference in sound intensity is analysed in the C.N.S. and provides the cue for the direction of the sound source. The magnitude of the sound shadow (and therefore the difference) is a function of the angle of incidence of the sound. Sound incident from directly in front of the head will be equal in both ears, whereas sound incident from one side will produce a maximum difference of about 10 dB. In mammals such as rats and mice, where head dimensions are much smaller, the wavelengths of the sounds used in communication are correspondingly shorter (figure 2.2 and Sales and Pye, 1974). Pinnae are probably a further elaboration of this strategy, but little is known about their function.

(ii) *Pressure-gradient receivers*. Many animals use communication sounds whose wavelengths are many times larger than the dimensions of the head (figure 2.2). Frogs, for example, communicate at around 900 Hz (wavelength 30 cm) whereas head width is 1 to 2 cm; the predominant frequencies in bird song are around 2 to 4 kHz (wavelength 17 to 10 cm), head dimensions being 2 cm or less. Structures of these dimensions can never produce sound shadows and interaural intensity differences of sufficient magnitude to allow unequivocal discrimination by the C.N.S. These animals resort to using a pressure-gradient system.

Frogs, reptiles and birds have interaural cavities derived, in the case of the frog, from the eustachian tubes and the pharynx, and in birds from the air spaces in the skull. The derivation of the connection in reptiles is not yet known, but it extends over the top of the skull. In all cases, these channels connect the inner surfaces of the tympanic membranes of each ear, and are transparent to sound, at least at some frequencies (Hill *et al.*, 1979; Coles *et al.*, 1979). As a result of the movement of (say) the

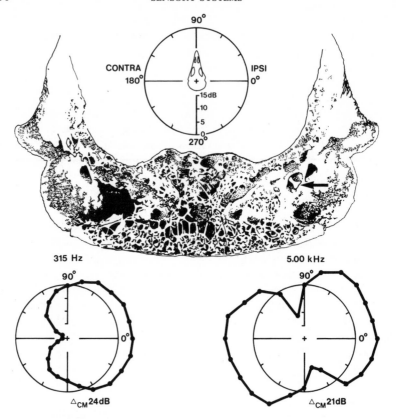

**Figure 2.11** Directional hearing in the quail. The pneumatization of the base and back of the skull allows the transference of airborne sound from one ear to the other, and the ears act as asymmetrical pressure-gradient receivers. The responses of a single ear to sound moved through 360° in the horizontal plane are also shown for two frequencies. The cardioid-type response at 315 Hz gives a maximum angular difference of 24 dB; at 5 kHz the figure-of-eight response gives a maximum difference of 21 dB (after Coles *et al.*, 1979).

right tympanic membrane, sound may be transmitted through these channels to the inner surface of the left tympanum (figure 2.11). At the same time, sound passes unimpeded around the head to the outside of the left tympanum. The movement induced in the left tympanic membrane is a function of the difference in the intensity and phase of the sound acting on the inner and outer surfaces of the membrane. Assuming no loss in the intensity through the head, and assuming that change in the phase of the sound passing through the head is equal to that around the head, then the sound pressure acting on each surface will be equal and opposite, resulting in cancellation. The membrane will not move because no *effective* sound pressure exists: the pressure gradient across the membrane is zero. By using this mechanism, the quail for example, can achieve interaural differences of up to 25 dB, even at frequencies of 315 Hz (wavelength 127 cm). The difference actually realized is a function of the angle of incidence of the sound (figure 2.11). However, the transmission of sound through the interaural channel is frequency-dependent and the quail shows distinct frequency bands where directional sensitivity is achieved, and these are interposed between frequency bands which provide no directional information.

(iii) *The insects*. The insects show examples of both strategies to achieve directionality in hearing. In female cicadas, the air bladders occupying the abdominal space between the ears are acoustically transparent, and the ears act as pressure-gradient receivers (Young and Hill, 1977). Crickets also use the tracheal system in this way, at least for the frequencies used in the species song (Hill and Boyan, 1977). At other frequencies the ears may act, as in the bush crickets, as mixed pressure/pressure-gradient systems (Larsen and Michelsen, 1978; Michelsen and Larsen, 1978; Lewis, 1974; Seymour *et al.*, 1978), since each ear has two inputs: directly from the exterior, and *via* the prothoracic spiracle and leg trachea (figure 2.12). Transmission down the trachea is, however, frequency-dependent. Similarly, transmission through the air sacs of locusts is frequency-dependent, and the ears are mixed pressure/pressure-gradient systems (Michelsen, 1971; Miller, 1977).

## Frequency discrimination and analysis

### (a) The visual system

Although animals perceive only a limited range of wavelengths as visible light, the capacity to discriminate between different wavelengths to produce colour vision is widespread among both invertebrates (Dethier, 1963; Waterman, 1961) and vertebrates (Duke-Elder, 1958).

In the visual system of vertebrates, distinction between the different wavelengths that make up the visible spectrum is associated with the retinal cones. It is best developed in the fovea. "Colourless" vision is

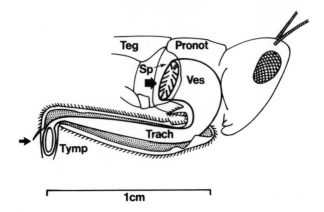

**Figure 2.12** A partial stereodiagram of the acoustic trachea in the right foreleg of a bushcricket. For clarity, the leg is drawn out of proportion to the body. The large prothoracic spiracle (Sp) opens directly into a vesicular air space (Ves) from which a horn-shaped trachea (Trach) descends through the leg to the region of the tympanal membrane (Tymp). The external surface of the tympanum is open to the outside via tympanic slits (not shown). Sound may therefore be incident on the membrane from two directions (arrows), the dominant entry being via the spiracle for most frequencies. The vesicle of one side abuts that of the opposite side but, in bush crickets, no acoustic transference occurs across the midline. In the crickets, on the other hand, the spiracle is partly closed by a lip, and acoustic transference across the midline does occur. Pronot, pronotum partly cut away to show the spiracle; Teg, tegmen or forewing (after Lewis, 1974).

mediated by the rods. There is little doubt at present that colour vision in man is fundamentally trichromatic. The existence of three cone pigments was demonstrated in the human retina by measuring the absorption spectra of single rod and cone cells. Human cone visual pigments include ones with maxima at 435 nm, 540 nm, and 565 nm. Cone visual pigments are called *iodopsins*. The normal fovea contains chlorolabe, the green absorbing pigment with maximal absorption at 540 nm, and erythrolabe, a red-absorbing pigment with maximal absorption at 565 nm; but the third blue-absorbing pigment, cyanolabe, is still being investigated. The direct measurement of the absorption spectra of cones cannot, as yet, be related to their electrophysiological activity.

The development of colour vision allows the use of colour in communication signals, and many examples exist, from the ultraviolet flower patterns used by bees, to the red rump of the baboon.

(b) *The auditory system*

The auditory spectrum within which animals are capable of frequency analysis ranges from below 100 Hz to over 100 kHz, though each animal is limited to a bandwidth well within this range (figure 2.2).

Two basic mechanisms occur for analysing the frequency content of acoustic signals: the *volley* (or telephone) *principle* and the *place principle*.

(i) *The volley principle.* By this mechanism, the responses of the receptor are locked to a particular phase of the sound; one or two action potentials are produced for each sine-wave of the sound. The frequency is therefore coded directly by the action potential repetition rate. To achieve this, the sound frequency must be lower than the maximum repetition rate of action potential production. Such responses occur below about 800 Hz in mammals and about 400 Hz in insects, e.g. the Johnston's organ, found in the second segment of the antennae of some insects, is excited when sound moves the flagellum. The Johnston's organ of mosquitoes responds to frequencies of 150 Hz to 550 Hz and is phase-locked to the incident sound. In the male *Aedes aegypti*, the maximum sensitivity corresponds to the flight tone of the female; the male flight tone, which is around 650 Hz, is above the limit of sensitivity and is not heard (Tischener, 1953; Risler and Schmidt, 1967). A similar mechanism occurs in *Drosophila* (p. 48) and in the whirligig beetle *Gyrinus* sp.; Johnston's organ is used to analyse surface waves on water.

(ii) *The place principle.* The place principle involves the coding of frequency by different cells placed in different positions on a vibrating membrane. The membrane may be resonant, or carry a travelling wave.

(I) Resonant membranes
In the locust, Michelsen (1971) has elegantly shown, using laser holography and electrophysiological recording, that different resonant patterns of vibration occur in the tympanic membrane in response to the different frequencies contained in the song. Responses are produced in four different receptor cell-groups which are directly attached to that membrane, thus establishing a simple form of frequency discrimination. This ability extends over a range of frequencies which include both the flight tone and the species song. In the bush cricket *Decticus verrucivorus*, a more sophisticated frequency analysis occurs (Kalmring, Lewis and Eichendorf, 1978). The ear of this animal has about 60 cells responsive to

airborne sound, and the results suggest that most of the cells respond to a different characteristic frequency extending over and beyond the range of the species song (figure 2.5). Here the mechanism underlying frequency analysis is still unknown; the receptor cells are not directly attached to the membrane; the membrane moves directly and in phase with the incident sound; no patterns of vibration comparable to those of the locust are established in the membrane. One clue to the mechanism may be suggested by the fact that the receptor cells decrease in dimensions (and therefore mass) distally along their linear arrangement. This change in mass of the cells may be a mechanism comparable to the change in mass of the mammalian basilar membrane.

(II) Travelling wave

Frequency analysis in the vertebrates is the result of vibration patterns in the basilar membrane. This membrane increases in mass as the distance from the stapes increases. The basilar membrane is displaced about its resting position as a result of the pressure wave developed in the scala vestibuli and scala tympani of the inner ear. This pressure wave is, in turn, the result of the movement of the footplate of the stapes on the oval window membrane. The travelling wave increases in amplitude as it moves apically in the cochlea, and reaches its maximum near the region where the resonant frequency of the basilar membrane corresponds to the frequency of the driving force. The amplitude of movement falls off rather rapidly beyond this point; a little distance beyond the position of maximum amplitude there is no significant movement. If the driving frequency is increased, the position of maximum amplitude travels towards the oval window; if the driving frequency is decreased, the maximum travels towards the apex (von Bekesy, 1960, 1970) (see figure 2.3). This mechanism allows the cochlea to act as a mechanical frequency analyser, because the extent of the activity and position of maxima vary as functions of frequency (cf. the locust). The upward and downward bulging of the basilar membrane results in a shearing action between the hair cells and the tectorial membrane, the maximum force being exerted at the position of maximum displacement. The bending of the hairs is the final and critical mechanical event in the mechanism of stimulation. At this point, the receptor membrane potentials are decreased, depolarization initiating action potentials in the auditory nerve fibres.

The innervation of the hair cells is complicated: a single nerve fibre innervates one to three of the inner group of hair cells; other fibres cross the organ of Corti to the external hair cells. Here each fibre innervates many external hair cells, but not every cell along its course; also, each cell typically receives more than one nerve fibre (see Bredberg, 1977, for review). Fundamentally, however, each hair cell, because of its precise position along the basilar membrane, is triggered maximally by a particular frequency. Frequency information is further sharpened by some unknown mechanism associated with the hair cells themselves (Russell and Selick, 1977) and by a lateral inhibition mechanism comparable to that of the retina. This information is retained in the separate units of the cochlear nerve as they pass into the C.N.S. (Johnstone, 1977; Evans, 1977).

## CONCLUSIONS

This brief consideration of the mechanisms for coding the complex stimulus parameters demonstrates the very considerable amount of analysis which may occur at the level of the receptor. It is only by investigating the response capabilities of the receptors physiologically that the contribution they make to the overall perceptual process can be assessed. The central nervous system cannot act on information it does not receive; of course, it may not act to produce an observable response anyway, but that is a problem for chapters 3 and 4.

It is also clear that the different modalities have to cope with quite different problems and principles in terms of the analysis and specificity of their inputs. On the one hand we can state that the greater the complexity of the receptor, the greater the probability of complex analysis occurring at the receptor level. On the other hand, the simpler the receptor, and the narrower its bandwidth, the greater its selectivity in sampling the environment.

In *Bombyx mori*, the silkworm moth, the male's olfactory receptors are tuned virtually specifically to the female sex attractant *bombykol*. Most of the receptors can only respond to that, or very·similar molecules. The only form of coding in this system will be "which afferents are active and by how much?"—that is, line coding. Even if very few of the olfactory receptors in the sense organ were specialized to respond to a particular pheromone, line coding is still sufficient to bring about response specificity.

In the auditory modality, frequency can to some extent be considered to be line coded—for here, too, it is which cells along the basilar membrane (for example) are active and by how much? But, in audition, intensity (coding both distance and direction) and temporal patterning, as well as frequency, can be coded, though not all of these may be necessary for species identification. Insects, for example, may not employ frequency as part of the species-specific code; it may be reserved for providing directional information, even though the receptor system is tuned to that frequency. As an illustration of the main points of this chapter we end with a detailed look at some particular examples of acoustic and visual communication.

### Acoustic communication in insects and birds

In insects, the major species-specific parameter is, in most cases, the amplitude-modulation pattern of the song. The amplitude-modulation pattern is an expression of the underlying motor activity. Consider the species-specific song pattern of the bush cricket *Homorocoryphus nitidulus vicinus*. The sound is produced during the closure of the forewings (or tegmina) of the male as a result of a fixed pattern of contraction of the "flight" muscles of the thorax. Each tegminal closure results in a syllable of sound. These syllables are regularly repeated at a species-specific rate of about 120 per second for extended periods of time. The underlying motor mechanism is, therefore, also species-specific in its output pattern. The sound is produced as a result of the impact of the edge (or plectrum) of the right tegmen against a row of teeth (or file) on the underside of the left tegmen. The energy of this impact is fed to a structure known as the mirror frame on the right tegmen, whose frequency of natural vibration determines the dominant (in this case) 16-kHz component of the song (see Lewis and Broughton, 1980, for references). Thus, the duration and repetition rate of the syllable are species-specific and provide the cue for the orientation behaviour of the female (Bailey, 1976). Support for this belief is also provided by much of the work in crickets (see Elsner and Popov, 1978, for references). This parameter in all orthopteran groups is directly coded as an action potential pattern in the tympanal nerve. The other parameters of the song, intensity and frequency, provide additional information for the receptive female: sound intensity is coded as the spike repetition rate in each unit of the tympanal nerve and, because sound is attenuated with distance, is an indication of the separation distance of the two individuals; the frequencies are coded as the activity in separate units (place principle and line coding) and are probably used to determine the direction of the incident sound. Thus, temporal features release, and intensity and frequency features orientate, the responses of the female insect. In this example, the role of the various parameters of the species-specific song in the release of behaviour can be understood on the basis of the physiological characteristics of the receptor. The analysis of this information, and the initiation and control of the motor acts during approach and copulation are, of course, the result of central mechanisms.

The differences between insect and bird songs are unmistakeable: birds

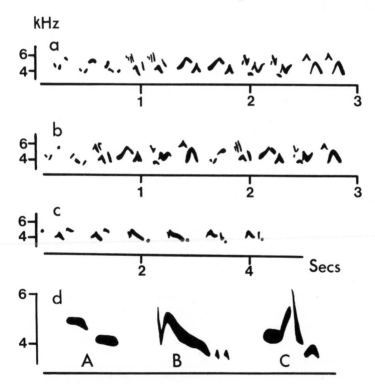

**Figure 2.13** Normal and experimentally modified songs of the indigo bunting *Passerina cyanea*.

   (*a*) Normal song

   (*b*) Repeated figures "respliced" into a non-paired sequence

   (*c*) Interfigure intervals at ×2

   (*d*) Song figures (scales increased) from which artificial songs were made up by repetition of the same figure; A does not incorporate large frequency sweeps and was not effective in eliciting responses; B and C do incorporate large frequency sweeps and did elicit responses (redrawn from Emlen, 1972).

use frequency modulation to a far greater extent. Emlen (1972) investigated the features of the indigo bunting song that conferred species recognition, by monitoring the levels of aggression shown by territorial males to tape recordings of the song. Initially, Emlen monitored the responses to the normal song. Using these as a baseline he measured the responses to songs whose "figures" had been unpaired (figure 2.13), i.e. AA B CC DD became A B C D, etc. This had very little effect on aggression levels, and Emlen next changed the "inter-figure" intervals of the song by inserting sections of blank tape at appropriate points (figure 2.13). There was a significant reduction of response by territorial males to this tape, but aggression levels were still higher than to the songs of other species. Finally, Emlen made a tape consisting only of those notes of the species song which did not have large frequency sweeps (figure 2.13). Virtually no aggression was shown to this tape. Emlen concluded that species recognition depended on phrases with large frequency sweeps (and these are typical of the indigo bunting song, giving it its harsh quality) and the interphrase interval. Since the experimental birds in Emlen's study were all wild adult males which presumably had already been exposed to the species song, the conclusions must be tentative. However, this kind of study has been carried out on a number of species and there can be little doubt that frequency plays an important role in conferring species specificity on the songs of birds. Thus, temporal patterning *and* frequency changes are both used as releasers of behaviour in birds, and indeed in the hearing vertebrates as a whole. But, in birds, physiological experiments have shown (Coles *et al.*, 1979) that the orientation of the response is likely to depend upon both the intensity and the frequency components of the song, as in insects. As discussed earlier (p. 49) accurate orientation to stimulus sources is the result of intensity differences at the two ears, at several different frequencies.

**Visual communication in the firefly and the stickleback**

In the visual modality, animals have the capacity for coding intensity, temporal patterning, frequency (colour) and spatial patterning (by line coding) to a sophisticated level. In addition, in some species, the plane of polarization of light may be discriminated. There are examples, mainly from bioluminescent forms, where only temporal patterning is employed in species recognition, e.g. the highly species-specific flash patterns of *Photinus* sp. But, the spatial position of the emitter must also be determined, and this is coded on the line principle of which ommatidia, in one or both eyes, are maximally stimulated. In addition, intensity, spectral composition, size and shape of luminescent organs may vary between species, and the firefly can control the spatial pattern of each flash by varying its flight path.

The early stages of courtship in the three-spined stickleback are visually mediated. The red underbelly, green eyes and zig-zag dance of the male induce attention and approach in the female. In turn, the male's behaviour is released by the silvery roundness of the female; details of shape are not critical, however, completely spherical objects proving adequate to release courtship in some males. The release of female approach and following is rather more closely specified: colour (frequency) and temporal patterning (the zig-zag dance) probably being the most important features.

## Comparison of visual and other modalities

The considerable advantage of the visual system over other modalities lies in its capabilities for form discrimination—in particular, patterns in space, or shapes. The complex organization of the receptor discussed above (p. 41), and of the higher levels of the C.N.S. (chapter 4), all contribute to the very sophisticated ability to locate an object accurately in three-dimensional space and to provide the maximum amount of information about its movement and appearance. Yet, even in animals with proven abilities of form vision, e.g. birds and mammals, the detailed shape of the releasers of behaviour seem to be relatively unimportant. Frequency and temporal patterning still seem to be the major parameters of the input that are relied upon. Frequency is line-coded, and temporal patterning can be coded relatively straightforwardly. One suspects that mechanisms for analysing visual inputs have been evolved to cope with extremely complex spatial information: the rapid and accurate fixation of objects in three-dimensional space, the shape and patterning of objects, movement detection, depth perception, constancy and stability, colour, etc. Thus, in communicative interactions, the production of a specific response to only a very specific spatial pattern may have been sacrificed during the evolution of these complex analytical processes. Specificity and rigidity on the one hand, and novelty on the other, may be exclusive. For the establishment of a particular visual pattern as a species-specific parameter, learning (with its necessary exposure to repeated signals) may be a fundamental requirement.

In this chapter we have shown how a knowledge of the physiological properties of receptors can complement the behavioural data. A full understanding of behaviour (in general) and communication (in particular) will only be achieved if both approaches proceed together. As stated at the beginning of this chapter (p. 27), knowledge of the sensory capabilities of an animal is also fundamental for the understanding of the central mechanisms of analysis and integration. In the next two chapters we consider these central mechanisms and discuss the ways in which they modulate and control communicative behaviour.

CHAPTER THREE

# EXTERNAL STIMULI, INTERNAL FACTORS AND BEHAVIOUR

## Introduction

At the beginning of chapter 2 we stated that an animal responds selectively to relatively few changes in its environment. This "selectivity of response" is due, in part, to the complement and capabilities of its receptors. In fact, the phrase "selectivity of response" is something of an understatement; animals can be extremely specific in their responses (especially in the context of communication), with particular stimulus configurations releasing one, and only one particular response. In *Stroll through the Worlds of Animals and Men*, von Uexküll (Hinde, 1970) describes the behaviour of the female tick. Once she has mated, she climbs the vegetation and clings there, perhaps for months, totally unresponsive to the changes around her, except for one: if she detects butyric acid in the air she will let go her hold. Butyric acid is a component of mammalian skin secretions, and her response to it ensures a reasonable chance of landing on a host. In fact, female ticks tend to move about in the vegetation quite a lot, and there are other stimuli to which they will respond. Nevertheless, the specificity of response to butyric acid is extreme and is probably conferred largely by the possession of many chemoreceptors which respond quite specifically to butyric acid. This is an example of *stimulus filtration* in the olfactory modality and can be accounted for by "line coding". In other cases, particularly when signals are in the visual modality, the filtration process cannot be ascribed so neatly to a peripheral phenomenon.

Stimulus and response are not always inexorably linked with each other. An animal's responsiveness can vary from time to time, even though external conditions, including the "releasing" stimulus, are held constant, e.g. the activity of the sensory nerves of the chemoreceptors on the feet of the blow-fly *Phormia* increases when they first come into contact with sugar, and then adapts. The time it takes to adapt and the initial rate of firing depend on the sugar concentration. The characteristics are the same whether the fly is fully fed or starving. However, a hungry fly will respond to a more dilute sugar solution than a fly which is recently fed. Dethier (1964) states that the fly's "acceptance threshold" varies with food deprivation, although its sensory threshold does not.

Thus, although the responses to a given sign-stimulus tend to be fixed, the *probability* of the appearance of such responses may vary, even over short periods. The inferred variable causing change of responsiveness in the blow-fly is "hunger", "feeding drive" or "motivation for food". We can say this because the acceptance threshold of the fly is correlated with the amount of time it has been deprived of food. There are many parameters of motivation apart from acceptance threshold or amount of food consumed that we could use, e.g. latency and amount of adulterated food consumed. Most of these parameters agree fairly well with each other, but agreement is never precise. The central problem is that motivation is something we can study only by inference, and motivations are used, not only to account for changes in responsiveness, but also to explain goal-orientated behaviour, spontaneity of behaviour, and the temporal clustering of particular behaviour patterns. It is an unwarranted assumption to use the same inferred neural processes to account for these different behavioural phenomena, but nevertheless we suspect that some aspects of the underlying causations must be the same.

Conventionally, stimulus filtration and motivation are regarded as unrelated functions of the nervous system. Sensory input is often regarded as arriving at "higher centres" in the C.N.S. relatively unchanged and certainly not affected by any modulating influences endogenous to the C.N.S. This is not the case and some of the modulating influences are discussed in the next section. If what we think of loosely as motivational systems are capable of modulating sensory input so that some stimuli have greater impact than others, then we do have a partial explanation of the changing thresholds to stimuli. It may be helpful to consider these motivational effects as a form of *gating* in the nervous pathways.

### Sign stimuli and the innate releasing mechanism

Many of the sign stimuli or releasers employed by animals are complex stimulus configurations. This is particularly true of releasers in the visual modality. Since responses tend to be highly specific, a number of ethologists have suggested that the recognition mechanisms must reside, not in the receptors but in the central nervous system. This line of argument was put forward forcibly by Tinbergen (1951) and relied primarily on two areas of investigation, both of them involving the behaviour of young birds.

## The alarm response to flying predators

Many birds apparently show an innate recognition of hawks and other birds of prey when these fly overhead. Depending on the species and/or circumstances, the observed birds will either freeze or run for cover. Characteristic vocalizations ("hawk calls") may accompany these responses. These alarm responses are not given when non-predatory birds fly overhead and the vocalizations, in particular, tend to be reserved for just one type of predator. The obvious conclusion is that recognition is quite specific and is probably innate. Lorenz and Tinbergen (quoted in Tinbergen, 1951) investigated this behaviour using penned goslings and a variety of game-bird chicks. Two-dimensional models of hawks were pulled over the penned birds and the alarm behaviour shown was extensive. When control experiments were conducted where the hawk shape was pulled backwards, so that the long tail now "became" the long neck of a goose-like bird, little alarm was shown. The young birds therefore seemed to be responding to two features of the stimulus: its shape and its direction of movement. "Recognition" of a stimulus configuration, where two independent parameters such as shape and movement are involved, cannot be accounted for by any known peripheral filtration processes.

## The begging response of the herring-gull chick

Herring-gull chicks induce their parents to regurgitate food by pecking at their bills. Initially the pecks seem to be aimed at a red spot (or patch) on the tip of the lower mandible of each parent. Tinbergen and Perdeck (1950) "dissected" this sign stimulus by presenting a series of two-dimensional models, some of which were an accurate copy of the parent head, others varying in shape and colour of head, location of the spot, or contrast of the spot against the bill. The chicks responded most frequently to models similar to the parental head, and least frequently to models lacking the spot. However, "intermediate" models tended to score equally well, the various factors such as spot position, bill shape and spot contrast being summed independently. This is "heterogeneous summation" and was not considered to be a likely capability of the avian retina. It was proposed that the recognition mechanisms for these sign stimuli required good computational ability and must therefore reside in the higher association areas of the C.N.S. Lorenz (e.g. 1950) called these mechanisms "Innate Releasing Mechanisms" (IRMs) and proposed a model (figure 3.1) where the IRMs acted as blocks in the path of energy flow to the motor mechanisms. The sign stimulus would thus act as a key turning in the lock of the IRM. This would release the dammed-up energy, and the relevant response would be activated.

The two studies which provided the main evidence used to support this model have been extensively criticized: the hawk-goose experiment because the geese were not naive, and because the responses of the flock rather than of each individual were monitored; and the herring-gull begging response because the height of the models and (in particular) the height and speed of movement of the mandibular spot were not taken into account. On the basis of more recent work, the balance of the evidence suggests that neither of the two releasers is as precise as was originally believed. The response to a hawk flying overhead is now suspected to be linked to the comparative novelty of the shape. Schleidt (1961) showed that turkey chicks were alarmed by any novel shape flying overhead, and that their alarm responses rapidly adapted to these shapes: the least presented stimulus, independent of its shape, tending to produce the most alarm. Hirsch *et al.* (1955) had already arrived at a similar conclusion from their work on white leghorn chicks. However, Melzack *et al.* (1959) and Green (e.g. 1968) indicate that there may be a more specific innate recognition of hawks by mallards. Novelty of stimulus is important

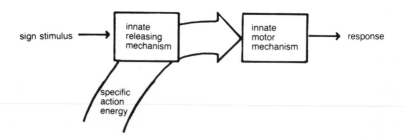

**Figure 3.1** Representation of early ethological "explanations" of response specificity.

here, too, but more activity is shown on first exposure to hawk than to other models.

Hailman (1969) has shown that naive herring-gull chicks respond equally well to conspecific or laughing-gull heads, and that they can be conditioned by feeding to prefer either. Hence, the preferences are only loosely specified at birth, and these could well be explained by filtration mechanisms at lower levels of the visual pathway (see chapter 2). It is perhaps unfortunate that Tinbergen and Lorenz chose to investigate the innate responses of birds, where parental care operates and where, under normal conditions, the young (precocious though they may be) have ample opportunity to fill-in details of these loosely-specified preferences by learning.

There are, however, a number of studies of cross-fostering species of birds, and results seem to indicate quite strong innate preferences based on complex input. Brown leghorn cocks when mature direct their court-ship preferentially not to models but to their own species; cockerels raised in isolation subsequently mate successfully with hens. Further, female Chilean teal mate preferentially with the species on which they have been imprinted whereas female mallards do not, preferring conspecific drakes. The mallard is much more sexually dimorphic than the Chilean teal.

Thus, there are indications that reasonably precise innate preferences do exist in the visual modality, at least in some species. There are also some very striking examples of response specificity from modalities other than the visual. But all these results do not tell us much about the details of the mechanisms, and we may be dealing with the combined effects of several displays. From chapter 2 it must now be clear that the different modalities have to cope with quite different problems and principles in terms of the analysis of their input. It is a mistake to talk generally about stimulus filtration and whether filtration occurs peripherally *or* centrally without reference to specific modalities.

Innate recognition of certain stimuli must be accepted, even for quite complex inputs, in the auditory and visual modalities. What we cannot accept in the Lorenzian arguments is that the recognition mechanisms are *discrete*. Present neurophysiological findings suggest that the filtration process is widespread, from receptor through every subsequent synapse. This argument is taken further in chapter 4. The point we want to make in this chapter is that a filtration process, widespread in the nervous system, is not physically discrete from involvement with other neural activity and should not, therefore, be regarded as functionally discrete.

## Intervening variables in behaviour

The distinction between "intervening variables" which carry no implications about underlying structures or processes and hypothetical constructs which do, has rarely been made, with the result that quite improbable mechanisms have been ascribed to the C.N.S. The principal critic of the earlier formulations of the energy concept is Hinde (1960), who points out that although the concepts of McDougall, Freud, Lorenz and Tinbergen differ in many details, all have the idea of a substance which is capable of energizing behaviour, held in a container and subsequently released in action.

Hinde criticizes the extent to which the energy models are considered by their authors to correspond to actual structures in the nervous system. McDougall (1923), for example, considered the energy released on the afferent side of the nervous system as being held back by "sluice gates" in the optic thalamus. Lorenz's model was initially based on behavioural data, but physiological data were later "fitted" to it. Tinbergen (1951), on the other hand, refers to his hierarchical system of Lorenzian reservoirs as "centres" clearly comparable to neural structures. The early "mechanistic" energy models place the analytical activity of the C.N.S. in discrete areas of the brain which act independently of other similar areas. Our present understanding of neurobiology does not allow such "pigeonholing". The interdependence of large areas of the C.N.S. also makes it difficult to equate "behavioural energy" with the properties of physical energy. For its activity, the C.N.S. uses potential energy in the form of action potentials, summative potentials and chemical transmitter molecules. Under normal conditions, such energy stores are not depleted during ongoing behaviour, as witnessed by a male rat walking away after copulation. The same muscles are used for both activities; there is certainly a change in motor *pattern* but not necessarily in motor *activity*. A given behaviour pattern is not terminated because energy is no longer available, but because the animal moves into a consummatory situation, or the eliciting stimuli are removed. In other words, a pattern of behaviour may be terminated by stimuli which the animal receives as a result of that behaviour, e.g. in *Drosophila*, female receptivity to the male courtship behaviour is inhibited by two mechanisms: the effect of copulation itself, which is probably mechanical, wears off after 48 hours; the effect produced by the presence of live sperms lasts until these are exhausted by egg-laying, usually 8 to 10 days. In the female grasshopper *Gomphocerus rufus*, the change from receptivity to defensive behaviour against further male approach is due to the presence of the spermatophore in the spermathecal duct, and the stimulus is probably mechanical. Finally, the waning of a response is often specific to the stimulus rather than to the response. In guinea pigs (Grunt and Young, 1952), substitution of a new female when a male has become sexually satiated produces a renewal of sexual behaviour. The substitution of a new female is more effective than the removal and replacement of the original female.

Whereas Lorenz's model (1950) of action-specific energy may only have been an analogy, Tinbergen's model (1951) is not: he writes of "thwarted energy sparking over" to another behavioural system when its discharge is blocked. "Sparking over" is, of course, quite out of the question, but there is now ample evidence that the performance of one activity may be associated with the simultaneous inhibition of others. Alternatively, inhibition of one pathway may result in the activity of others. Kennedy's (e.g. 1974) studies of the relationships between flying and settling in *Aphis fabae* show such phenomena at the behavioural level. This insect flies for a while after becoming adult and then settles on a leaf to feed. The elicitation of each of these activities has an inhibitory effect on the other. When one activity ceases, however, the previously-inhibited activity may appear with either an enhanced (antagonistic induction) or reduced (antagonistic depression) strength. Which of these effects occurs depends on the precise conditions, such as the nature of the leaf surface, the strength of the settling response at previous landings, and the length of time the insect has been flying. Kennedy suggests that it is not the performance of one activity which has the inductive and depressive after-effects on the other, but the stimuli which elicit it. He suggests that the stimulus, in eliciting one activity, simultaneously inhibits the antagonist; this inhibition then produces the after-effects. Similar mechanisms are suggested by Samways (1977) for the disruption of the species song of the bush cricket *Platycleis intermedia* when this insect is caged with an individual *P. affinis* (figure 3.2). The normally homogeneous series of disyllabic sound emissions (chirps) of *P. intermedia* can be thrown by the long emissions of *P. affinis* into an inhibition/excitation cycle involving post-inhibitory rebound. The chirp duration, which is species-specific, is the most behaviourally mutable song component, and such interspecific acoustic interactions illustrate the extent to which variation of song components takes place without involving long-term changes in physiological and environmental conditions. However, whereas Kennedy's aphids were reacting to an independent extraneous stimulation, Samways' bush crickets were interacting, so that the animal's response to the stimulus, in

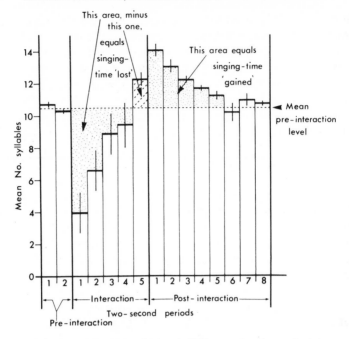

**Figure 3.2** Mean time singing (syllables produced per 2 s) by *Platycleis intermedia* before, during and after a duet with *P. affinis*. Analysis of thirty duets from one song sequence of one pair of bush crickets. The singing time "gained" at the postinteraction was c. 85% of that "lost" during the interaction (from Samways, 1977).

effect, changed that stimulus, since the two species produced a perfect alteration of duets and inhibitions.

A "threshold" type of model has often been used to explain short-term switching between alternative behaviour patterns (see Dawkins, 1969, for references) and for the addition of more complex sequences into a behaviour pattern. Dawkins used the example of a chick presented with two food sources. Since the chick cannot peck simultaneously at two targets, Dawkins suggests that it could go into a state of being equally likely to peck at either. Which food source is pecked may then be determined by which target the chick is oriented towards, i.e. the probability of occurrence of a particular behaviour may be determined statistically on a "threshold" basis. The predictions of such a statistical model (concerning the proportions of different types of choice) do show good agreement with data obtained from experiment. Another "threshold" model was suggested by Bastock and Manning (1955) for *Drosophila* courtship, because of the way in which three behaviour patterns were "super-imposed" on each other. Orientation was the low-threshold activity and could occur by itself; wing vibration only occurred if orientation also did; and "licking", with the highest threshold, only occurred super-imposed on vibration and orientation. This model is based on experi-mental observation and implies that these behavioural sequences may be arranged as a hierarchical sequence within the C.N.S., the higher threshold activity being triggered as a result of the stimuli obtained from the per-formance of the lower-threshold pattern. The model says nothing about the mechanisms gating the appearance of each sequence, and cannot there-fore "explain" the behaviour (but cf. mechanisms of motor control, p. 115).

"Threshold" models have proved quite popular in recent years; switch-ing from one behaviour to another and general changes in responsiveness can both be predicted by such models. A number of neurophysiological phenomena have been observed which may, in part, account for such changing thresholds of response.

*Selective attention*

The phenomenon of selective attention usually refers to a limitation of responsiveness such that some stimuli control the organism's behaviour to the exclusion of others. Peripheral filtration mechanisms based on receptor capabilities play a large part in this.

Sense organs are not mere passive transducers of the incident stimula-tion. Peripheral control of receptor activity occurs when we attend to a sound: the head position is adjusted, and the tensor tympani muscle sets the eardrum tension. In the visual system, the eyes are converged on the selected object, the lens is focused, the amount of light is adjusted by changing the diameter of the pupil, and eye movements occur to overcome retinal processes of inhibition and to maintain activity in the visual path-ways. Single touch receptor activity in isolated skin areas of the frog is facilitated by stimulation of the sympathetic nerve supply to that region. They are also facilitated by local application of epinephrine or norepine-phrine, or by introducing these hormones into the circulation. Evidently these receptors are subject to both generalized and local sympathetic control. Similar sympathetic influences are known to occur across neuro-muscular junctions, so that both the peripheral sensory and peripheral motor parts of the reflex arcs relating to touch are under some degree of central control. This influence may be a general one, since all sensory receptors receive a sympathetic supply.

Another clear example of peripheral facilitation by a hormone has been shown by Pfaff *et al.* (1974). They demonstrated that the lordosis reflex in rats was initiated when the male made contact with the back, flanks and ano-genital area of the female as he mounted her and started pelvic thrusting. Input from these areas is mediated in part, by the pudendal nerve. When previously ovariectomized females were treated with oestrogen, the receptive field of this nerve increased to include the posterior border of the rear leg. The effect could not have been a centrifugal one, because the pudendal nerve had been severed before its entry into the spinal cord.

Some stimuli are much more effective in eliciting a response than are others. The nature of the stimuli that prove to be effective makes it certain that something more than receptor mechanisms is involved in many instances.

### Centrifugal control

In many cases, the external stimuli received by an animal may be the result of its own activity, and such strong signals may cause damage, or may "blunt" the receptors' sensitivity to subsequent, much fainter signals. If the animal is able to predict when intense stimuli are going to occur, it can turn down the sensitivity of the system at a level which is peripheral enough to prevent damage to the receptors. This mechanism has been called *overload protection* (Collett, 1974). The hair cells of the lateral line of fish and amphibia are inhibited during movements of the animal and most, but not all, neuromasts (figure 2.9) receive at least one inhibitory nerve fibre. Bats emit intense cries when chasing insects and are guided to their prey by faint echoes. Henson (1965) showed that to prevent temporary deafness being produced as a result of the emission of an intense sound, which would mask the much fainter echoes, the stapedius muscle of the middle ear (figure 2.3) contracts some 4 to 10 ms before the pulse is emitted; the contraction is maximal just before the onset of the pulse. Henson calculated that this mechanism provided about 15 dB attenuation of the emitted sound. Suga and Schlegel (1972) have demonstrated another neural mechanism of attentuation in the auditory system of bats. This mechanism is located distal to the inferior colliculus. In their experiments it provided an estimated 25 dB attenuation of hearing during sound pulse emission. There is no evidence, however, for attenuation in the *auditory nerve of bats* during pulse emission, despite the known fact that centrifugal fibres passing out to the hair cells are inhibitory. These fibres occur in all mammals investigated; they arise in the region of the superior olive and terminate in the contralateral cochlea. Stimulation of the medulla of the brain, in the region of the superior olive and along the course of the olivocochlear bundle, results in the suppression of auditory nerve responses elicited by standard "click" stimulation (Galambos, 1956).

The anterior commissure of the brain of mammals contains efferent fibres which arise in the basal areas of the rhinencephalon and pass out to the olfactory bulb. These fibres are believed to terminate on granule cells and in the periventricular and external plexiform layers (figure 4.4) where they may be associated with the synaptic junctions between receptor cell processes and bulbar neurones. Indeed, there are several central inputs to the olfactory bulbs. For example:

(*a*) Large, but relatively few axons from the Diagonal Band of Broca, a distinctive band of cells in the medio-caudal telencephalon.

(*b*) Many fine axons from the anterior olfactory nucleus (some ipsi- and some contralateral via the anterior commissure).

Although these centrifugal fibres are basically inhibitory in their effects, the overall result of their activity may be either inhibitory or excitatory, depending on whether they terminate directly on principal neurones or on intrinsic cells. If they terminate on principal neurones, they may exert a direct inhibition; but if they terminate on intrinsic inhibitory cells they may achieve facilitation of the effects of primary neurones by inhibiting the inhibition.

Granit (1955) induced an augmentation of the spike frequency of individual ganglion cells in the mammalian retina when the midbrain tegmentum was stimulated, although occasionally inhibition was elicited from the same general region. Both the facilitatory and inhibitory effects are conveyed by fine efferent fibres to the retina. The central origin of these fibres is not established, but their effects are most readily initiated by stimulation of the midbrain reticular formation.

The centrifugal control of the avian retina has recently been resolved and is now amongst the better-understood systems (see e.g. Miles, 1972). In the bird, the centrifugal innervation of the retina comes from a nucleus in the posterior midbrain, the isthmo-optic nucleus (ION) which, in turn, receives its input from the optic tectum, the principal destination of the optic nerve (figure 3.3). The retina projects topographically onto the tectum and the tectum is then mapped onto the ION, the cells of which project back to that region of the retina from which, indirectly, they receive their inputs. This centrifugal system therefore forms a short feed-back loop (p. 76). The most characteristic property of the retinal ganglion cells is the organization of their receptive fields—an annular inhibitory area surrounding a small disc-shaped central area (p. 42). The main effect of the centrifugal fibres is to disrupt the surround inhibition.

The centre/surround organization of the retina is established as a result of the lateral inhibition of the retinal bipolar cells (produced by the activity of the horizontal cells, figure 2.7), and the inhibition of the retinal

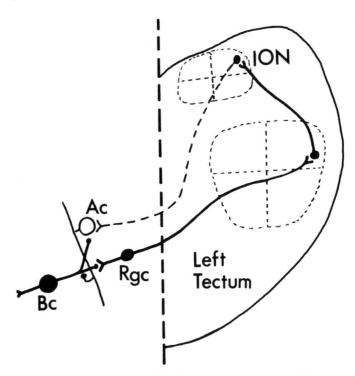

**Figure 3.3** Fibre pathways associated with the centrifugal inhibition of the avian retina. Only one half of the tectum is shown, and the optic region and the isthmo-optic nucleus (ION) are drawn out of proportion to demonstrate the topographical organization which corresponds to the contralateral retina. The isthmo-optic tract (broken line) exerts its inhibition primarily on the amacrine cells (Ac) of the retina (cf. figure 2.7). Bc, bipolar cell; Rgc, retinal ganglion cell.

ganglion cells by the activity of the amacrine cells. The amacrine cells receive their inputs from bipolar cells and provide inputs to other amacrine cells and back to bipolar cells, in addition to their inputs to the ganglion cells. It is thought that the pathway from bipolar cells is a short negative feedback loop (see p. 76). Its purpose is to cut off the bipolar input to the amacrines and to the ganglion cells, so that they respond only to transient changes in the stimulus, such as movement or brightness changes. It is believed that those ganglion cells which give a tonic response to illumination receive a sustained inhibitory surround mediated by horizontal cells; those ganglion cells with phasic responses have surrounds which show only transient inhibition, probably mediated by amacrine cells.

The centrifugal fibres in the bird terminate mostly on the amacrine cells. Electrical stimulation of the ION tract results in inhibition on the amacrines so that by a process of disinhibition (i.e. inhibition of the inhibitory amacrines) the ganglion cells become much less selective about the sort of stimuli that activate them. Miles (1972) states that these ganglion cells then become much more useful in detecting objects than in discriminating contours. This may be a way of inducing a transient increase in sensitivity when, for example, the bird turns to inspect a new area of its surroundings.

In addition to their effects on the surround area, in a small percentage of cases the centrifugal fibres have been shown to have a modulating effect directly on the centre response. In these instances, the discharge of a ganglion cell to a centrally-located light spot is facilitated; but the same ganglion cell never shows both central facilitation and surround disinhibition. The local facilitatory system will come into operation when a new stimulus comes into view or moves over a different region of the retina. The localized centrifugal discharge produced by such a stimulus will call attention to it by enhancing the response of the retinal ganglion cell. As Collett (1974) points out, this is filtration, not on the basis of a stable attribute of the stimulus (like colour or form), but on a transient one (its newness).

In addition to the control of peripheral sense organs, modulation of the activity of sensory systems also occurs within the C.N.S., e.g. in the mammals, the lateral geniculate nucleus (LGN) is the main thalamic area of synapse and relay of the retinal ganglion cell input. Centrifugal cortico-thalamic axons synapse directly onto the principal neurones of the LGN or indirectly affect LGN principal neurone output by facilitating intrinsic cell activity. The centrifugal-LGN synapses are primarily excitatory, hence the direct effects on the principal neurones will be facilitatory and the indirect effects inhibitory.

Centrifugal control may therefore occur at all levels of sensory input. In many cases, centrifugal fibres merely complete short feedback loops and may therefore act as "sharpening mechanisms". In other cases, however, the effects may be more profound. Paralleling the ascending tracts of afferent neurones from the receptor to the cortex is a descending system which links the same synaptic relay stations from above downwards. This descending system undoubtedly contributes to the perceptual process and is probably involved in the mechanism by which the amplitude of the sensory-evoked responses can be modified. This mechanism, which exerts its effects within each of the classical sensory pathways, probably acts principally by way of the brain-stem reticular formation, which is known to exert modifying influences upwards upon the cerebral and cerebellar cortex and downwards upon both sensory and motor synaptic relays (figure 3.4). However, the complexity of the neural connections in this region makes it impossible to conceive of a simple "input pathway—output pathway" arrangement. Its role must be one of modulation. The end-result of its activity may be facilitatory or inhibitory, but for many central relays it appears to be predominantly inhibitory, e.g. stimulation

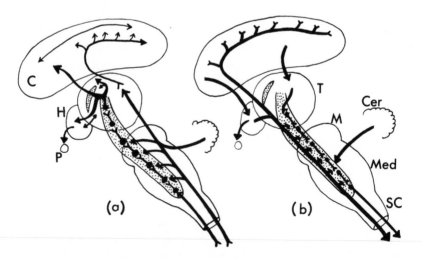

**Figure 3.4** The ascending (*a*) and descending (*b*) fibre pathways (tracts) associated with the brain stem reticular formation (dotted area). C., cortex; Cer, cerebellum; H, hypothalamus; M, midbrain; Med, medulla; P, pituitary; SC, spinal cord; T, thalamus.

of the mesencephalic reticular formation causes a marked reduction in the amplitude of auditory-evoked responses recorded from the dorsal cochlear nucleus. This occurs even when the electrical responses recorded from the round window in response to the same sensory stimuli are unaffected.

The reticular formation may be the site of two (not independent) functions:

(i) The behavioural and neurophysiological evidence suggests that the sensory pathways are plastic rather than fixed in the transmission of afferent information. Regions such as the reticular formation may provide an "active organizing principle" which selects and further modifies sensory messages. In this way, the involvement of the higher levels of the C.N.S. with those signals of least significance to the individual may be decreased.

(ii) To this consideration should be added the fact that there is no physiological boundary between central sensory and motor mechanisms. Each central pattern for the initiation of movement has its neuronal repercussions upon central sensory patterns, and each performed movement introduces alterations in sensory input patterns. In this way, sensory and motor mechanisms are bound together both internally and externally, e.g. the signals received from the touch receptors of the finger-tips while an object is being manipulated, or the texture of the surface is being explored, will depend upon the kind of movements made, their speed and their extents. Furthermore, exploratory movements made, may in turn, depend both on what the sensory input is and also on one's hypothesis of what the sensory input represents (see p. 115). The reticular formation is well placed to perform such interactions between sensory and motor activity.

Barlow (1961) has pointed out that most sensory messages contain a great deal of redundancy and could advantageously be compressed before recognition is attempted. If the redundancy in the messages was reduced in stages, the result of which was reversible and dependent upon the relevant parameters, the complexity of the perceptual process would be greatly reduced. As an example of a redundancy-reducing mechanism, Barlow cites lateral inhibition, where there is evidence that the existence of the mechanism is related to the existence in the input of the very sort of redundancy it removes. Thus, lateral inhibition does not occur in the dark-adapted retina of mammals, but does under conditions of uniform background illumination. It therefore seems to be a consequence of the correlated activity of many receptor cells. Comparable mechanisms could exist at higher levels of the C.N.S., each dealing with a specific form of redundancy in the animal's environment. Thus, making new discriminations may be the result, not of establishing new pathways to deal with "novel" stimuli, but of redefining strategies for the removal of any accompanying redundancy. The strategy used will be determined by the stimulus situation itself. Barlow suggests that constant features (always present) in the stimulus situation cause particular types of redundancy in the sensory messages, and the nervous system modifies its code appropriately to eliminate them. Broadbent (e.g. 1971) has proposed that the sensory information must pass through a series of "limited-capacity filters" before it is fully analyzed. This concept is comparable to that of Barlow if it is accepted that the filter capacity is determined by the stimulus situation itself. In any case, the higher levels of the C.N.S. will receive qualitatively-valid but quantitatively-reduced information about the stimulus situation, making recognition much easier (cf. the examples of central integration given on pp. 103–115).

The clamp or inhibition of a particular pathway by these mechanisms becomes the "result" of the patterning mechanism which, on the basis of internal and external cues, determines which stimuli will be "attended to" and which responses will be "allowed" to occur. The reticular formation is ideally placed to perform such integrative functions.

*Feedback control*

At the level of specific pathways, whether sensory or motor, general principles of feedback control may also operate. These mechanisms have been reviewed by McFarland (1971; for a general treatment of feedback control see Ashby, 1958, 1960).

The output of a system may depend only on the input; when the output in no way influences the input, the control mechanism is said to be "open-loop". An important property of open-loop systems is that they allow a direct and rapid change of output with change of input. It is found in rapid eye and limb movements in humans and prey-catching movements in invertebrates such as cephalopods and mantids. However, when the output does influence the subsequent input by feeding its information back to the input stage, "closed-loop" control operates. Such a closed-loop system provides constant information about ongoing activity in the output stage, so that the effect of the input can be modulated. "Positive feedback" occurs when the consequences of the output *increase* the subsequent output. An example is the effect of the release of the milk from the mother's breast as a result of suckling by the baby. The very act of suckling increases the amount of sensory information being passed back into the C.N.S. from receptors in the nipple; the effect of this increased activity is to increase the flow of milk. When the consequences of the output *decrease* the subsequent output, on the other hand, "negative feedback" occurs. Since the effect of the initial stimulus is decreased under negative feedback control, such systems tend towards stability and equilibrium. Most of the physiological processes in the body achieve their homeostatic characteristics by means of negative feedback control.

The mammalian muscle spindle responds to changes in the length of the skeletal muscle (figure 3.5). Extension of the muscle (extrafusal fibres) pulls on the muscle spindle lying in parallel and gives rise to afferent impulses which excite the skeletal muscles' own motor neurones to bring about reflex contraction of that muscle. The spindle system provides a

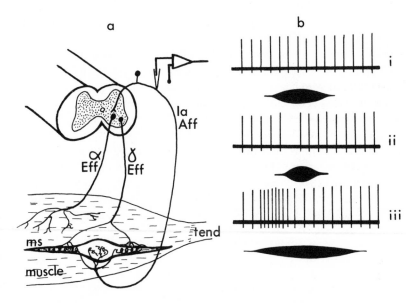

**Figure 3.5**   The mammalian muscle spindle and its responses.

(*a*) The innervation of the muscle and muscle spindle (ms). The muscle spindle lies in parallel with the skeletal muscle fibres, and its extensions are themselves contractile. These regions are innervated by the $\gamma$-efferent fibres; the skeletal muscle is innervated by the $\alpha$-efferent fibres. The sensory endings of the muscle spindle are of two types: the annulo-spiral endings in the contractile portions, and the nuclear bag endings in the central region.

(*b*) The responses of the Ia afferent fibre under three different skeletal muscle states. In (i) the muscle is at rest, the muscle tone producing a low background level of activity (upper). Voluntary contraction of the muscle (ii) "unhooks" the spindle, and activity ceases for a short time until the contraction state of the spindle readjusts. In (iii) the muscle is passively stretched, producing an increased pull on the spindle; this results in an increase in spindle response until the system is "reset". The spindle can, therefore, provide information about the state of the skeletal muscle.

negative feedback in a closed-loop system. The adjustment of graded voluntary movement depends upon the fact that the equilibrium length of the muscle spindles is adjustable. The ends of the spindles are themselves contractile (intrafusal fibres), receiving a motor supply (the $\gamma$-efferents) from the ventral horn of the spinal cord (Granit, 1975). If the efferents cause the ends of the spindle to contract, the sensory "nuclear" portion will be stretched and its rate of discharge will increase. As a result, the muscle reflex will be initiated and the extrafusal fibres will shorten until the increased rate of discharge of the intrafusal fibres is offset. Skeletal muscles can therefore be made to contract either through the activity of the $\gamma$-efferents and the feedback loop, or directly by the activity of motor fibres. In reality, the system is far more complex, since extrafusal muscle contraction is also modulated by the activity of Golgi tendon organs which lie in series with the extrafusal fibres, in the tendons of the muscles. The Golgi tendon organs' activity is increased during passive stretch and during active contractions; they inhibit the activity of motor neurones. Further inhibition may occur *via* the small Renshaw cells in the ventral horn of the spinal cord. Collateral branches from the motor neurones themselves feed back to form excitatory synapses with the Renshaw cells. These, in turn, exert an inhibitory influence on the motor neurone pool to which they distribute.

The precise mechanisms of motor control are therefore extremely complex and are still the subject of intensive investigation.

### The "reafference" principle

Sensory feedback as a result of movement is often needed to ensure that the movement is made in accord with the original command. In a scheme elaborated by von Holst (1954), the nervous system predicts the sensory consequences of a movement and subtracts an equivalent signal from the resultant sensory input. A signal of zero appearing after the subtraction means that the movement was made correctly, while any departure from zero will suggest either an additional stimulus or an incorrect movement. Hinde (1970) has used the term "Sollwert" (or "the should-be value") to define the condition of equilibrium between the predicted value and the resultant sensory input. In the control of motor activity by the muscle spindle described above, the Sollwert is achieved when the lengths of muscle and muscle spindle bear a certain relation to each other. In the control of skilled movements, the cerebellum plays a part in comparing an actual movement, as indicated by proprioceptive feedback, with a Sollwert received from the cerebral cortex (see also p. 119). Such control mechanisms may therefore occur at all levels of the nervous system.

The model has also been applied to the orientation of animals to their environment. When a fly is placed on the axis of a cylinder painted with vertical stripes and the cylinder is rotated, the animal will turn in the same direction. This is known as the optomotor response. The same movement of the image on the eye occurs during locomotion and does not effect optomotor turning movements. The difference in behaviour in these two cases depends essentially on the distinction between "exafferent" stimuli produced by movement of the external world, and "reafferent" stimuli which are the result of its own movement (von Holst and Mittelstaedt, 1950). They suggested that the mechanisms by which the cause of the retinal displacement are correctly interpreted can be understood if we accept the existence of a "comparator" mechanism within the C.N.S. (figure 3.6). This comparator receives information from two sources: one, which is a copy of the command to move the eyes, and two, which is the movement perceived by the eye. If the eyes move to the right, the transformed copy of the motor signal will be compared with a signal caused by the displacement of the retinal image to the right. If the two signals are equal in value, the output of the comparator is zero, and no environmental movement is apparent. If, on the other hand, the environment moves, no motor commands occur and the comparator interprets the environmental movement as "real".

Similar phenomena occur in mammals, and the levels at which such comparisons are performed are just beginning to receive attention. Horn and Hill (1969) studied the preferred orientation of simple cells in the visual cortex of the cat (p. 112) when the head and body were rotated. These cells respond to bars or edges in a preferred orientation. When the cat was tilted, some of the units showed compensatory changes such that the preferred orientation did not rotate with the eye. This compensatory response may be mediated by a vestibular input to the visual cortex.

It should now be apparent that the level of the responsiveness of an animal may be the result of a number of factors: hormonal influences, both peripheral and central; threshold changes and modulation of the activity of receptors and sensory pathways by centrifugal control; modulation of motor activity by central and peripheral feedback mechanisms; and central mechanisms of analysis which compare the sensory and motor activity. The short and long-term changes in an animal's responsiveness to a given stimulus can therefore be explained, to a large extent, by

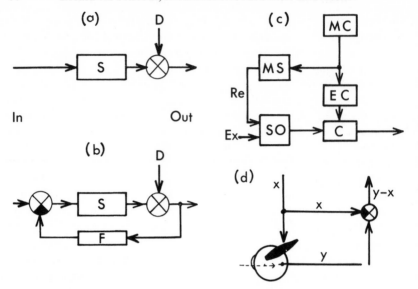

**Figure 3.6** Simple open (*a*) and closed (*b*) loop systems. S, system characteristics; F, feedback information; D, displacement.

(*c*) A simple reafference system in block diagram form. MC, motor centre; MS, motor system; SO, sense organ; EC, efference copy of motor output; C, comparator.

(*d*) The reafference principle as applied to the control of eye movements: the efference copy (x) is compared with the input from the retina (y). See text for further details.

known mechanisms that are not entirely located within the C.N.S. In other words, many of the "intervening variables" of behaviour become perfectly "admissible" when considered at a neurophysiological level.

A problem we have not yet considered, however, concerns the mechanisms which actually *determine* the level of responsiveness. What actually *sets* the levels of activity in these variable control systems? In other words, what sets the gate level for behaviour? As stated on page 62, this phenomenon has been "explained" as being due to "motivational state". We shall now consider whether this term can be more rigorously applied.

## Motivational gating

A wide variety of behavioural phenomena has been described whereby the existence of motivational factors can be inferred, e.g. some species of cichlid fish, when in the parental phase, may guard or "lead" *Daphnia* as if they were their offspring. In this state they respond to the characteristics that *Daphnia* share with their young rather than to their food characteristics. The influence of the strength of external stimulation (measured by the size of the female) and the internal state (measured by the colour pattern of the male) was determined for the courtship behaviour of male guppies *Lebistes reticulatus* by Baerends *et al.* (1955). They showed that the same response pattern (posturing, sigmoid intention, full sigmoid, in increasing values of response strength) may appear with a range of combinations of internal state and external stimuli. Similarly Leong (1969) found that different components of the colour patterns of territorial males of cichlid fish *Haplochromis burtoni*, painted on dummies, were additive in their effects upon attack rates. The consequence of these findings is that, as motivational factors increase, objects having fewer and fewer characteristics in common with the natural object are adequate to produce a response of given intensity; the range of effective stimuli therefore increases. Aggressive behaviour is normally directed towards another individual and is elicited by visual, auditory and olfactory stimuli (or a combination of these) received from another individual. Further, in most species, fighting occurs only in spring when the gonads are active and sex hormones are being released. But additional short-term changes may also occur, even when external factors are apparently constant. A male bird may at one moment be feeding quietly on his territory in the company of other individuals, but the next moment he may fly to his song position and attack any bird within a considerable distance. We must therefore assume that temporary central states occur independently of the more long-term hormonal changes.

The occurrence of high levels of circulating male or female sex hormones is also an important factor in controlling courtship behaviour. Marler (1961) argues that an understanding of the stimuli eliciting male courtship in the jumping spider is difficult except in terms of a motivationally-dominated response-specific mechanism for stimulus selection. The strongest responses occur to visual patterns with a certain size and orientation, divided into thorax and abdomen, with legs having a particular size and orientation to the body, and with the black-and-white species pattern on the abdomen. Outside the breeding season, however, the response disappears and all models evoke either prey-catching or avoidance behaviour, depending on size.

The action of oestrogen on the C.N.S. was first demonstrated by the implantation of stilboestrol or oestradiol into the brains of ovariectomized cats, when sexual behaviour was totally restored and even augmented to the level of nymphomania (Harris *et al.*, 1958). The genital tract remained in complete anoestrus, so that the hormones must be assumed to have acted directly on the nervous system. Comparable data are available for rats (Lisk, 1962). Implantation of oestradiol in the medial-basal preoptic and anterior hypothalamus regions of spayed rats produce behavioural sexual receptivity. Androgens may influence male sexual behaviour by acting specifically on the same regions. We must stress yet again that these regions cannot be called sex areas: the hormone controls (or modulates) the probability of occurrence of sexual behaviour, but it does *not control its form*. (A good introduction to the role of sexual hormones in behaviour is given by Slater, 1978.)

Numerous examples are also available on the elicitation of recognizable behaviour patterns by intracranial electrical stimulation. By way of illustration we shall consider the work of Flynn *et al.* (e.g. 1970) who chronically implanted electrodes in the brain of awake and unrestrained cats. Two types of behaviour could be elicited by stimulation. One, termed "affective attack", was characterized by piloerection, hissing and growling; the other, termed "quiet biting attack" was more direct and rarely accompanied by the type of display seen with affective attack. The anaesthetized rats made available to the cats during brain stimulation were usually killed by a nape-bite at the end of a quiet biting attack, whereas they were scratched and bitten at other places during an affective attack. Quiet biting attack equates more with behaviour shown during a predatory attack, while affective attack equates more closely to behaviour shown in intraspecific encounters and defence. Quiet biting attacks were elicited by stimulation of regions in the thalamus, hypothalamus and midbrain; affective attacks from the stria terminalis, hypothalamus and midbrain. The hypothalmic sites from which quiet biting was obtained tended to be more lateral than affective attack sites, indicating that each kind of attack is mediated by distinct neural substrates (figure 3.7). Simulation *sites* must not be taken to mean control *areas*. Electrical stimulation of an unpatterned nature can activate ascending or descending pathways just as easily (and with greater likelihood) as integrative centres. The fact that the same behaviour pattern can be elicited from (at least) three sites of the brain should be an indication of the care that must be taken in the interpretation of the data.

When other sites in the brain were stimulated concurrently with hypothalamic sites that elicited attack, it was shown that various regions of the amygdala, hippocampus and midline thalamus had either facilitatory

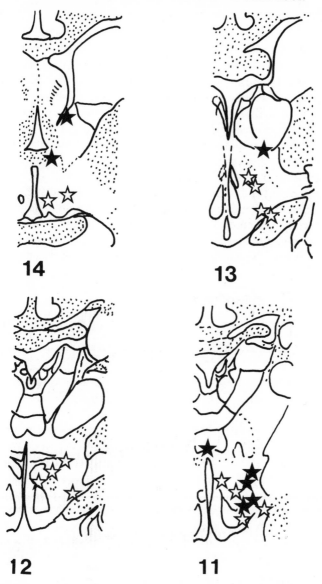

**Figure 3.7**   Some of the hypothalamic sites from which quiet biting (☆) and attack with display (★) could be elicited in awake and un-restrained cats. Numerals refer to number of millimetres anterior to horizontal plane through external auditory canals (redrawn from Flynn *et al.*, 1970).

or inhibitory effects on the attack behaviour, depending on the particular locus of stimulation within these areas. Areas that influenced elicited attack behaviour in this way (but which did not, when stimulated alone, elicit attack behaviour) were termed *modulating mechanisms*.

Flynn *et al.* (1970) also found a number of effects of hypothalamic attack site stimulation on the sensory and motor mechanisms involved in the attack, e.g. when the motor nucleus of the trigeminal nerve was stimulated to bring about jaw closure, concurrent stimulation of the hypothalamus increased the effect quite dramatically (figure 3.8). Stimulation of hypothalamic sites other than those that would elicit attack did not increase the strength of trigeminal nucleus-elicited jaw closure.

Influence on the sensory input by the hypothalamic sites was shown by experiments where the lips and facial area around the mouth were probed while hypothalamic attack sites were stimulated. With increasing hypothalamic stimulation, the field around the mouth that, when probed, resulted in head turning and biting, increased in size (figure 3.9). When

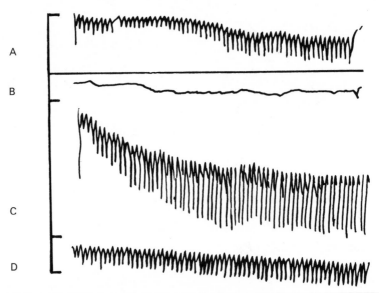

**Figure 3.8** Closing movements of the jaw in cats subject to:
    A. Stimulation of the motor nucleus of the trigeminal nerve.
    B. Stimulation of an "attack site" in the hypothalamus.
    C. Combined effect of A and B.
    D. Combined effect of A and stimulation at a non-attack site in the hypothalamus (modified from Flynn *et al.*, 1970).

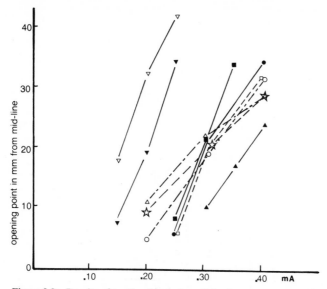

**Figure 3.9**   Results of tactile stimulation of the lips concurrent with hypothalamic attack site stimulation (9 cats). A tactile stimulus was moved from the corner of the cat's mouth towards the midline. The first point at which mouth opening occurred was measured for various intensities of stimulation of the hypothalamus. The mean distance from the midline increased with increasing stimulation. The entire region from the midline to the opening point was effective for the elicitation of jaw opening (modified from Flynn *et al.*, 1970).

the probe was moved inwards from the corner of the mouth to the midline during low-intensity hypothalamic stimulation, the mouth opened when the probe came level with the upper canine of that side. At higher intensities of hypothalamic stimulation, touching the corner of the mouth was sufficient to induce opening.

"Biases" in the visual system were also shown to occur during stimulation of the hypothalamic attack sites. The influence of the reticular formation was eliminated in this case by lesioning large areas of the mesencephalon. Subsequent recordings from the visual cortex showed that the responses of cortical neurones to moving slits changed as a direct result of concurrent hypothalamic stimulation.

As a result of this and other work, Flynn *et al.* (1970) formulated a general scheme of how brain stimulation brings about attack behaviour in unrestrained cats (figure 3.10). Since areas such as the lateral hypothalamus, central midbrain grey and the reticular formation have multi-

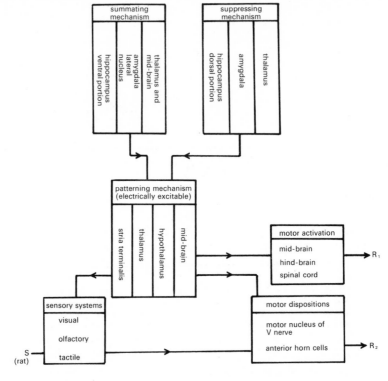

**Figure 3.10** Central nervous areas implicated in elicited attack behaviour in cats (after Flynn *et al.*, 1970).

synaptic connections with both ascending sensory and descending motor systems (p. 74), electrical stimulation of "attack sites" in these areas is thought of as putting a particular bias on these neural systems. These biases form a particular pattern (hence the term *patterning* mechanism) that increases the probability of a particular response (attack) being given to a particular input (sight of rat). The motor mechanisms bringing about attack are influenced in two ways by the patterning mechanism: first, there is direct activation of certain motor elements (elements of affective display such as ear flattening can be elicited even from anaesthetized cats); second, there is facilitation or a predisposition towards the performance of other motor elements, provided that a target is present. Furthermore, the patterning mechanisms effect a gating of particular sensory inputs such as to enhance behaviours orientated to a relevant target.

A similar concept probably applies to the generation of the species-specific song pattern in crickets (Gryllidae). There is now strong evidence (see Huber, 1974, 1975, 1978 for reviews) that chirp and syllable rhythms of the song are programmed entirely within the thoracic nerve cord. However, the calling, courtship and aggressive songs can be elicited by stimulation or lesioning of the mushroom body and central complex of the brain (figure 4.5). Low-intensity stimulation elicits calling; with increasing stimulation intensity, calling song may be changed to courtship, and then to aggression. The early interpretation of the results of these experiments suggested that the descending motor "command" fibres' activity was patterned in the brain and then delivered to the motor neurone pools of the thoracic ganglia. However, it has since been established (Huber, 1975, 1978, and Bentley, 1977) that the activity in descending command fibres is not temporally-patterned according to the song type. Electrical stimulation of an identified premotor interneurone induces normal calling song pattern in the fight muscles, and the stimulus need not contain any timing cues for the song pattern. The role of the mushroom body and central complex cannot therefore be the establishment of the song *pattern*. Rowell (1963) suggested that the results obtained from early stimulation and lesioning experiments were primarily caused by the experimentally-induced alteration of the animal's responsiveness to sensory inputs. Although the ascending acoustic interneurones have not yet been traced directly to the mushroom body, other sensory inputs (e.g. from the antennae and eyes) have; the inputs from the acoustic neurones may be indirect, *via* small-diameter fibres not yet isolated. It has been suggested that the roles of the mushroom body and central complex may be to change the ongoing behaviour pattern to another, this change being the direct result of a change in the total sensory input and the level of inherent activity in feedback loops (Lewis and Broughton, 1980).

Thus, in both vertebrates and invertebrates, motivational mechanisms may be involved in the process of stimulus filtration, biasing the input and output so as to increase the probability of occurrence of relevant responses.

### Conclusions

In our discussions of motivational gating we have briefly referred to only a few of the behavioural and neurophysiological studies relevant to this area. Motivational gating has been put forward from evidence gained primarily from a series of studies on elicited aggressive behaviour in cats.

Supportive evidence from studies on other "motivational systems" (and the purist must forgive us for using this convenient "shorthand" term) is not strong. However, there is no reason to suppose that motivational systems as diverse as, for example, aggression and drinking, should operate in similar ways.

One common feature of many studies in the neural substrates of behaviour is the apparent involvement of the hypothalamus. It has been implicated in a variety of "motivational systems" in many vertebrates. At one time, for example, a "satiety centre" in the ventromedial hypothalamus and a "feeding centre" in the lateral hypothalamus were thought to control feeding behaviour in mammals. However, it is now suspected that most of the effects brought about were the result of interference, not with hypothalamic neurones, but with fibres of passage through the hypothalamus, in particular, tracts between midbrain and telencephalon. It is becoming increasingly unlikely that motivational centres, as such, exist at all. In fact, even thinking in terms of "motivational circuitry" is probably a gross oversimplification. Any activity above the reflex level probably involves extensive and widely separated areas of the nervous system.

Animals rarely attempt the performance of incompatible activities at any one time. This would be maladaptive. Competitive inhibition between activated "systems" in the nervous system is one way of promoting this "singlemindedness of action". Competitive inhibition is an established mechanism in certain parts of the nervous system and is discussed in chapter 4. The struggle to direct ongoing behaviour would be won by the most highly activated competitor. The biasing of the input is a feasible method of producing enhanced input of a certain kind that would, in turn, produce central biases that would tend to swing competition in a particular direction. However, we do not think that biasing an input can explain features of motivated behaviour such as its spontaneity and apparent goal directedness; there are many ways of biasing central nervous activity other than by direct sensory input.

So far, we have very limited evidence regarding the nature of centrifugal and allied effects on sensory input in invertebrates. There are, as yet, no firm grounds for suggesting that behaviour is controlled in the same ways in invertebrates and vertebrates, though there must be a very limited number of similar ways. The semi-autonomous role of the ventral ganglia in invertebrates results in a degree of localization of filtration mechanisms that has no correlate in the vertebrates.

We started this chapter with a consideration of an early model put forward by ethologists to account for stimulus filtration and changing levels of responsiveness. The Lorenzian model made an important contribution in that it organized our thinking about innate behaviour. In the light of our discussions in this chapter, it is of interest to see where we have now come to differ.

First, we now believe that stimulus filtration results from activity at the receptor and at every synapse in the sensory pathway. A discrete mechanism, the IRM, is no longer a necessary part of the model.

Second, we have very different ideas about "motivational systems"; they are not represented by discrete areas of the C.N.S. and, although we have used the term "motivational system", we suspect that this itself is a gross oversimplification of processes involving changing temporal and spatial patterns of activity in the nervous system, no two of which will ever be identical. The buildup of particular *kinds* of activity in the C.N.S. predisposing towards the performance of certain *kinds* of behaviour is probably the result, not of "specific action energy" building up in a reservoir, but of input from many sources: external events, internal cues and other activities in the C.N.S.

Scanty though the evidence is at present, it is a distinct possibility that particular kinds of activity in the C.N.S. can, *via* centrifugal and feedback mechanisms, bias input in such a way as to enhance further the level of that particular kind of activity. Setting of gate levels in this way may also be a feature of motor systems and, if this is so, we have a possible partial explanation of both changes in response threshold and the neural mechanisms underlying response specificity.

# CHAPTER FOUR

# INTEGRATION AND THE CONTROL
# OF BEHAVIOUR

## Introduction

The contribution of the sense organs to the overall filtration ability of the nervous system was outlined in some detail in chapter 2. In chapter 3 we showed that the appearance of a behavioural response to a stimulus is dependent upon "motivational" factors, over and above stimulus reception. These modulating influences rely heavily on the filtration and gating mechanisms available to the nervous system. In this chapter we shall consider how the C.N.S. actually performs this filtration of information and gating of behaviour.

The basic mechanisms of filtration and integration are common to all the modalities and are present because the nervous system, in all animals, is composed of the long processes (or axons) and cell bodies of nerve cells, and the supporting cells. Typically, information transfer over long distances occurs along the axons, the information being carried as a pulse code of action potentials. Action potentials are produced as a result of a transient change in axonal membrane permeability specifically to sodium ($Na^+$). The energy for the action potential is provided by the gradient of $Na^+$ concentration from the outside of the cell to the inside. It is therefore a physical process; ATP is necessary only for maintenance of the original gradient and for the recovery from depolarization. Because of this, the amplitude, duration and conduction rate of the action potential is said to be the same over the whole length of the axon. In other words, it is all-or-nothing (i.e. non-summative), non-decremental, and of constant speed. In the majority of cases, the axons make functional, but not structural, contact with the succeeding cell, in a manner usually considered to be a hierarchical sequence. Most of the central analysis and integration of information occurs at these junctions (or synapses), since these are the regions where the non-decremental action potentials can be modified. The classical understanding of the integrative action of the nervous system relies on such synaptic processing. However, in recent years, our understanding of the activity of the nerve fibre during the transmission of information has resulted in a re-interpretation of the belief that the axon is the "fundamental unit" of the nervous system. Thus, our first consideration of the mechanisms of integration and the control of behaviour must be at the level of the nerve fibres.

Understanding these mechanisms will then allow us to consider some examples of the complex integrative properties of the olfactory, auditory and visual systems. As we shall see, the complexity of organization of the central sensory pathways is such that we are forced to this conclusion: the amazing feature of the nervous system is not that behaviour varies from time to time but that, by all measureable criteria, the same behaviour pattern can ever be repeated. The questions we must ask then are: what are the mechanisms that bring about this repeatability? can we pinpoint specific generating mechanisms governing particular patterns of behaviour? how is it that the same muscles used in flight, walking and singing in insects, for example, can have these different patterns imposed on their activity?

## Mechanisms of filtration and integration

### Synaptic processes

In the informational sense, nervous transmission is a binary code. Changes in this binary code can occur (in the main) only at the junctions between neurones, because of the all-or-nothing non-decremental nature of the action potential (p. 30). These junctions, or synapses, can be classified into two main types:

(i) Electrical synapses or ephapses, where contact between neurones is either direct physical contact or *via* gaps of less than about 10 nm.

(ii) Chemical synapses, where the larger gaps (15–60 nm) and the large surface area (and therefore high resistance) of the postsynaptic membrane, compared to that of the pre-synaptic process, prevents direct electrical transference. Instead, synaptic transmission is effected by the release of chemical transmitter molecules.

Many specific transmitter substances have been isolated from central nervous systems, but for our purposes they can be divided into two groups: excitatory and inhibitory (for an extended consideration of synapses see Cottrell and Usherwood, 1977). A common excitatory transmitter in the C.N.S. is acetylcholine (ACh), gamma-amino-butyric acid (GABA) being an inhibitor. All transmitters are released from the vesicles present in the terminal endings (boutons) of the presynaptic fibre and diffuse across the synaptic cleft to the postsynaptic membrane where, by becoming attached to receptor sites, they change the membrane permeability to ions. The minimum amount of transmitter that can be released is that contained in one vesicle; synaptic transmission is therefore said to be *quantal*. The sequence of events which follows the reaction of a transmitter molecule with a receptor site depends upon whether the synapse is excitatory or inhibitory. Excitatory cholinergic synapses usually result in a change of postsynaptic membrane permeability to sodium and potassium ions, but not to chloride, the net result being a decrease in the transmembrane potential towards zero. This potential change is called an excitatory postsynaptic potential (EPSP). Inhibitory transmitters result in IPSPs brought about by an increase in postsynaptic membrane permeability to either potassium or chloride—the membrane potential increases to a value greater than the resting potential, i.e. the cell becomes hyperpolarized. In all cases calcium ions are necessary for adequate synaptic functioning.

All postsynaptic potentials have characteristics similar to those of receptor potentials: they are summative and decremental. The post-synaptic membrane therefore differs from that of the remainder of the nerve cell membrane in being electrically inexcitable. Neurones make their synaptic contact with each other in a variety of ways: synapses occur between axons (axo-axonal synapses), axons and somata (axo-somatic synapses), axons and dendrites (axo-dendritic synapses), and between dendrites (dendro-dendritic synapses). On the other hand, action potential production, for forward propagation to the next synaptic level, occurs at some distance from the synaptic cleft. In the frog skeletal muscle, the non-synaptic membrane adjacent to the synapse is capable of generating an all-or-none action potential, but in the majority of central neurones (e.g. most motor cells) the site of spike production is the axon hillock region or the first node of Ranvier.

Neurones with profusely-branched dendritic processes, such as the pyramidal cells on the mammalian cerebral cortex, receive synaptic inputs from hundreds or even thousands of other neurones. This principle of *convergence* (Sherrington, 1909) is of general applicability in the nervous system, as indeed is the complementary principle of *divergence*, whereby one neurone diverges to send processes to many nerve cells (figure 4.1 and p. 103). The existence of a large number of synaptic inputs to the post-synaptic cell, each of which may have origin in a different source or modality, has important implications for the functioning of the central nervous system. In the first instance, it is clear that the output of the postsynaptic cell will be the integrated result of previously independent activity. However, not all this activity will be equally effective. The spatial arrangement of the synapses on the postsynaptic cell (i.e. the distance between an active synapse and the spike initiating region) is of fundamental importance because of the decremental nature of the postsynaptic potentials; the greater this distance is, the greater the likelihood that the postsynaptic potential will diminish in amplitude to a subthreshold value by the time it spreads to the spike-initiating region. A subthreshold potential at this position will not, of course, trigger spike production. On the basis of the spatial arrangement alone, all other factors being equal, those synapses furthest from the spike initiating region are least likely to trigger an action potential. The inputs to the postsynaptic cell are therefore weighted in "importance" (figure 4.2).

However, all other factors are not equal. The summative characteristic of the postsynaptic potential means that two excitatory postsynaptic potentials occurring together in time or space can sum to produce a larger EPSP, whose amplitude at the spike-initiating region may now be above threshold value (figure 4.2). The output of the cell is now the result

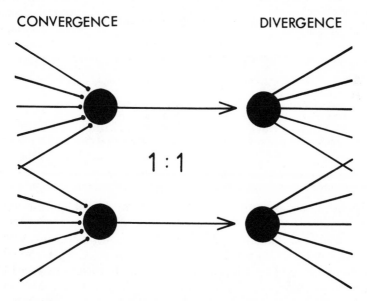

**CONVERGENCE**                **DIVERGENCE**

1 : 1

**Figure 4.1**    Convergence and divergence of neural connections within the C.N.S.

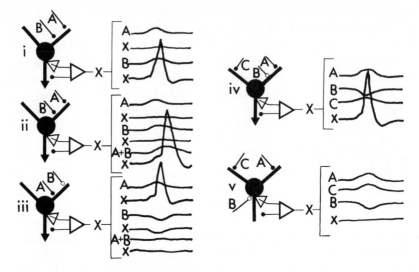

**Figure 4.2** Synaptic integration in the C.N.S.

(i) An action potential is produced in the postsynaptic cell (X) only when excitatory input B is active; excitatory input A is considered to be so far from the spike-initiating region that the EPSP it produces is subthreshold at the spike-initiating region.

(ii) Temporal summation of A and B is necessary for spike production.

(iii) Input A alone results in spike activity in X; input B is inhibitory, and temporal summation of A and B results in spike inhibition.

(iv) The addition of another excitatory input (C), however, restores spike activity.

(v) Inhibition at the spike-initiating region (B) effectively shuts off the cell (X) regardless of the activity of excitatory inputs A and C. The resultant activity shown here is only diagrammatic; the actual output of a given postsynaptic cell will depend upon the magnitude of the excitatory and inhibitory input and on the spatial organization of excitatory and inhibitory synapses. The figure represents some possible conditions.

of the spatial arrangement of synapses and the number of excitatory synapses active.

Temporal and spatial algebraic summation also occurs between excitatory and inhibitory synapses when the effect is the prevention or termination of spike production (figure 4.2.). If such activity occurs sequentially in time, or if the spatial arrangements of the excitatory and inhibitory synapses are not comparable, then the resultant output of the postsynaptic cell will be determined by:

(i) the spatial arrangement of excitatory and inhibitory synapses;
(ii) the number of excitatory and inhibitory synapses active at a given time;
(iii) the temporal sequence of excitatory/inhibitory synaptic activity.

Such complex integrative activity by a postsynaptic cell within the central nervous system requires that the spike-initiating region be divorced from the integrating region. This is probably why spike production occurs on the final common pathway—the axon base. Inhibition at this point will therefore shut off the cell totally, regardless of the input; alternatively, presynaptic inhibition of a single input modulates the activity of the postsynaptic cell by turning off that input alone; inhibition at the base of one dendrite will turn off that dendrite; and so on (figure 4.2). A precise arrangement of synaptic inputs is therefore necessary to produce the required output in *each* postsynaptic cell.

*Axonal processes*

Until recently, all modification of neuronal activity was thought to occur at synaptic junctions. Although this region remains of prime importance, recent studies of the physiology of axonal transport indicates that the propagation of the action potential along a single axon is not an unchanging phenomenon. Changes in rate, duration and amplitude have been shown to occur in regions of special geometry, such as branch points and points of sudden change in axon diameter (figure 4.3). Further, the channelling of different information into different branches or sections of a single axon depends on the past history of the axon's activity. Such modifications are not especially surprising when the underlying mechanisms of action potential production are understood, but they have, nevertheless, taken a long time to become recognized.

The magnitude of the resting potential of a neurone is the result of the ionic gradients and the surface area of the membrane. The larger the surface area, the larger the current necessary to achieve depolarization, and the larger the amplitude of the action potential. The smaller the diameter of the axon, the greater the resistance to current flow, and the slower the speed of propagation. The current generated by an action potential in a small-diameter region of the neurone will therefore depolarize an adjacent large-diameter region only with difficulty. However, if as a result of a build-up of current in the region of diameter increase, the larger region is depolarized to threshold, the regenerative mechanisms in the membrane produce a spike of larger amplitude and

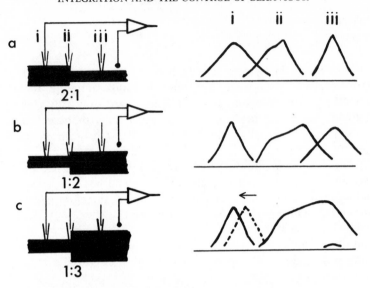

**Figure 4.3** The changes in the action potential shape with changes in axon diameter. The action potential is represented as having been recorded at three different positions along the axon (i, ii, iii). Electrode (ii) is at the position of the change in axon core diameter. The responses recorded at the three positions are shown on the right. Complicated changes in action potential shape occur at the transition points: with a step increase of less than 1:3 (*b*), the action potential is propagated in a forward direction, but when the increase is 1:3 or greater, forward propagation fails. The long duration of the potential change at the transition point means, however, that the refractory period of the narrower portion is over and reverse propagation then occurs (data after Golstein and Rall, 1974).

greater duration, which is then propagated distally at a faster speed (Goldstein and Rall, 1974). If a step increase in diameter of more than three times the narrow region occurs, forward propagation may fail. However, the arrest of the action potential that occurs in this region, with the consequent build-up of charge, may occupy a time greater than the recovery period of the smaller-diameter portion. If this is the case, reverse depolarization may occur and a decremental potential or an action potential may be propagated backwards (antidromically). Forward propagation of a single action potential may therefore depend on a volley of action potentials of high repetition rate arriving at the step increase in diameter; a slower volley or a smaller number of spikes may be blocked or propagated antidromically. A filter mechanism is therefore built into the axon itself. A decrease in axonal diameter has opposite effects. The events occurring at branching points of the neurone depend initially upon the diameter of the branches relative to the diameter of the main axon, and the results are similar to those obtained at a step increase or decrease of axonal diameter. In addition, however, other factors such as the relative diameters of each branch and the membrane sensitivity of each also play a fundamental role.

Conduction block of impulses has now been demonstrated in several preparations (Spira *et al.*, 1976; Yau, 1976; Kalmring *et al.*, 1978), e.g. at many branch points of the acoustic axons of the ventral nerve cord of *Locusta migratoria*, the responses may undergo spatially and temporally variable modifications, which are conducted along the side branches. These modifications depend on the geometry of the axonal region (spatial variability) and also on the "previous history" of impulse transmission, i.e. on the number and discharge rate of the action potentials that have already passed (temporal variability). Often the "filter properties" of axonal expansions and branches are not constant in time.

The established belief that the fundamental unit of central nervous activity is the axon therefore requires modification—our present understanding of axonal function demonstrates that regions of special geometry have the capacity to change the pattern of impulses, a property classically assigned to chemical synapses. Indeed, because of the existence of regions of conduction block, portions or branches of an axon may perform integrative activity quite independently of the remainder or even of the main branch of that axon.

*Non-spiking interneurones*

It is generally assumed that all communication between nerve cells is by action potentials. Furthermore, present hypotheses for integrative mechanisms within localized regions of the nervous system are dominated by the idea that action potentials are generated in the interacting neurones. However, recent data (see Pearson, 1976, for review) show that graded changes in potential in some neurones can influence the activity in others, and that neurones occur that function normally without ever generating action potentials. Because of the extreme resistance to current flow in very small neurones, their function may be one of modulation, by graded potentials, of adjacent cells, and this may be especially true of small neurones without distinct axonal processes, e.g. the horizontal cells (figure

2.7) of the vertebrate retina (as well as the photoreceptors and bipolar cells) do not generate action potentials. Retinal amacrine cells do show spiking characteristics, but it is possible that the slow graded potentials that occur in these cells are also of importance in the integration of visual information. The dendro-dendritic contacts between the axonless granule cells and the mitral cells of the mammalian olfactory bulb are reciprocal synaptic connections. Experimental data suggest that the mitral-to-granule connection is excitatory and the granule-to-mitral connection is inhibitory (figure 4.4). A system of non-spiking interneurones is responsible for the central patterning of walking behaviour in the cockroach. The membrane potential of interneurone I oscillates with a slow depolarizing phase that occurs during flexor activity. Another interneurone inhibits flexor activity when depolarized and shows membrane oscillations during rhythmic leg movements which are 180° out of phase with those of interneurone I. It has no effect on activity in the extensor motor neurones. Two other interneurones specifically affect the extensor motorneurones; one causes excitation of these motorneurones when depolarized, while depolarization of the other inhibits extensor activity.

Anatomical and physiological studies have shown that transmission at most junctions between non-spiking cells and other neurones is mediated chemically. There is little reason to believe that the synaptic mechanisms differ from those which occur at junctions where there are action potentials in the presynaptic terminals. The graded input from a non-spiking neurone may be an advantage for simple neuronal systems when the output of a "following" neurone is to be controlled from a single input. Furthermore, if spiking inputs from many regions converge directly onto output elements, the temporal patterning of the input may be reflected in the temporal patterning of the output. This may be disadvantageous when the output is to be related to the *net* level of the input rather than to its temporal patterning. One solution is to interpolate non-spiking cells between the input and output, e.g. in the olfactory system of mammals, the non-spiking granule cells of the olfactory bulb receive inputs from wide-spread areas of the C.N.S. The graded activity in the granule cells then controls the degree of tonic inhibition to the mitral cells which are the output elements of the bulb. Thus, overall sensitivity of the olfactory system is continuously regulated by the graded activity in the granule cells.

There is no doubt that information is propagated over long distances to, from and within the C.N.S., only by means of action potentials. However, the information, coded by the volley of spikes, may be modified during its progress along the axon and by such integrative changes as may occur at the synapse. Branching and changes in axonal diameter have profound *filtration* effects on the spike volley. At the synapses, complex processing involving convergence, divergence, excitation and inhibition, acts to determine the activity of the postsynaptic cell. A precise spatial and temporal pattern of inputs is necessary to produce a given post-synaptic response. Filtration of "incorrect" combinations of inputs must be a common feature at these junction points. As a further feature, the response level of a postsynaptic cell may be determined by the activity of small non-spiking local interneurones, i.e. the response probability of a postsynaptic cell may be a function of the modulating influence of non-spiking cells: the *gate* (or threshold) level may be set by the activity of such cells which may, in turn, be modulated by further neural and/or hormonal influences. The complexity reaches an incredible level when we appreciate that such processing may occur at each synaptic level of the nervous system, from the receptor to the cerebral cortex, and back again to the muscles.

Thus, to produce a given response in the postsynaptic cell, a precise combination of spatially- and temporally-arranged inputs is necessary and, to repeat, this occurs at each synapse. It should not be surprising then, that in many cases specific stimulus configurations are necessary in order to produce a specific behavioural response in the recipient. Equally, it is understandable that, because of the modulation of the activity of the central neurones (and the consequent changes in their thresholds), be-havioural responses may not appear even for the presentation of the "correct" sign stimulus. We are far from understanding the details of these modulating mechanisms, but some of the principles by which such effects can be mediated are known.

So far we have concerned ourselves with the "fixity" of the postsynaptic response, with the implication that the sources and spatial organizations of the synaptic contacts it receives are genetically determined. Before con-sidering examples of central integration, a word of caution is necessary. Many animals have a considerable capacity for learning. Although the neurophysiological mechanisms of learning are outside the scope of this book, they are the subject of intensive research (see Rosenzweig and Bennett, 1976, for review), and one thing, at least, is clear: much of the connectivity of the nervous system is plastic, i.e. it is capable of being modified and adapted in response to the animal's experience. Changes in connectivity may continue throughout life or may be restricted to critical periods of development. Whichever is the case, the genetically-determined connectivity patterns may be highly modified by the experience gained as a result of exposure to the environment. The two influences on the development of the nervous system (and therefore behaviour) cannot be isolated. Thus, in addition to specific, repeatable and stereotyped activity, the nervous system retains the potential for adaptability and variability (see Gaze, 1974, for a review of neuronal specificity, and Blakemore, 1974, for plasticity).

## Examples of central sensory integration

The amount of information entering the central nervous system via the sensory nerves is, even in the less-complex animals, quite immense. In the vertebrates, the cranial nerves conduct olfactory, visual, tactile, temperature, auditory and gustatory information from the head, while somatic and visceral sensation ascend the spinal cord from the body. These sensory inputs can be traced, in the form of sensory projections, to the telencephalon and midbrain structures, such as the optic tectum. The sensory projections are relatively distinct anatomical features of vertebrate nervous systems and can be recorded relatively easily. In the invertebrates, the organization is not so clear-cut.

Reorganization of input occurs at every level in the projections of neurones and tracts, in both vertebrates and invertebrates, and neurophysiologists have successfully monitored many of these effects. However, we still know very little about the processes occurring within the areas of termination of the sensory pathways. In particular, we would be interested in why some features of input are successful in spreading their excitation (to put it rather crudely), while others are not; but the answer still seems to be conceptually beyond our grasp. Even so, the changes that occur at the various levels of organization of the sensory projections are illuminating and help us to shape our thinking about the processes of sensory integration. Accordingly, we shall consider some established mechanisms in the olfactory, auditory and visual systems.

### The olfactory system

The fineness of olfactory axons and the location of the olfactory tracts in the base of the forebrain make recording difficult (figure 4.4.). Further, "time locking" of olfactory stimuli is not readily achieved. However,

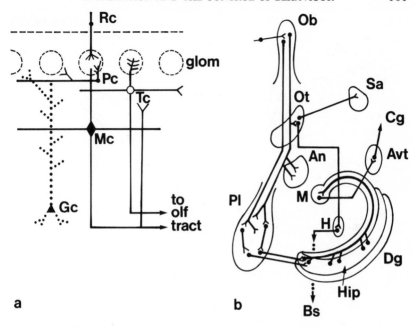

**Figure 4.4** The olfactory system of a mammal.

(a) The general arrangement of the cells in the olfactory bulb of the brain. Activation of the mitral cell (Mc) produces responses in the granule cell (Gc) which synapses back onto the mitral cell to produce long-lasting inhibition. The periglomerular cells (Pc) are also inhibitory. Tc, tufted cells.

(b) Some of the major fibre pathways (tracts) of the olfactory system. An, amygdaloid nucleus; Avt, anteroventral thalamic nucleus; Bs, brain stem; Cg, cingulate gyrus; Dg, dentate gyrus; H, habenula; Hip, hippocampus; M, mammillary body; Ob, olfactory bulb; Ot, olfactory tubercle; Pl, piriform lobe; Sa, septal area.

some progress has recently been made, e.g. in the insects, the major olfactory receptors occur on the antennae. The axons of the peripherally-placed receptor cells pass into the brain (or supraoesophageal ganglion) and synapse with the cells of the mushroom body (figure 4.5). The axons of these postsynaptic cells branch in the mushroom body stalk; one branch passes to the β-lobe, and a collateral passes to the α-lobe. The axons are arranged in strata, and their position in one lobe is precisely repeated in the other lobe. The output of the β-lobe connects with the suboesophageal ganglion and the ventral nerve cord, but a collateral branch passes back to the α-lobe. Howse (1974) believes that the mush-

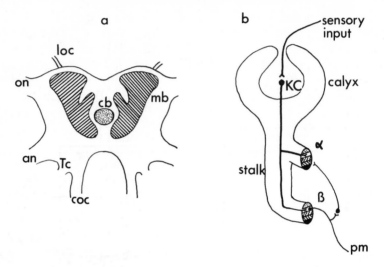

**Figure 4.5** (*a*) Cricket brain showing the positions of the mushroom bodies (mb) and the central body (cb); an, antennal nerve; coc, circumoesophageal connective; loc, lateral ocellar nerve; on, optic nerve.

(*b*) The organization of the mushroom body. The sensory input to the calyx excites Kenyon cells (KC) whose axons project to specific positions in the β-lobe; collaterals of these axons pass to equivalent positions in the α-lobe. Premotor fibres (pm) arise from the β-lobe and descend the ventral nerve cord. A short feedback loop passes back to the α-lobe from these premotor fibres, but their precise destination in the α-lobe is not yet known (data for (*b*) from Howse, 1974).

room body neurones are organized to respond to specific patterns of sensory stimulation as a result of which they "unlock" certain behaviour patterns. The correct input will trigger the appropriate output, e.g. the smell of a male or female cricket could trigger the production of the aggression or courtship song respectively. Mushroom body function is very complex; in addition to the antennal input, it also receives visual and (probably) auditory inputs, and it is not surprising that the role of the feedback loop to the α-lobe and the details of the integrative mechanisms are yet to be understood.

In the mammalian olfactory bulb, the three major types of nerve cells are arranged in discrete layers (Shepherd, 1972, 1978). The principal output-path neurone is the mitral cell which has a long axon projecting to the olfactory cortex (figure 4.4). Its dendrites are of two types: branched secondary dendrites that extend laterally from the cell body and a long primary dendrite. The dendrites receive incoming axon terminals from the olfactory cells within a small spherical region called a *glomerulus*. One of the intrinsic neurones of the olfactory bulb, the periglomerular cell, sends a small dendritic tuft into a glomerulus and gives rise to a short axon that terminates in an adjacent region. The third type, the granule cell, lacks an axon but sends out two dendrites in opposite directions.

Antidromic stimulation of the mitral cell axon results in its subsequent inhibition, which lasts for up to several hundred milliseconds. The arrival of an impulse in the mitral cell triggers the activation of excitatory synapses from the secondary dendrites of the mitral cell onto the dendrites of the granule cell. This excitatory synaptic input depolarizes the granule cell and activates inhibitory synapses back onto the mitral cell to produce the long-lasting inhibition. The graded (non-spiking) depolarization is conducted electrotonically throughout the dendritic tree of the granule cell, so that inhibitory synapses onto adjacent mitral cells are activated as well. The periglomerular cells also make reciprocal excitatory-inhibitory synapses with the dendrites of the mitral cell inside the glomerulus.

These inhibitory processes shape the responses of the mitral cell. The ability to distinguish one odour from another may depend on these interactions, since odour stimulation is associated with spatial patterns of activity in the olfactory bulb.

In the rabbit, there are about $5 \times 10^7$ olfactory cells which synapse with the $5 \times 10^4$ or so principal neurones (mitral cells) of the olfactory bulb, a convergence of $1000:1$. In many respects the olfactory bulb can be regarded as playing the same role in olfaction that the retina does in vision. However, the input:output relationships of the retina show much less convergence ($100:1$ for rods:retinal ganglion cells and $5:1$ for cones: retinal ganglion cells).

*The auditory system*

A relatively simple example of central processing of acoustic information was described by McKay (1969) for a large central auditory neurone in the bush-cricket *Homorocoryphus* sp. She found that over the range investigated (2 kHz to 40 kHz) the response of this unit increased with increased stimulus intensity, except for a narrow band of sound around 15 kHz, when the activity was diminished. 15 kHz is the dominant frequency of the species song, and the decrease in response at this frequency was postulated to be the result of inhibitory mechanisms.

A clearer example of central inhibition has been described by Kuhne *et al.* (1979) for a large central auditory neurone in *D. verrucivorus* (figure 4.6). This unit responds to the species song over a wide intensity range, by producing a single spike for each syllable; the volley of spikes per syllable produced in the primary acoustic unit is integrated to result in the single spike output of the central neurone. The unit's characteristic response is always produced, except when the fore-legs are vibrated at 1000 Hz, when the response in inhibited. The function of such an inhibitory mechanism is not known, though it may mediate a termination of movement in response to the species song when the substrate is vibrated as a result of, for example, the approach of a predator: the insect's cryptic coloration would then make it difficult for the predator to locate it.

The responses of other central neurones to more than one song parameter have been described by Roeder (1966, 1967) for moths, by Kalmring (1975) for the locust *Locusta migratoria*, and by Rheinlaender (1975) for *D. verrucivorus*. Complex processing by central neurones has recently been reviewed by Elsner and Popov (1978) and Lewis and Broughton (1980), e.g. in his study of *D. verrucivorus*, Rheinlaender (1975) reports that the responses of all ventral cord units are different from those of receptor units—a transmission of the simple "relay" type as described by Roeder (1966) for moths was not found. The ventral cord neurones receive input from several receptor units of the same side, and in many cases from the opposite side as well. As a result of unilateral and bilateral facilitation and inhibition mechanisms, responses at the ventral cord level are enhanced or degraded. One ventral cord unit produced a maximal response over a narrow frequency band, 20 kHz–30 kHz, but then only when the sound intensity was 50–70 dB; outside these frequencies and sound pressure levels the response was inhibited. The region of maximal response thus amounts to an island, in a field of inhibition, and the response characteristic of this unit is therefore extremely specific.

Studies of the central auditory pathways in mammals have been directed principally towards its *tonotopic* organization, even though the greater number of neural elements cannot be demonstrated to be frequency-responsive (Ades, 1959). The coding of frequency by the cochlea is sharpened at the cochlear nuclei and the superior olivary complex, so that in the higher regions of the pathway frequency-dependent units are more frequency-selective than those in the cochlear nerve. The frequency-dependent units are tonotopically organized at all levels of their ascent to the cortex, but the only auditory function that seems to have been linked

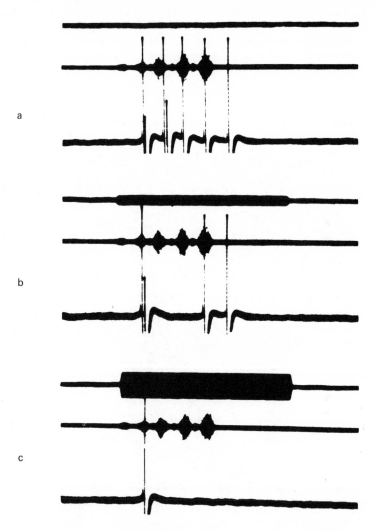

**Figure 4.6** Responses of a single ventral nerve cord acoustic unit in the bushcricket *D. verrucivorus*.

(*a*) Responses to one chirp of the species song.

(*b*) The spike responses to the species song are partially inhibited when the leg is also stimulated with low-intensity 1000-Hz vibration.

(*c*) With higher vibration intensities, inhibition of the acoustic response is almost complete; the species-specific response pattern is lost. Duration of vibration stimulus, 100 ms (from Kuhne, Lewis and Kalmring, unpublished data).

with the cortex is the discrimination between two three-tone patterns. Many other ascending units, though not frequency-selective, do respond to complex sounds such as clicks and noise, and it has been suggested that the analysis of the various parameters of auditory signals occurs in parallel. The cochlear nuclei certainly contain at least three projections or replicas of the organ of Corti. Crossing of the auditory pathway occurs at the trapezoid body near the entrance of the cochlear nerve (figure 4.7). It is also at this level that the superior olivary complex, by

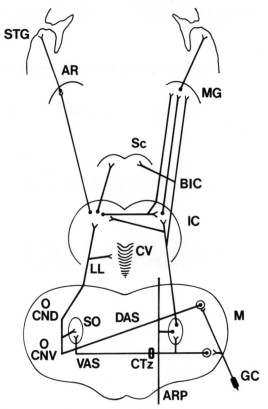

**Figure 4.7**    The afferent auditory pathways (tracts) of the mammal. AR, auditory radiation; ARP, acoustic reflex pathways; BIC, brachium of inferior colliculus; CND, dorsal cochlear nucleus; CNV, ventral cochlear nucleus; CTz, trapezoid body; CV, vermis of cerebellum; DAS, dorsal acoustic stria; GC, cochlear ganglion; IC, inferior colliculus; LL, lateral leminiscus; M, medulla; MG, medial geniculate; SC, superior colliculus; SO, superior olive; STG, superior temporal gyrus of cerebral cortex; VAS, ventral acoustic stria.

virtue of its bilateral input from cochlear nuclei, provides many of the ascending fibres of the lateral leminiscus which represent either ear.

*Topological organization* has received much less attention. It is, however, clear that when sound is presented to one side in the free field, the cortical response is greater in the (crossed) contralateral than in the ipsilateral hemisphere. When sound is in the median plane, the cortical activity is equal in both hemispheres. However, auditory localization is not abolished by destruction of the auditory cortex, so that binaural interaction must be established at lower levels, perhaps at the inferior colliculi.

Topological organization has been intensively studied in recent years in birds, especially owls. Knudsen and Konishi (1978) investigated a region in the barn owl's (*Tyto alba*) midbrain auditory area known as the nucleus mesencephalicus lateralis dorsalis (MLD) which is the avian homologue of the inferior colliculus of mammals (figure 4.8). This region contains units that respond to sound only when it originates from a small area of auditory space. Furthermore, these units are arranged systematically within the nucleus according to the horizontal and vertical position of their receptive fields, so that they form a physiological map of auditory space. These MLD units sense a limited area of space that is largely independent of the intensity or nature of the sound stimulus. Knudsen *et al.* (1977) also found auditory units in the telencephalic auditory region, field L. These units could be segregated into three groups:

(i) Space-independent units which responded to sound stimuli, usually of low frequency, regardless of location.
(ii) Space-preferring units which responded best to sounds located in a particular area of space (preferred area), but the borders of their receptive fields were poorly defined and varied considerably with sound intensity
(iii) Space-dependent units which responded only when a sound was located within a well-defined receptive field, the borders of which were distinct, regardless of intensity.

The peripheral mechanism of directional sensitivity in birds (p. 49) is very frequency-dependent, so that it is not especially surprising that Knudsen *et al.* (1977) showed that most of their units preferred a particular type of sound. Thus, to excite most space-preferring and space-dependent units, both the spatial and spectral properties of the sound had to be adequate.

## The visual system

Lateral inhibition between peripheral and central areas of the receptive field of a retinal ganglion cell of the mammal, as outlined in chapter 2,

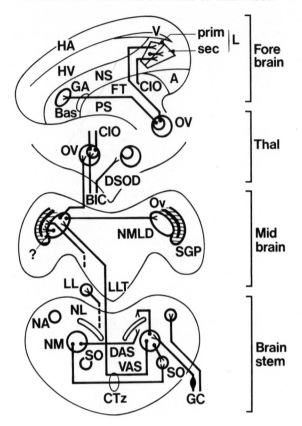

**Figure 4.8**   Auditory receiving areas and associated fibre pathways
(tracts) in the bird. Dotted lines indicate that the origins of the fibres
are not known. The forebrain is shown in lateral view, the remainder
as transverse sections. A, archistriatum; Bas, nucleus basalis; BIC,
brachium (inferior colliculus); CIO, cisterna internalis occipitalis; CTz,
trapezoid body; DAS, dorsal acoustic stria; DSOD, supraoptic
decussation; FT, fronto-thalamic tract; GA, field GA; GC, cochlear
ganglion; HA, hyperstriatum accessorium; HV, hyperstriatum ven-
trale; LL, lateral leminiscus; LLT, lateral leminiscus tract; NA,
nucleus angularis; NL, nucleus laminaris; NMLD, nucleus mesencephalicus dorsalis; NM, nucleus magnocellularis; NS, neostriatum;
OV, nucleus ovoidalis; Ov, optic ventricle; Prim, Sec, L, primary and
secondary field L; PS, paleostriatum; SGP, stratum griseum et
periventriculare; SO, superior olive; V. ventricle; VAS, ventral acoustic
stria (original data from R. B. Coles).

helps to accentuate boundaries between differently-illuminated parts of the field. This effect is not limited to vertebrates. Hartline (1949) illuminated a single ommatidium of the lateral eye of the king crab *Limulus* (Order Xiphosura), recording the spike response from the corresponding fibre of the optic nerve. A few seconds later, an adjacent ommatidium was also illuminated, and the discharge from the first was found to decrease. When the order of illumination was reversed, the inhibitory effect was found to be reciprocal. The mechanism depended upon the integrity of a plexus of nerve fibres lying in the region behind the ommatidia (Hartline and Ratliff, 1956).

The principle that the visual pathways contain units responsive to qualitatively different parameters of the stimulation is of widespread applicability. In the optic nerve of the crab *Podophthalmus vigil*, information is carried by a variety of types of fibre. They differ according to:

(i) The area of the visual field to which the fibre responds, ranging from the whole to quite small portions of the field.
(ii) The type of stimulation eliciting the maximal response, ranging from fast-moving large objects to changes in the intensity of stationary illumination.
(iii) The amount of contrast necessary for maximal response.

In this species there are also numerous fibres running to the eye and responding to visual stimulation of the other eye and/or tactile stimulation of various parts of the body. Visual information is integrated with information arriving from other sources (Wiersma *et al.*, 1964).

Units responsive to complex visual stimulation are also known in insects. The "novel movement" detectors from the locust tritocerebrum show a directional selectivity: they are most responsive to stimuli moving in one particular direction (see Rowell, 1970, for references). The response of these units also decreases with successive presentation of the stimulus (i.e. they habituate). The value of detection of novel elements in the environment is obvious and can, at least partially, be achieved by habituation in the sensory pathway.

A large number of different visual interneurones can be recorded from insect brains. Horridge (e.g. 1968) grouped those of the optic lobes and protocerebrum of locusts into three classes: classes A and B, with rather simple properties, do not habituate and are commoner in the optic lobes; C neurones are found more commonly in the protocerebrum and have more complex features. They show habituation to single visual stimuli and periods of up to hours are required for the recovery of a completely waned response.

Current understanding of the vertebrate visual system blossomed when Lettvin *et al.* (1959) suggested that stimulation of the frog's retina by point sources of light could tell us little about how the eye functions normally. By using complex stimuli, Lettvin and others were able to identify five types of ganglion cell in the frog's eye.

   (i) Sustained-contrast detectors
  (ii) Convexity detectors
 (iii) Moving-edge detectors
 (iv) Net-dimming detectors
  (v) Absolute-darkness detectors.

The first four types each project in an orderly way onto the optic tectum of the brain, each type projecting into a different layer. In each of these layers there is an exact topological mapping of the retina, and hence of the entire visual field. Responses of contrast detectors can be recorded in the superficial layers, the convexity, moving-edge and dimming detectors at successively deeper layers; the absolute-darkness detectors are found in the same level as those of the moving-edge detectors (figure 4.9).

Through these four layers project dendritic branches of the deeper-lying optic tectum cells, each of which is influenced by the several properties of one particular area of the retinal field. The image is thus perceived as a combination of the various qualities registered by detectors.

The thalamic-pretectal region is the second major destination of fibres from the amphibian retina and provides what has been called a "caution" system. Four main types of neurones have been identified. They are activated respectively by:

   (i) movement of objects extended perpendicularly to the direction of motion ("enemy" stimuli)
  (ii) movement of an object towards the eye
 (iii) large stationary objects
 (iv) stimulation of the balance receptors by tilting.

In general, these thalamic neurones are activated principally in situations that tend to require evasive movements (Ewert, 1974).

Thus, on the basis of retinal ganglion-cell input, the optic tectum "tells" the toad where in the visual field a stimulus is located, how large it is, how strongly it contrasts with the background, and how fast it is moving. The connections from the tectum to structures in the thalamic-pretectal region enable the toad to discern the significance of the visual signals to its behaviour. The basic filtering process for the prey-enemy differentiation can be conceived as passage through a series of "window discriminators"

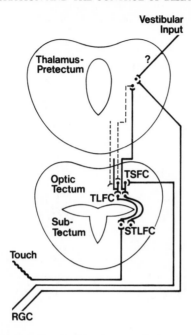

**Figure 4.9** The central visual projections in the frog. The fibres from the retinal ganglion cells (RGC) pass through the optic chiasma to the opposite side of the optic tectum and directly to the thalamus. (Only one side is represented in the figure.) The thalamus also receives an indirect input from the cells of the optic tectum. In the tectum there is an exact topographical mapping of the retina and therefore of the visual field. On the surface of the tectum, cells with small receptive fields (TSFC) occur; these project to large field cells (TLFC) in deeper layers which, in turn, project to subtectal large field cells (STLFC). These latter also receive inputs from touch and vibration receptors in the skin of the same side of the body as the visual input. Projections from the tectum to the thalamus are excitatory. In turn, the cells of the thalamus, which also receive a vestibular input, exert an inhibitory effect (broken line) back onto the tectal cells.

or specific filters. Each ganglion cell acts as a vertical window that codes extension perpendicular to the direction of movement. The retinal analysis is repeated and amplified in the thalamic-pretectal region. Extension in a horizontal direction is coded primarily by Type I tectal cells which respond to the net-convexity detectors of the retina. The Type II tectal cells show a response which decreases with increase in the vertical parameter of the stimulus. This response is the result of an excitatory input from Type I cells and an inhibitory input from the thalamic-pretectal region; it acts as the trigger stimulus for the orientation movement (figure 4.9).

The cat, unlike the frog, has little differentiation at the retinal level (see chapter 2) but a much greater differentiation at the cortical level.

A greater complexity is already evident in the lateral geniculate nucleus. Although the cells are generally similar to those of the retina, there is an

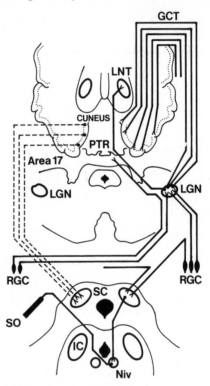

**Figure 4.10** The afferent visual fibre pathways (tracts) of the mammal. Retinal ganglion cells (RGC) and their projections from one half of each retina only are shown. The reflex pathways to the external eye muscles are represented by the pathway to the IV cranial (trochlear) nerve. Parts of the occulomotor nuclei (III cranial nerve) are also related with corresponding regions of the superior colliculi (SC). The projections to the pretectal region (PTR) subserve the pupillary light reflex. Visual sensation is mediated via the topographic projections of the geniculo-calcarine tract (GCT) on the striate cortex. Efferent fibres (broken lines) are also shown as descending from the cuneus to the superior colliculus (SC). IC, inferior colliculus; LGN, lateral geniculate nucleus; LNT, lateral nucleus of thalamus; SO, superior oblique muscle.

enhanced capacity of the surround of the receptive field to inhibit the effects of the centre. The cells of this nucleus are therefore even more responsive to spatial differences in retinal illumination, and certain of the cells receive inputs from both "on" and "off" centre units.

In the visual cortex, too, the cells mostly have mutually-antagonistic excitatory and inhibitory regions, though none have circular receptive fields. The patterns to which they respond become increasingly complex, and some respond only to certain orientations of line stimuli or direction of movement. Most cells are influenced by both eyes. Hubel and Wiesel (e.g. 1965a) recognized at least four cell types:

(a) *"Simple" cells*: These cells respond to line stimuli at a particular location and oriented in a particular direction. The receptive fields are elongate with strongly antagonistic on/off areas. A line stimulus oriented along and just covering the central area produces a strong response; a line at right angles to the central area produces no response.

(b) *"Complex" cells*: These cells respond to line stimuli moving in a particular direction. An appropriately oriented edge anywhere in the field will cause the unit to respond with an increase or decrease in rate of firing.

(c) *"Hypercomplex" cells*: The adequate stimulus is a line falling within a given region, oriented in a particular way, and of a limited length, so that it does not fall on an adjacent region.

(d) *"Higher-order hypercomplex cells"* respond optimally to line stimuli of limited length in either of two orientations at right angles.

It has been suggested that these cells are arranged in a hierarchical sequence: several geniculate cells converge on one simple cell; several of these on to one complex cell, and so on, the brain literally building up a picture by synthesizing the inputs of increasingly complex cells. Hubel and Wiesel (e.g. 1965 for references) have shown that cells in the cortex are not arranged haphazardly, but that cells with similar physiological properties (e.g. orientation) may be grouped together in columns. This has been taken as supporting evidence for the hierarchical arrangement. However, the complex cells have been shown, in many cases, to have latencies of activity shorter than those of the simple cells. Further, whereas many cells are influenced by both eyes, in the regions adjacent to the visual cortex, cells occur which respond specifically to binocular discrepancies (Hubel and Wiesel, 1965b). These are ideal for coding depth perception. It is probable that future work will show parallel systems of analysis rather than a simple hierarchical arrangement.

*Multimodal integration*

Units responding to more than one modality have been described in the insects. Horridge *et al.* (1965) report that their classes A and B visual interneurones do not have mechano-receptive inputs, while those of class C do, wind on the head being especially effective. Bacon and Tyrer (1978) have described a similar unit in the tritocerebrum of the locust *Schistocerca gregaria*. It extends from a cell body in the brain through the suboesophageal and all thoracic ganglia. It responds with a phasitonic response to wind and a phasic response to changes in light intensity on the ipsilateral side. Behaviourally, either of these stimuli (wind on the head or a sudden change in light intensity) is sufficient to initiate flight. Other bi- or multi-modal units have been described (e.g. Rowell, 1970). Horridge (1964) and Horridge *et al.* (1965) report large audiovisual units in the optic lobes of *Locusta migratoria*. These units could be adapted to one type of stimulus without marked effect upon their sensitivity to the other. The simplest explanation of such a phenomenon is that the different sensory inputs act on widely different regions of the unit from which the recordings are made. O'Shea (1975), for example, has shown two sites of axonal spike production in a bimodal interneurone. The same results are found when wide-field visual units are habituated in one small fraction of their field and then tested in another fraction; they behave as if they have ramifying dendrites between which there are few interactions.

Under natural conditions the amphibian's behavioural response to a visual stimulus can be influenced by sensory modalities other than vision. If, for example, a beetle crosses the toad's field of vision, its orientation reaction can be accelerated or retarded by simultaneous vibratory and tactile stimuli. The area for producing such changes in behavioural activity appears to be the sub-tectal region where multimodal integration is achieved. In the area below the third ventricle of the midbrain there are large-field neurones with response fields similar to those of the large-field tectal cells. The sub-tectal neurones receive additional inputs from vibratory and tactile stimuli. The mechano-receptive field of one of these bimodal neurones always occurs on the same side as the visual receptive field. The additional inputs from non-visual neurones could serve to lower the threshold of a part of the visual field in which a visual stimulus is anticipated and thus to raise the level of visual alertness (Ewert, 1974).

All the sensory systems discussed in this section show one clear trend: convergence of many receptors onto relatively few C.N.S. neurones at the first synapse, and then a relay (i.e. $1:1$) to areas which have, in many cases, higher numbers of neurones concerned with that input. For example, in the visual system of man, the 1 million or so lateral geniculate principal neurones relay directly or indirectly to many times that number of visual cortex neurones. There are (very approximately) $5 \times 10^8$ visual cortex neurones, but not all of them project directly to the lateral geniculate nucleus neurones.

Another general feature of sensory input is that the axons concerned supply widely-separated areas of the C.N.S. Thus, the retinal ganglion cell axons, before synapsing in the lateral geniculate nucleus, give off collaterals to the suprachiasmatic nucleus, the optic tectum, pretectal nuclei, reticular formation and possibly other areas. Mitral cell axons divide many times, supplying the anterior olfactory nucleus, olfactory tubercle, prepyriform cortex, amygdala and the transitional entorhinal cortex. The principle is clear: initial convergence (and presumably basic reorganization) is followed by divergence to areas serving different functions. It is therefore not possible to define specific areas as being solely concerned with the analysis and integration of sensory information in a particular modality. As a consequence, it is not possible to define a single sensori-motor interface where sensory information initiates motor activity: "pontifical neurones" probably do not occur within the C.N.S.

Finally, it is clear that the messages analysed by the receptors and the central nervous system are not single independent stimulus parameters; they are not, for example, pulses of sound or spots of light. The message is highly organized and interpreted by the receptor, and further organization occurs at each successive level. The nervous system must be considered to be a "pattern discriminator". But is it also a "pattern generator"? Certainly, for effective communication the sender and the receiver must have an agreed-upon code. Both time and effort is saved if this code is partly or wholly genetically determined; the receptors of the recipient should be adapted genetically to respond maximally to those complex stimulus parameters that are of adaptive significance and the complex stimuli produced by the sender should evolve into forms that are best perceived by the intended recipient. The motor mechanisms underlying signal production concern us for the remainder of this chapter. The major question to be considered is the extent to which complex motor activity is independent of environmental or feedback control.

### The motor system and behaviour

In order to understand the basic motor mechanisms underlying overt behaviour, we need to know how the C.N.S. commands the muscles to contract during sequences of motor activity. What determines the order, the timing, and the relative emphasis of individual movements during the sequences? Most behaviour is highly variable and hence is not suitable for neurophysiological investigation. There are, however, certain units of behaviour which appear in more or less the same form from performance to performance; these units are commonly termed "fixed action patterns". Certain fixed action patterns used in signalling behaviour are not only relatively stereotyped in form but are repeated time and time again for long periods.

Clearly such repetitive sequences of behaviour are far more easily studied at the neurophysiological as well as at the behavioural level. Observations of such FAPs immediately suggest that the underlying neural network is also fixed and patterned, in such a way that once activity is initiated, the entire sequence is read out from "stored information". Hoyle (1976) states that the single, most important aspect of ethological study is the inherited FAP, and much of the attention of neuro-ethologists has been directed at answering such questions as: what are the properties of the neural pattern generators involved? to what extent are they innate, and to what extent are the patterns established within the C.N.S. modified or controlled by feedback information?

The behavioural term *fixed action pattern* is, of course, rather general, and a number of recent discussions in the literature (e.g. Barlow, 1977) are posing certain problems. Let us therefore first examine this concept, "the discovery of which", Lorenz regards as his "most valuable contribution to science" (Lorenz, 1974).

### The fixed action pattern—a valid concept?

When a particular behaviour is labelled as a fixed action pattern it usually means that it incorporates recognizable elements that transcend variation in timing, extent and completeness. The three main features traditionally used in the diagnosis of fixed action patterns are the following:

(i) The components appear in a predictable temporal sequence (cf. p. 68). Thus, a pattern consisting of elements A, B, C and D may, at low intensities, occur as A, AB or ABC but never as ACB, ACD, etc. The sequencing is thus fixed, the only variation being in the degree of completeness.

(ii) The components of a fixed action pattern all depend on the same causal factors. In other words it cannot be split into successive responses which depend on qualitatively different external stimuli. In practice this is very difficult to prove and amounts to a statement of faith.

(iii) The stimulus releasing a fixed action pattern is merely a trigger, and exercises no further control over the performance of the pattern. The performance is thus "free running", although "directing" stimuli may still influence the *orientation* of the behaviour.

The basic pattern of coordination is not, in fact, always separable from its orientation or "taxic component", despite Hinde's (1970) assertion that, "By definition, the form of a fixed action pattern is independent of the environment". For example, the head stand display of the three-spined stickleback is *only* recognizable by its orientation. Furthermore, there is a wide variety of displays, particularly those shown in agonistic encounters, where the intensity of the display is continuously modulated as a result of changing external factors. In the Orange Chromid *Etroplus maculatus*, the degree of spreading of the fins, the angle at which the body is held, and the presence or absence and timing of head jerking, are constantly being modulated in response to changes in the behaviour of the opponent (Barlow, 1968).

There are probably many units of behaviour that do not conform to these three diagnostic features of the fixed action pattern. Further, the very term "fixed action pattern" is misleading in that it overstates the stereotyped nature of most units. "Stereotyped action patterns", or perhaps better still, "modal action pattern" (Barlow, 1968, 1977) are better descriptions. But it should still be borne in mind that these descriptions probably embrace a heterogeneous assemblage of behaviour units and *do not imply similar underlying neural mechanisms*.

Despite these objections, the concept of the fixed action pattern has been one of the main unifying themes in ethology. In fact much of what is said in this book depends to some extent on the concept, so let us reassert what can be said with confidence about the general features of innate behaviour patterns.

First, many behaviour patterns have been shown to be inherited to a greater or lesser extent, in a form recognizable from one generation to the next, e.g. the adult crickets that emerge first in the spring have no opportunity of learning the species song from their parents; in the majority of cases, adults do not overwinter (see p. 138).

Second, on what little information we have at present, behaviours that are innate tend to be shown by all members of the species. In the same way that we can recognize eyes, limbs, etc., we can recognize complex units of behaviour and, just as for "compound" morphological features, the genetic control of complex units of behaviour involves many loci on the chromosomes. Some sexual dimorphism in behaviour does exist but again, as for anatomical features, it is under hormonal control, at least in the vertebrates. Hence it is possible to "masculinize" female rats with a single injection of testosterone if this is given soon after birth. Such masculinized females show many of the aggressive and copulatory patterns normally associated with male behaviour. Conversely, male rats can be feminized by removal of the testes immediately after birth; when older, these animals not only show female mating behaviour but also a range of maternal responses including pup retrieval, nest building, and crouching over the pups (McCullough *et al.*, 1974).

Third, inherited behaviour does show variation between individuals in the same population but, as stated earlier, we have little information on the extent of this variation. Just as eyes, limbs, etc., tend to be uniformly present throughout the population, so too are most units of behaviour. But just as details of the eyes and limbs will vary, so will the details of the behaviour.

*Reflex control*

Reflexes have often been considered to be the fundamental units of behaviour. They are repeatable and stereotyped: a knee jerk is always elicited by a tap on the patellar tendon; a sharp prick to the sole of the foot always results in the withdrawal of the leg. Such "simple" behaviour may seem far removed from the complex activity seen during communication, but many of the properties of reflexes are shared by complex patterns (see Manning, 1979, for a summary), and Sherrington (1906) showed that simple reflexes could grow into more complicated sequences as a result of "motor recruitment", e.g. Sherrington (1917) describes what he calls the cat's "pinna reflex". Repeated tactile stimulation of the cat's ear initially results in the ear being laid back. If stimulation continues, the ear is fluttered, then the head is shaken, and finally the cat brings up its hind leg and scratches. The effect of the stimulus therefore spreads within the nervous system, recruiting more and more motor units. But much more is involved than just the activation of more motor nerve fibres. A behaviour pattern is not the result of the contraction of single muscles, but of the integrated activity of groups of muscles, both flexors and extensors. In ear fluttering, head shaking and scratching, patterns of movement are recruited in a sequence which is determined by their relative thresholds. Nevertheless, Sherrington maintains that these patterns are built up from the same basic reflexes that occur in the knee jerk, with the additional concept of central "reciprocal inhibition". Sherrington showed that excitation of either a flexor or an extensor muscle of a joint resulted in the inhibition of its antagonist. But, as the antagonist becomes stretched, the activity of its muscle spindles and tendon organs is increased; the net result is the reflex contraction of this muscle and the reciprocal inhibition of the original contractor. In other words, reciprocal inhibition, together with feedback control from muscle spindles and tendon organs, can account for the oscillating flexion and extension of a joint as found during a scratch reflex. Sherrington showed that inhibition of antagonists was not restricted to those of the same joint. The activity of all the joints of the same limb were integrated, as were those muscles located on opposite limbs which have antagonistic effects during locomotion. When the flexors of one limb contract, the flexors of the opposite limb are inhibited, and similarly for the extensors. The "simple" reflex arc can therefore account for quite complicated behavioural sequences whose appearance is repeatable and stereotyped. The fundamental requirement for reflex control is feedback information from peripheral receptors. Given this factor, the only other requirement may be the identification of the stimulus which evokes the reflex response!

What then of the role of the higher levels of the nervous system in the vertebrates? Eccles (e.g. 1973) states that the principal organ concerned in the control of movement is the cerebellum, especially in the control of complex and subtle movements such as playing musical instruments. Originally, the cerebellum was designed for processing the information from lateral line and vestibular systems in fish, subsequently exerting its control over swimming movements. In the higher vertebrates, it becomes increasingly involved in the control of the complex motor activity underlying skilled movements, receiving its inputs from a variety of receptors and from other parts of the brain. It exerts its control during bird flight and in the walking patterns of mammals (integrating the changing inputs from the eyes and vestibular systems) and also in speech; but it is a form of control which is learned to a large extent (in the higher vertebrates at least). In such a way, during the course of evolution, it has come to exert an increasing control over both innate and learned motor activity. Its enormous growth in mammals, and especially in man, testifies to the greatly increased capacity for learning motor skills. The inherited components of FAPs may therefore be much more difficult, or even impossible, to isolate in the higher vertebrates.

*Control by central pattern generators*

Reflex control was once the generally-accepted and only hypothesis for the neural control of behaviour. For complex activity, it has now largely been replaced by the idea of central pattern generation. With few exceptions, the role of sensory feedback seems to be one of adjustment and modulation of a preprogrammed or learned central activity. Even in the cerebellum, the sensory inputs are not considered to determine the pattern of the motor outflow, but only to trigger such activity as is already laid down. To do full justice to the concept of pattern generation would require a book in itself, and we can do no more than outline the main points. Detailed accounts are given in the appropriate chapters of Usherwood and Newth (1975) and Fentress (1976).

Strong evidence for central programming in the absence of any specific timing of sensory inputs was first obtained for the basic flight pattern in locusts (Wilson, 1961, 1970). The generator is located within the thoracic ganglia where about 80 motorneurones control the activity of the muscles driving the two pairs of wings. It has been shown to be composed of (at least) four subsystems, each of which consists of two reciprocally active populations of neurones responsible for the up- and down-stroke of one wing. Central patterning of wing stridulation in crickets was first demonstrated by Bentley (1969). He recorded from the mesothoracic motorneurones, interneurones and motor nerves of *Gryllus campestris* after the removal of all peripheral inputs to the thoracic nerve cord. He was able to correlate the activity of the neurones with the closer and opener systems of the stridulatory muscles which act antagonistically during sound production. Although this "song pattern generator" receives input from the brain and from the genital apparatus, this input is used as a trigger command and for power control (and may also modulate the ganglionic excitatory state), and does not determine the pattern of the output.

Wilson and his colleagues suggested that the alternating bursts of activity in elevator and depressor muscles, and the correct phase relationships between bursts, could be generated by sets of reciprocally inhibitory neurones and was a fundamental property of the network. Alternatively (see Selverston, 1976, for references), within any network there may be one (or more) cells that has an intrinsic capacity to burst and which acts as a driving force for the whole network. The correct phase relationships in the outputs would be established by synaptic connections among the cells in the network. Evidence is accumulating for both mechanisms.

The available evidence suggests that the motorneurones themselves are not part of the generating system; the oscillator, whether a single cell or a network, is believed to be presynaptic to them (Burrows, 1975).

In the vertebrates, certain behavioural sequences proceed wholly under central control. In the cat, various forms of deafferentation have no effect on the motor discharge underlying purring. In the frog, the "release-call", produced by a male when clasped by another male, is independent of afferent feedback information. It can be released by electrical stimulation of the midbrain focus, even after total denervation of the brain stem, but the ease with which it may be elicited depends upon the circulating level of the hormone testosterone. The same is probably true for the species-specific courtship song which is commonly evoked by the call of another frog. It is also likely to be true in birds, once the full song has been established, but a learned component may be involved here (see Doty, 1976, for references).

*Command neurones*

Many oscillatory networks are not active continuously, and the way in which they are turned "on" and "off" is poorly understood. A change in the sensitivity of such networks could result from a change in level of some hormone or from the activity of specific excitatory inputs. Little is known about the hormonal effects within the C.N.S. (but see p. 81), and most of the attention has been directed at specific neural control mechanisms. Such inputs to the networks have been called *command neurones* and are widely assumed to be the pathways by which the higher levels of the nervous system *trigger* the appropriate sequence. Command neurones have been most intensively studied in invertebrates and have been reported to promote walking movements, swimmeret beating and stridulation.

Descending command fibres trigger cricket chirping. For the courtship and aggressive songs, these fibres receive inputs from the antennal receptors (see p. 101), and their activity is passed into the network of thoracic neurones controlling stridulation. The courtship sequence in the male grasshopper *Gomphocerripus rufus* is an extremely complex FAP. It starts with a gentle rocking and weak stridulation, proceeds through strong head rocking, and ends with a violent backward flick of the antennae and a loud song. The motor activity underlying this FAP has been determined by Elsner (see Elsner and Popov, 1978, for references) by recording the electromyographic activity of all the involved muscles. No subroutine of this sequence is used in any other context, and the leg stridulation (at least) is temporally organized by neurones in the metathoracic ganglion. The initial orientation manoeuvre is triggered by the visual input received from the female. This contains information about the female's position relative to the male, the movements of the female or of her appendages, and of the female's "Gestalt". Huber (1975) states that this "Gestalt" is a complex recognition parameter. However, even when the complex eyes and ocelli are covered, males may still perform the whole sequence as soon as they hear the song of the conspecific female. This indicates that either visual or auditory signals can trigger a very complexly-timed motor command which differs in its temporal structure from any of the triggering inputs.

The demonstration of such command fibres in vertebrate nervous systems is more difficult because of the greatly increased complexity. A similar system may occur between the cerebrum and the cerebellum. What happens during ordinary movements in mammals is that the cerebrum gives a general command which the cerebellum takes over, and then organizes the fine details. Such "generalist" activity from the cerebrum may be analogous to the command activity in invertebrates, but the system is much more complex. The activity of the cerebellum is subsequently returned to the same area of the motor cerebral cortex whence it came, so further modifying the descending activity in the pyramidal tract (Eccles, 1973).

Although there are undoubtedly fibres which pass through the brain of invertebrates (and probably vertebrates, too) to the motor or premotor neurone pools, and whose activity determines the onset of patterned behaviour, the concept of *the* command neurone has recently been criticized and reviewed (Kupfermann and Weiss, 1978). The outcome of this discussion seems to be whether one, or more than one, descending neurone is necessary for the production of a full behaviour pattern, i.e. whether they should be termed command neurones or command systems, but there seems little doubt that they occur.

### Conclusions

The behavioural term *stimulus filtration* has clear and precise correlates at the neuronal level. Mechanisms along the nerve axon and at each synapse are sufficient to manifest this phenomenon at a behavioural level. What is not yet clear is how those factors which determine neuronal connectivity and response specificity produce their effects. Genetic control of growth and connectivity is certainly of major importance in this context, and the growth of connections in the visual system (for example) has been described in detail (see Gaze, 1974, for references). However, plasticity must also be a feature of nervous systems since, as Blakemore (1974) has pointed out, many neuronal connections are established as a result of learning and experience. The main question is this: to what extent are specific connections within the C.N.S. established genetically, so that a given sign stimulus always tends to evoke a specific response? Our present knowledge of the details of synaptic connectivity (such as the spatial arrangement of presynaptic terminals on a postsynaptic cell) does not yet provide an answer to this problem. This is because of the technical difficulties of tracing presynaptic terminals back to axons whose origin and physiological state are also known. Until this can be done, the relative importance of the numerous presynaptic terminals can only be deduced from circumstantial evidence.

Present neurophysiological techniques only allow the investigation of the larger neurones; small cells are mostly inaccessible, even though they provide the bulk of the population in the C.N.S. Their numbers suggest a very fundamental function, a supposition which is supported by the known activity of some axonless non-spiking neurones (p. 97). The activity of the larger neurones may be very dependent upon the excitation level established by the smaller fibres. Modulation of activity and threshold changes may be a fundamental feature of nervous activity. The term "motivational gating" *may* eventually come to mean the activity state of local populations of small nerve cells, for example; but, in the absence of known causes, the term is descriptive and not explanatory.

The complexity of the analytical process within the C.N.S. indicates that no one area or "centre" can be considered to "control" the output (and therefore a behavioural activity). Different regions of the nervous system extract and analyse different features of a complex sign stimulus (e.g. the frog visual system described on p. 110); further interactions of the results of such processing occur in yet other regions, and so on until the final activation of the appropriate musculature. The neurophysiological correlates of an "innate releasing mechanism" must therefore be all those receptors, axons and synapses, systems and analytical regions that are interposed between the stimulus and the response, and whose activity and connectivity are genetically determined. As a descriptive short-hand term for the stimulus-specific activity of the nervous system, it may be behaviourally useful, but it cannot be more than this and it cannot be placed in any one "higher centre" of the C.N.S. As an explanatory term it is neurophysiologically so broad as to be useless. The questions asked about the neural control of behaviour must be far more specific.

In principle, there are two extreme ways and a number of intergrades by which an animal might control its motor output.

(i) Once a pattern is initiated, the muscles contracting later in a sequence may be activated by feedback effects from those contracting earlier. In this case, the form of the movement is a closed-loop chain-reflex pattern, without central preprogramming.

(ii) The sequence by which the muscles are contracted may be determined solely by established motor patterns within the C.N.S. so that, once initiated *via* command fibres, the movement is independent of sensory stimuli. Because there is no feedback from the ensuing movements, such a control system is termed open-loop or motor-tape control (Hoyle, 1964).

(iii) Intergrades. A first preprogrammed sequence may control only a discrete portion of the whole, the second and subsequent fractions being initiated only after sensory feedback from the first.

Perhaps the most important alternative to either of the extremes is one in which there is continuous computation of the output required to achieve the desired movement by comparing the actual sensory input and a Sollwert (see p. 78) of that associated with the correct performance. This type of error-correcting system involves the reafference principle of von Holst (1954) and has been called *sensory-tape control* by Hoyle (1964).

It is, however, often difficult to categorize precisely a particular behaviour pattern, e.g. movement of a pianist's fingers may occur too fast to involve control by proprioceptive feedback, so that it cannot be included in (i). Equally, the pattern is not inherited (ii), but learned. Studies on the learning of motor tasks by primates, including man, suggest that they rely heavily on sensory input to control new movements during acquisition, but that as they learn, they shift progressively towards using motor-tape programmes triggered by the appropriate stimulus. Little is known about the neural processes that underly such learning mechanisms.

# CHAPTER FIVE

# SIGNALS AND THEIR EVOLUTION

## Introduction

That certain elements of behaviour are inherited is beyond question. Provided that some variation in these elements exists between individuals of the same species, then natural selection will operate and behaviour will evolve. Ethologists have been highly successful, using the comparative approach, in tracing the phylogenetic development of certain of these inherited elements. An example of this kind of study is Lorenz's (1941) work on courtship behaviour in the Anatidae. "Mock preening" by the drake has evolved along several lines from the original form. In the mallard *Anas platyrhynchos*, the display resembles normal preening, the bill being drawn along the underside of the partly-lifted wing producing a loud "Rrrrr" sound. At the same time a bright blue feather, the speculum, is revealed by the lifting and separation of the wing feathers. The mandarin *Aix galericulata* mock-preens with an exaggerated wing movement, where the wing is raised like a sail to display the large red tertiary feathers. At the same time a bright orange secondary is touched by the bill, but no sound accompanies this display. The shelduck *Tadorna tadorna* has elaborated the acoustic components, producing a low rumbling sound with a powerful bill stroke along the shafts of the wing quills. The "fixed action pattern" of courtship preening thus appears to show the same kind of radiation that numerous anatomical features show. However, the basic tenet of evolutionary theory is that natural selection operates gradually on small differences within interbreeding populations and it is, perhaps, anomalous that Lorenz chose to emphasize the invariant species-specific nature of the fixed action patterns that he studied. Fixed action patterns are *recognizable* from individual to individual, but this does not mean that there is no variation. Measurement of such variation is difficult because, unlike morphological features, behaviour will not be identical from performance to performance by the same individual. Nevertheless, to a greater or lesser extent, variation in behaviour between individuals of the same species will be there.

Several attempts have been made to assess this variation, although in many cases inter-individual differences are masked by variation in the performances of the same individual, e.g. Dane *et al.* (1959) analyzed film sequences of courtship displays of the goldeneye duck, a species whose courtship is generally regarded as highly stereotyped. Bearing in mind that Dane *et al.* did not distinguish between within-individual and between-individual variation, most of the displays showed a standard deviation in duration of 10% to 20% of the mean duration. The one non-signal movement measured was the wing stretch, and this showed much greater variability in duration. Temporal duration is, of course, only one parameter of many possible ones. Extraction of between-individual differences in this type of situation is clearly a mammoth task. However, Rothblum and Jenssen (1978), in a study of head bobbing in the iguanid lizard

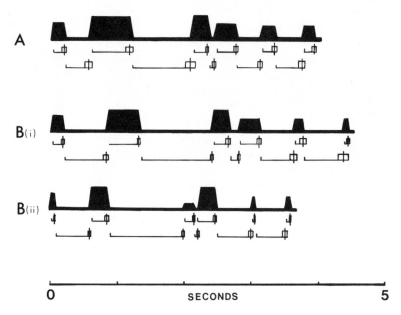

**Figure 5.1** Head bobbing in the lizard *Sceloporus undulatus hyacinthinus.*

A, Generalized type A display.

B (i) and B (ii), Type B display shown by two individuals.

Vertical axis of graph shows relative head amplitude movement and the horizontal axis gives display duration. Unit statistics are shown below the graph: horizontal line, unit duration; vertical line, unit mean; outer edges of white boxes, 99% confidence intervals of unit mean (from Rothblum and Jenssen, 1978).

*Sceloporus undulatus*, were able to investigate the between-individual variation in one type of display. They showed that there were two distinct bobbing displays: Type A is "highly stereotyped" and probably serves for species recognition; Type B shows high intra-individual stereotype, but each individual has its own unique variation of the display. Figure 5.1 shows the displays of two *Sceloporus* individuals. Temporal patterning and head amplitude show differences significant at the 99% confidence limit. The individual distinctiveness of Type B displays is probably the result of the need for individual recognition. In other vertebrates, however, individual recognition seems to depend more on morphology than on behaviour. The quantification of between-individual variation for most displays is therefore likely to prove more difficult than for *Sceloporus*. Furthermore, the amplitude and form of most movements are generally not so easy to measure.

Despite the paucity of information, it seems a reasonable assumption that inter-individual differences in behaviour are widespread and, if this is so, the laws of natural selection will operate on behaviour in a fashion comparable to their action on morphological elements. As a general principle, therefore, it is feasible that behaviour patterns that are inherited have, and will evolve into, different forms. Some of these forms develop communicative function, and the processes which bring this about are one of the themes of this chapter. Most of the studies on these processes have concentrated on signals in the visual modality. As we have stated before, overgeneralization should be avoided and we therefore now consider some examples and certain problems of the evolution of signals in the different, distance, sensory modalities.

### Chemical signals and their evolution

Living organisms probably developed responsiveness to chemicals in the external environment as a means of locating and identifying both food and sexual partners. Even animals equipped with highly developed vision, hearing and other senses, still in the main employ the chemical sense for final identification of food and mates. It may well be that chemical signalling is the most primitive of the distance signalling systems.

Chemical signals are used by both plants and animals. Thus the female gametes of the brown alga *Ectocarpus siliculous* produce a chemical, allo-cis-(cycloheptadien 2', 5'-yl)butene-1 which attracts male gametes. The pheromone, acrasin, which promotes cellular aggregation in the slime moulds is now known to be 3′, 5′, cyclic AMP (Konijn *et al.*, 1968). A likely origin of this molecule is intracellular metabolism, and it may initially have become effective as an aggregational signal because of leakage across the cell membrane in some individuals, with consequent interference in the metabolic processes of adjacent individuals. This is surmise, but we have stronger evidence regarding the origins of chemical signals in certain animal species. Thus, in the bark beetle genus *Ips*, aggregational pheromones may well be metabolites of host tree resins, e.g. myrcene found in pine tree resin is probably a precursor of the pheromone molecule ipsdienol. In turn, ipsdienol is probably the precursor of ipsenol, another of the pheromone molecules found in the quite complex blend of molecules that make up the aggregational signals of *Ips* species (Hughes, 1974) (figure 5.2.).

In general, metabolites make poor signals as their concentration tends to depend on the metabolic state of the animal. Nevertheless Wynne-Edwards (1962) suggests that mammalian pheromones have all developed from metabolites excreted onto the surface of the skin or into the urino-genital and intestinal tracts. Chemical signals that may well have originated as metabolites are androsterols which give boars and certain other mammals their musky odour. Androsterols may have originated as by-products of the catabolism of male sex hormones. In boars, the salivary glands appear to be the target organs for androgen, and it is in these glands that androsterols are produced to be secreted into, and dispersed on, the breath. Amouriq (1965) suggests that the sex attractant of the female guppy is probably oestrogen, which is released through the gono-pore. This may account for the persistent nipping that some males direct at this region in the early stages of courtship.

A number of alarm odours appear to have derived from defensive secretions. Thus the chemicals released during stinging by honey bees serve also to alarm and increase the probability of attack by other workers.

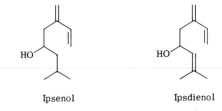

Ipsenol                    Ipsdienol

**Figure 5.2**  Representative chemicals that have been implicated as pheromone components in *Ips* species.

Honey bee stings tend to be clustered in the pelt of the victim because of this.

Although chemical signals form the basis of most species communication systems, there are several drawbacks, e.g. no case of information transfer by frequency and amplitude modulation of chemical emissions is known for any species: one chemical (pheromone), one message seems to be the rule. But, increase in information by chemical transmission may be accomplished in two ways. First, the number of pheromones may be increased; honey bees are "walking batteries" of exocrine glands, each gland producing a different pheromone. Second, the chemical signal may be increased in complexity by the incorporation of a number of different molecules which form a "mix", the variation in details of which may give extensive information about the emitter. Gas chromatography of the distillate of tarsal gland secretions of the black-tailed deer *Odocoileus hemionus* reveals the secretion to be a complex mix of molecules which differs between adults and juveniles, and males and females (figure 5.3).

The tarsal glands are the glands most involved in age, sex and individual identification in black-tailed deer, and clear differences in age and sex obtain. Certain insects also employ chemical mixes. The females of some closely-related species of moth release blends of chemicals as a means of conferring species distinctness. The main molecule, which is identical for several species, is accompanied by other molecules which potentiate the blend for conspecific males, while inhibiting responsiveness in other males (Comeau and Roelofs, 1973). Another ploy developed in the Lepidoptera is variation in concentration specificity. Thus the females of both the cabbage looper moth and the alfalfa looper moth secrete cis-7-dodecenyl acetate: high release rates attract male cabbage loopers, while low release rates attract male alfalfa loopers (Kaae *et al.*, 1973). But, only a few examples of "complex" odours and specificity of response to odour concentration have so far been found among insects, in contrast to what is proving to be the rule in mammals. This contrast may reflect general differences in central nervous system organization (p. 100); on the other hand it may reflect the greater opportunities available to mammals to learn the detailed characteristics of particular signals.

Wilson and Bossert (1963) suggested that airborne pheromone molecules would fall within particular ranges of carbon number and molecular mass. Below a carbon number of 5 and molecular mass of 80, relatively few compounds can be readily manufactured and stored. Above carbon numbers of 20 and molecular masses of around 300, molecular diversity reaches such high levels that further increase in size is unnecessary: species

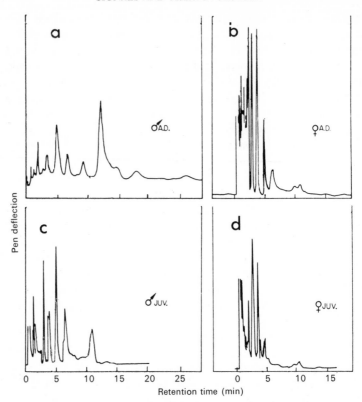

**Figure 5.3** Gas chromatograms of tarsal gland secretions of black-tailed deer. Attenuation of peaks is not shown. (*a*) adult male; (*b*) adult female; (*c*) juvenile male; (*d*) juvenile female (modified from Muller-Schwartze, 1971).

distinctiveness would already have been achieved. Wilson and Bossert predicted that chemicals serving as alarm signals, because they need not be species-specific, would tend to have lower molecular masses than, for example, sex attractants. Present findings now support these predictions. Thus, among the insects, the molecular masses of most alarm pheromones fall between 100 and 200, while most sex attractants fall between 200 and 300.

The same rules apply to water-borne chemical signals but differences arise in emission rates. Vapour pressure falls off steeply with increasing molecular mass, and upper limits on molecular size of air-borne chemical signals may therefore be set because of this. This rule does not, however, apply in water, and hence we see greater use of proteins (which have very low vapour pressures but which are often soluble in water) in the aquatic medium. This contrast between the chemical communication systems of aquatic and terrestrial animals may have posed problems during the colonization of land. Chemical "blindness" or, at the very least, "short-sightedness" would have been a highly likely result of emergence on to land.

However, provided that suitably volatile chemicals could be produced and responded to, there were certain bonuses for chemical communication in air, e.g. the speed of diffusion in air is between $10^4$ and $10^5$ times greater than in water. This results in increased speed of communication, but it also results either in the necessity to emit more molecules per unit time, or in the necessity to increase the sensitivity of the recipient to the molecule, if the "active space" of the emission is to be of the same order of magnitude as for water-borne chemicals. The active space of a pheromone is given by the ratio $Q/K$, where $Q$ is the emission rate ($\mu$g/second) and $K$ is the response threshold ($\mu$g/cm$^3$ of air). This ratio holds true only in still air. In moving air, the active space is, of course, skewed to one side of the emitter, and is, in part, determined not only by $Q$, $K$ and wind speed, but also by the degree of turbulence. The following formula was used by Wilson and Bossert (1963) to calculate a theoretical mean maximum distance of chemical communication in moving air:

$$x = \frac{8Q}{vK} \cdot \frac{4}{7}$$

where $x$ = communication distance in cm
$v$ = wind velocity in cm/s
$Q, K$ = as above

Typical responses to distance chemical signals are to head up wind (anemotaxis) or current (rheotaxis) until the molecule is no longer detected. When this happens, the receiving animal increases its rate of change of direction until the molecule is once more detected. If emitter and received are far apart, and if wind speed is high, then considerable amounts of pheromone may have to be released before emitter and receiver make contact. (The rate of vaporization of a molecule is proportional to the rate of air movement over the emission surface.) Production of large amounts of pheromone must be energetically expensive, and hence high wind speeds, notwithstanding the concomitant increase in turbulence, are not to the advantage of species employing chemical communication. A partial solution to this problem seems to have been found by the cabbage looper moth. The female apparently monitors the prevailing wind velocity and adjusts the duration of her pheromone release periods accordingly (Kaae and Shorey, 1972). At very low wind speeds, she exposes her pheromone-producing glandular surfaces for about 20 minutes, whereas at wind speeds approaching 3 metres/second exposure time goes down to about 5 minutes. Many other Lepidoptera simply do not give off pheromones unless wind conditions are suitable.

The effects of turbulence have not been discussed in detail because very little is known about them. However, a likely explanation of the dichotomy in distance signalling between day- and night-flying Lepidoptera is the fact that air turbulence increases during daytime as the result of local warming of the air. Thus, moths employ chemical signals over long distances, whereas chemical communication in the day-flying butterflies is largely employed only over short distances. Of course, visual signalling is greatly enhanced in daylight and is the main distance-signal employed by the butterflies, and this may also, in part, account for this dichotomy.

Thus only in a few cases can we even guess at the origins of chemical signals. However, some general trends are discernible. The pheromones of unicellular forms may have become the hormones of the Metazoa. These, in turn, have come, occasionally, to serve as pheromones. Other pheromones have probably originated as metabolites of various catabolic processes. Thus the androsterols of boars and perhaps other mammals are probably metabolites of androgen; and the pheromones of several species of insects (e.g. beetles of the genus *Ips*, and Danaid butterflies, see chapter 6) are metabolites of certain chemicals obtained from plants.

The chemical structures of a variety of pheromone molecules are now known. This is particularly true of lepidopteran pheromones. Despite this, no phylogenetic trends can be clearly discerned. Different taxonomic groups tend to employ different basic types of molecule, and different species tend to employ molecules that differ in some respect or other. However, the trends are reversed in too many instances to be given the label of "rule". Mammalian "odours" seem generally to be more complex than the exocrine gland secretions of, for example, the insects. However, we are not yet certain how many of the molecules making up mammalian odours actually have information value and so, even here, no emphatic statement can be made.

**Acoustic signals**

*Characteristics of the acoustic channel*

The consideration of acoustic signalling immediately raises the problem of what we mean by sound. To say that sound is what we hear is unfortunately, no help, and leads us into a circular argument:

Sound is what we hear; if we hear it, it's sound.

Pumphrey (1940) discussed this problem and emphasized the difficulty facing a human observer when he attempts to distinguish between "phonic" and tactile senses in an animal; the tendency is to analyze the responses in terms of the observer's own sensory experience. The distinction between hearing and tactile senses is often based only on the intensity factor and may be quite arbitrary, e.g. in insects many "tactile" hairs (e.g. on the cerci) are used as "hearing" organs if the intensity of the air-borne sound is high. It is often difficult, also, to distinguish between sound and ground vibration. Generally the morphology of vibration receptors differs little from those responding to air-borne sound. The only distinction in this case is the medium through which the pressure waves are transmitted. The question is further compounded when we talk of sound transmission in water.

It is, in fact, not possible to distinguish between vibration and sound; the characteristics of the signal are determined by the medium in which it is propagated. Water, like air, is an elastic medium, and the mode of sound propagation is identical in both cases: it is propagated by means of compressional waves. But water is much less compressible than air, and thus the amplitude of the oscillations is (with an equal intensity) 60 times smaller; but the sound pressure is 60 times greater in water than in air. This must be taken into account when considering transmitting and receiving devices, whether these are loudspeakers and microphones, or of a biological nature, e.g. a loudspeaker built to work in air has a low efficiency in water, because it is made to vibrate with great amplitude and work at low sound pressure. The same is true for microphones. Underwater transducers are therefore much more rigid, and the hearing organs of animals are adapted in the same way. Further, the speed of propagation of sound in air is approximately 344 m/s; in water it is about 1500 m/s. This means that for a given sound frequency, the wavelength in water is about five times that in air. The very low compressibility of earth further compounds these problems. Measuring the wavelengths of earth-borne

waves and referring these to airborne *frequency* (or *vice versa*), will produce quite erroneous values unless the compressibility of the medium is
taken into account.

For the maximum transfer of energy from the vibrator to the environment, the mass of the vibrator must be equal to that of the medium. In
detail: the important vibrator factors are its mass, its compliance (the
reciprocal of stiffness) and its mechanical resistance to displacement.
These factors introduce an *impedance* into the system which is a function
of the oscillator itself. The medium also acts as a load on the oscillator
which is called the *radiation impedance* and which must be added to the
mechanical impedance of the oscillator. The radiation impedance is also
a complex quantity. It consists of a reactive part, which may be represented by a thin layer of the medium next to the oscillator and which
moves with it, and a resistive part, which represents that which the
oscillator has to overcome in the radiation of energy. Thus, in any driven
system, with a constant driving force, maximum energy output is obtained
when the radiation impedance equals the internal impedance of the
vibrating structure (Beranek, 1954). In media with different masses, com-
pliances and resistances, different values apply.

Substrate-borne vibration (e.g. in soil) can only be used for short-
distance communication because of the high degree of attenuation (6 dB
cm$^{-1}$). But this attenuation may be exploited for orientation purposes.
Markl (1968, 1970) has shown that leaf-cutting ants (*Atta* sp.) produce
trains of clicks by pulling the file on the gaster forwards beneath the
scraper on the post-petiolar tergite. This forces the cuticle of the whole
body into vibrations at frequencies between 1 kHz and 3 kHz when they
are buried in soil. Because of the high degree of attenuation, there may
be up to 18 dB difference in intensity of the vibration arriving at the fore-
and hind-legs. This gradient is further magnified because the campaniform
sensilla in the joints of the forelegs are 4 to 5 times more sensitive than
those of the middle and hind legs. These factors allow soldier ants to locate
and release an individual buried up to a depth of 5 cm (Markl, 1970).

In air and water, two parameters are available to exploit in communication: medium displacement and pressure (see chapter 2, p. 47). In
the near field (i.e. within approximately one wavelength of the sound),
medium displacement is at an advantage because of the greater increase
in particle displacement as the source is approached, over the increase in
pressure; but delicate vane-like structures are necessary to monitor
medium displacement, whereas pressure receivers can be sunk below the
body surface to some extent. However, monitoring of medium displace-

ment is potentially easier in an aquatic environment than in air, since the mass of the tissues is comparable to that of water. Displacement of the water molecules can therefore be transferred directly to the cells. The lateral line systems of fish (p. 47) exploit this principle and monitor the movement of other individuals in their near field. Such receptors are likely to have evolved, in the first instance, in order to monitor medium displacement produced as a by-product of movement. Such mechanisms are of clear advantage for shoaling species.

Acoustic communication by monitoring medium displacement also occurs in *Drosophila*. The problem is an order of magnitude greater in air than in water, because the tissues have a greater mass than the medium. The receptors of *Drosophila* are the light feathery antennae, at the base of which the sensory cells are grouped together to form the Johnston's organ. Displacement of the antenna by the medium results in a receptor response which is phase-locked to the periodicity of the incident stimulus. The signal, produced by a male standing within 1 cm of a receptive female, is the result of a "flicking" motion of one wing. The rate of wing flick is species-specific and may be between 160 Hz and 400 Hz. Patterns are also established by inserting longer pauses at intervals. Because of the smallness of the wing and the very low frequency of emission, little *sound* is produced, but near-field displacements are very large (Ewing and Bennet-Clark, 1968; Bennet-Clark, 1975). The courtship of *Drosophila* must therefore be a very private affair, occurring within about 1 cm of the emitter.

However, beyond about one metre in water or air, communication usually involves reception of pressure waves. In water, sudden movements, movements of bones and joints during swimming and feeding, the impact of jaws and teeth during feeding, all produce a variety of sounds. These sounds are incidental and do not involve specialized emitters, but they may be of communicative value by evoking responses from other individuals appropriate to the presence of food, predators, etc. It is probably from such sources that specialized sound-producing and sound-receiving equipment and specific behavioural responses may have evolved. In the Scinenidae (Pisces), for example, sounds are associated with spawning areas and seasons. Often only males are capable of sound production. Moulton (1956) suggests that the "staccato" call of the sea robin (*Prionotus* sp.) may function in species discrimination and may be related to breeding behaviour. A remarkable example of adjustment of vocal behaviour to long-distance transmission of acoustic signals in an aquatic medium is provided by the whales. By using very low-pitched sounds and placing themselves at an intermediate depth in the ocean, in the so-called "deep sound channel", humpback whales are thought to be able to hear each other calling over hundreds of kilometres. Because of the refraction of sounds by the thermocline near the ocean's surface and by the compression layers deep in the ocean, sound waves are trapped within this channel, retaining much more energy than they would if they impinged on the surface and on the ocean floor (Payne and McVay, 1971; Payne and Webb, 1971).

## Mechanisms of sound production

Since water and living tissues are of approximately equivalent mass, Griffin (1955) suggested that a fish is, in a sense, "transparent" to sound and that an air-filled chamber, such as a swim bladder, serves as an acoustic discontinuity and will thus aid in sound reception. Swim bladders are also involved, directly or indirectly, in sound production. Their direct involvement is shown in the toadfish *Opsanus* sp. Here the swim bladder is thin-walled, tightly distended and possesses intrinsic musculature. The interior is divided into two chambers by a thin membranous transverse partition. Muscular contraction sets this membrane into vibration by changing the air pressures within the chambers. In the sea bass family, Serranidae, the swim bladder is thin-walled, non-muscular and functions only indirectly in sound production. Any blow against the body resonates within the bladder and is therefore amplified and extended in duration. Drum-like thumps are produced by the pounding of the operculae against the cleithra and other pectoral supporting bones. In the sea catfish *Galeichthys felis*, a creaking sound is produced when the enlarged pectoral spines are moved on their sockets, and this sound is amplified by the swim bladder (Moulton, 1963).

In the terrestrial environment, two main mechanisms have been used to produce sound: expulsion of air through a small orifice, and cuticular displacement. In the main, these two mechanisms are restricted to the vertebrates and the invertebrates, respectively.

The expulsion of air from the respiratory tract is designed to set membranes or cords into vibration. The fundamental frequency of vibration of these structures may be considerably modified by cavity resonance and/or harmonic emphasis. Further, two or more membranes may be used (as in the syrinx of some birds), in which case the membranes may, or may not, have the same fundamental mode of vibration; their sound frequencies may interact to produce harmonic distortion and extensive side bands;

and they may be capable of independent activity. Sound production due to expulsion of air, although occurring mainly in the vertebrates, also appears sporadically in the invertebrates. It occurs in cockroaches which produce a whistle through partly-closed spiracles when they are picked up, a response which is probably protective in function. The death's head hawk moth *Acherontia atropos* produces two different sounds alternately. The first is a broad-band sound which is produced when the roof of the pharyngeal cavity is raised and air is sucked in over a crescent-shaped flap, the epipharynx, which then vibrates. The second sound is a shrill whistle and is produced when the pharynx is relaxed, the epipharynx raised, and the air is forced out (Busnel and Dumortier, 1959).

In the vertebrates there is a clear adaptation of the ventilatory system for acoustic signalling. But more than this, the syrinx of birds and the larynx of mammals are highly complex mechanisms that have evolved specifically for the purpose of communication by means of temporal, amplitude and frequency modulation of the acoustic signal.

The existence of the external cuticular skeleton in insects inevitably results in sound production whenever any two parts are hit together, and it is not surprising that acoustic signals are mostly made in this way in this group. Sound is produced in the grasshoppers (Acrididae) when the hindleg is rubbed against the forewing (or tegmen). A plectrum on the tegmen (in Copiphorines) or the femur (in Oedipodines) is drawn across the series of teeth (the file) on the opposing structure. Each tooth impact results in a pulse of sound. A similar mechanism occurs in the crickets (Gryllidae) and bush crickets (Tettigoniidae), except that in these insects the plectrum and file are situated on the two tegmina (p. 15). Sound is produced usually during the closure of the tegmina, the opening phases being silent. Thus, a period of sound alternates with a period of silence. The repetition rate of this sound period or "syllable", is species-specific and is the direct result of the rate of limb movement (p. 56).

Once such patterns have evolved, the possibilities of variation in their amplitude modulation are almost infinite, especially if the rate of movement can also be varied (figure 1.5). The song of crickets has been divided into:

(i) Trills, where the syllable repetition rate is stable and continues for extended periods of up to hours.

(ii) Chirps, where the syllables are further packaged into discrete groups known as chirps.

The situation becomes even more complex in the grasshoppers that have, in effect, two sound emitters—the two metathoracic legs. The phase

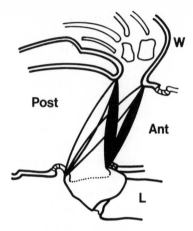

**Figure 5.4** The synergistic/antagonistic action of flight/walking muscles in insects. To move the leg (L) forward, the shaded muscles must contract synergistically, but to move the wing (W) up or down the same muscles must contract antagonistically. Similarly for the unshaded muscles.

relationship between the two legs may be fixed either in, or varying degrees out of, phase when the silent interval between each single leg sweep may be filled by the sound produced by the movement of the other leg. Alternatively, the phase relationship between the two legs may change during the single sweep, resulting in extremely complex sounds (Elsner and Popov, 1978; Lewis and Broughton, 1980).

*Evolution of song patterns in Orthoptera*

There is little or no overlap of generations in the orthopterans of the temperate zones. The young that emerge first therefore have no opportunity to learn the species song. Furthermore, individuals reared in isolation in the laboratory produce the full species song, and we can therefore state with confidence that singing in the Orthoptera is under genetic control. The question that arises is whether the rhythms of the song have evolved *de novo*, or whether the underlying neural mechanisms developed earlier in evolution for some other function, and have subsequently been modified for sound production. Flight and walking patterns are the most likely cyclically-occurring behaviours (chapter 4, p. 121). Without doubt, acoustic communication in *Drosophila* (discussed above) has evolved from flight, but the signal is produced by only one wing at a time and may be patterned. These additional features suggest that further neural patterning mechanisms are superimposed on the basic flight system. Flight and stridulation are also phylogenetically related in crickets and bush crickets (see Elsner and Popov for references). The wing-beat frequency in *Gryllus campestris* (and *G. bimaculatus, Acheta domesticus*) during flight is 20 to 30 Hz and is almost precisely the same as the frequency of tegminal movements during stridulation. Only minor changes in the flight motor programme are necessary to convert the up-and-down movements of the wings during flight to the to-and-fro movements of stridulation. In most crickets the main difference between flight and stridulation is the chirping nature of the songs compared to the continuous nature of flight (figure 1.5). Clearly, the chirping species have evolved further than the trilling species such as *Pteronemobius heydeni*. In the course of such further evolution, other oscillators must have been incorporated to modulate the basic pattern.

In the acridids, leg movements such as those of walking, jumping and defensive activity have been suggested as possible bases for the development of leg stridulation. Clearly, any movement that produces sound may have been exploited for communication purposes. On the other hand, neurophysiological evidence exists for the phylogenetic origin of sound from flight in several grasshoppers. In *Chorthippus mollis, Ch. biguttulus, Gomphocerippus rufus*, for example, the basic stridulatory rate is 50 Hz, which is exactly the flight frequency. In other species (e.g. *G. sibiricus, Ch. brunneus, Stauroderus scalaris*) the individual movements of stridulation occur in steps which follow each other at full, half or double the flight frequency.

The involvement of flight mechanisms in leg stridulation is not as strange as may appear at first sight. The muscles moving the wings also move the legs; the motor units are *bifunctional*. Confusion is prevented by a switchable synergistic/antagonistic relationship (figure 5.4). Bifunctional muscles which are attached to different sides of the leg (moving it forward and back) are inserted on the *same* side of the wing (moving it either forward or back, but not both). Similarly, muscles inserted on the same side of the leg are attached to different sides of the wing. Thus, whether the leg or wing is moved depends upon the coordination of these motor units.

In *Ch. brunneus*, a flight frequency of stridulation (50 Hz) is superimposed upon a slower rhythm of half that frequency. In *Ch. biguttulus* the flight rhythm is interrupted, every third cycle of up-and-down strokes producing a "chirp-like" structure (Elsner and Popov, 1978). This "chirping" disappears in time if the sensory nerves are cut in the femora on both sides. The pauses are inserted less and less frequently, and after 10 days disappear almost completely. The song is thus reduced to the unmodified flight rhythm. The flight rhythm appears to be the basis from which the song is built up.

In the light of these findings, Elsner and Popov (1978) suggest that, whereas the flight pattern is fixed, "stabilization" of the additional motor patterns which underly stridulation has only reached an intermediate stage as far as independence from peripheral control is concerned, since only in the short term is peripheral input unnecessary for the patterning of the song (see p. 123).

## Further considerations

The two groups of animals in which acoustic signalling is most highly developed are the insects and the terrestial vertebrates. Preadaptations for sound production probably existed in both groups: the heavily sclerotized exoskeleton in the insects and the ventilatory apparatus for moving air in and out of the lungs in the terrestrial vertebrates. Only in the vertebrates, however, do we see exploitation to the full of *frequency modulation* of acoustic signals. This presumably reflects the fact that only in the terrestrial vertebrates is sound frequency analysed to such a high degree, although frequency modulation of sound may be more difficult to effect with the type of sound-producing apparatus used by the insects.

Modification of emitted signals as the result of learning probably does not occur in the chemical modality, but is a feature of sound production in some birds and some mammals. Certain species of bush crickets have been shown to modify their songs as the result of interaction with other individuals (Broughton, 1965; Samways, 1977) but these modifications are not the result of learning *per se*.

Cultural transmission of song has been shown for a number of species of birds, both in laboratory conditions (Thorpe, 1958; Marler and Tamura, 1964; Immelman, 1969) and in the field (Marler and Tamura, 1962; Nottebohm, 1970; Jenkins, 1978). The abandoning of rigid genetic control over song at first sight seems to lack any significant strategical advantage, but one possibility is that dialects serve to reduce gene flow between locally adapted groups of birds. However, in the semi-flightless passerine *Philesturnus carunculatus*, Jenkins (1978) suggests another possible selective advantage of dialect formation. *Philesturnus* shows permanent pair bonds, and is also relatively long-lived. The risk of in-breeding is high, and dialect formation may serve to ensure *outbreeding*. Jenkins reports that males showed a strong tendency to avoid the parental dialect area and a tendency to settle in areas where conspecifics had a different song dialect. Such males then acquired the local song dialect. This phenomenon has not been reported for other species of birds in which song dialects have been known. Indeed two species, the zebra finch and bullfinch, show strong tendencies for juvenile males to sing the same song as their fathers. Both of those latter two species also form long-term pair bonds, yet show a distinct difference from *Philesturnus* in the way that the song "dialect" is transmitted. It would be interesting to know more about the ways in which *females* choose mates in these species.

Cultural transmission is also a feature of the sound emissions of Primates and, of course, is extremely well developed in humans. The amount of information conveyed in primate vocalizations is potentially immense, and bird song dialects seem to fare poorly in comparison. It should, however, be remembered that bird song is a signal serving just a few specialized functions; those of territorial signalling and mate attraction. Other vocalizations of birds are, in general, more variable and probably contain comparable amounts of information to those of the Primates. Human language, as opposed to non-verbal vocalization, is a rather special case and, although it is of course culturally transmitted, we feel that it falls outside the scope of this book.

Of all the signalling modalities, the acoustic modality seems to show the greatest potential for individual modification. Unlike, for example, visual signalling, complex acoustic signals have been specifically developed for communication purposes, and hence, being free of competing selection pressures, we might expect higher levels of specialization to be attained.

## Visual signals and their evolution

It is a truism, but nevertheless necessary to say, that visual signalling develops hand in hand with visual ability. With the ability to perceive movement and form arose signals *employing* movement and form, and with the ability to discriminate frequency came signals employing colour. More than with any other sensory modality, "nascent" signals, in the form of existing morphology and behaviour, must have been ready and waiting. Support for this assertion can be found in spider courtship behaviour. Web-building spiders employ mainly tactile signals during courtship. Thus male argiopids initiate courtship by vibrating the webs of females in highly characteristic rhythms. Thereafter, the approach towards the "short-sighted" female is slow and careful. Contact is made with outstretched forelegs and palps, and the male follows this by clambering over the cephalothorax of the female and inserting his pedipalps into the paired openings in her genital plate.

All male spiders, before they go in search of a female, "charge" the pedipalps with sperm deposited in a sperm web spun specifically for that purpose. The pedipalps of male spiders have thus become specialized storage and insertive devices (figure 5.5) and are readily distinguished from those of the female because of their increased size and complexity.

A number of families of spiders, e.g. the Lycosidae (wolf spiders) and the Salticidae (jumping spiders), have good form vision, presumably developed in conjunction with their active hunting habits. The pedipalps and/or the extended forelegs are used by the males of these families as visual signals when females are first encountered. Thus a feature showing strong sexual dimorphism (the pedipalp) has come to serve the additional function of a display feature. The tendency for the forelegs to be used in display is also interesting. Most male spiders extend the forelegs towards the female during the approach to her. In the web-building spiders they constitute a tactile signal, but in many species possessing well-developed form vision, they have come to serve as a visual signal. The males of many species of lycosids and salticids twitch, wave, or tremble the pedipalps and/or forelegs in a highly characteristic manner. The males may be vividly coloured on the legs, pedipalps or body, and the movements of the appendages, coupled with this coloration, produce displays which are often spectacular in the extreme and hence minimize the chances of being mistaken for potential prey by the female.

In the fly family, Empididae, the males of some *Empis*, *Empimorpha* and *Rhamphomyia* minimize the risk of being eaten by the female, by holding out a previously caught prey animal during their courtship approach. While the female is occupied with consuming the prey, the male achieves a copulatory clasp in safety. Some *Hilara* and *Rhamphomyia* males catch prey prior to courtship, but then join in an aerial dance with other conspecific males. The resultant swarm acts as an attractant to females who fly in and are copulated. In other species of empids, the dancing males add silk to the prey to enhance the visual effect of the swarm. In yet other *Empis* species, the prey is wrapped in a complete cocoon of silk. The amount of edible prey presented to the female now

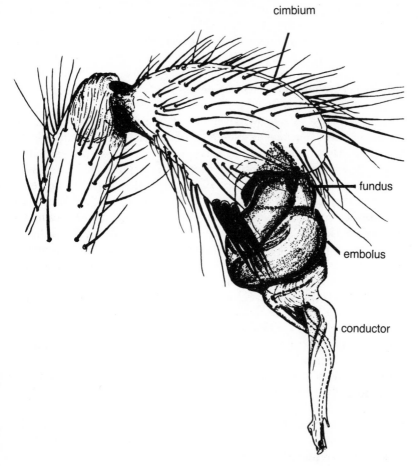

**Figure 5.5**   Lateral view of a palp of a male spider *Hypochilus gertschi* (from Kraus (1978) *Symp. Zool. Soc. Lond.* **42**, 235–254).

starts to dwindle because the males tend to feed on the prey before they cocoon it. Finally, in *Hilara granditarsus* and *H. sartor*, the males spin cocoons without enclosing any prey. The original ploy of food presentation during courtship seems to have evolved into an elaborate visual signal (Kessel, 1955; Wilson, 1975).

The amount of information potentially available in visual displays is probably greater than for any other modality, and the strong tendency of all groups that have well-developed eyes to employ visual signalling is undoubtedly linked with this factor. In particular, the *location* of the signaller and the wealth of contextual information that accompanies his display are *automatic* concomitants of visual signals.

## Origins and evolution of vertebrate signals

Some of the most interesting developments in ethology have centred on the ways in which signals originate and become "fixed" in an animal's behaviour. Most of this work has concentrated on "fixed action patterns" and their employment in communication. An example of this kind of work is Lorenz's studies on courtship behaviour in the Anatidae, described briefly at the beginning of this chapter (p. 125). In the minds of many people, the terms *visual signal* and *display* are synonymous, and this probably reflects the impact of the work of Lorenz, Tinbergen and others on the readily discernible visual signals of birds and fish. In fact, the term *display* can be used more generally to describe signalling in any modality. Some authors (e.g. Smith, 1977) have gone so far as to suggest that the term *display* be confined to *behaviour* that is employed as a visual signal, but we cannot subscribe to that view. However, it is no accident that many of the theories to be discussed below apply only to visual signals. Animals engaging in "social intercourse" of one kind or another frequently find themselves in a state of "internal conflict". In this state they may oscillate between approach and retreat, or engage in seemingly irrelevant behaviour, such as feeding, grooming, or thermoregulatory behaviour. In most cases, it is only in the visual modality that these activities will be perceived by the social partner(s). The following discussions relating to the origins of vertebrate signals therefore apply almost exclusively to visual signals. However, whatever the source of a signal, once communicative function has been acquired, natural selection operates to enhance the effectiveness of that signal. Later sections on ritualization, etc., are therefore relevant to signals in all the sensory modalities.

Evolution occurs gradually as a result of selection acting on small differences between individuals over a long period. This holds true for genetically controlled behaviour. New innate patterns of behaviour do not suddenly arise out of thin air. At first sight, the bizarre displays of courting and fighting vertebrates would seem to suggest that here, at least, the rules have been broken; that behaviours that are undoubtedly inherited have arisen spontaneously—from nowhere, as it were. However, the comparison between behavioural units and morphological features can only be taken so far. A behavioural unit can be shown by the same individual in different contexts, with different orientations, and perhaps with small changes of form. Context and orientation are vital clues employed by ethologists in the categorization of behaviour and, if these and form also change, then the category will also be changed. Extensive interspecific comparison of certain displays, as conducted by Lorenz on duck courtship, for example, has revealed that some displays are modified forms of behaviour normally shown in a different context. Hence, behaviour such as preening could also be used as a basis for courtship display. The process by which a behaviour normally shown in one context can come to be used for different functions (e.g. as a display) was originally termed *displacement*. However, the term *displacement behaviour* (or *displacement activity*) is now used more narrowly (see p. 152) and the overall process of "displacement" is therefore referred to as *derivation*.

The high frequency with which the process of derivation seems to have occurred in display behaviour is interesting, and Tinbergen (1953) and others proposed that derivation occurs as the result of mutually incompatible underlying tendencies coming into prolonged conflict. The tendencies referred to are the tendencies to be aggressive, to flee and, if it is a courtship situation, to mate. If mutually incompatible tendencies attain effective equality, then they may "cancel" each other out and allow less highly activated tendencies to express themselves as overt behaviour. Thus, an animal engaged in courtship may show the apparently irrelevant behaviour of preening, and in time this "irrelevant" preening may come to serve as a signal. Preening that occurs out of context in this way is a displacement activity in the narrow sense of the term, but displacement activities are not the only result of conflicting underlying tendencies.

### Behaviour resulting from "conflict" of underlying tendencies

Under most circumstances conflict between incompatible tendencies is readily resolved, e.g. an animal given the choice of two food sources may hesitate initially, but will eventually head for one or the other of the two sources. As one food source is neared, the less likely is he to backtrack to the other food source. In other words, this "conflict" is short-lived and unstable. The same holds true of conflicts over food *v.* water, food *v.* mate, etc. However, external events can bring about a less readily resolved conflict of tendencies, as Miller (1959) showed for the laboratory rat. The rats were trained to obtain food from one arm of a T-maze. After this initial training period, fleeing tendencies were induced in the rats by subjecting them to an electric shock just before they reached the food (figure 5.6). Adjustment of the level of intensity of electric shock and length of food deprivation to "approximate equivalence", resulted in the rats repeatedly running back and forth in the starting arm of the maze. The rats would approach the goal arm of the maze but, before reaching the point at which they had previously received an electric shock, they would turn and run back down the maze. On reaching the end of the runway, they would retrace their path towards the food and repeat the whole performance again. Eventually, many of the rats sat down and groomed themselves at some point in the starting arm. Miller proposed that the oscillation of the rats in the maze could be explained if the incompatible tendencies to approach and avoid the "feared goal" were not of equal gradient (figure 5.7).

He postulated that avoidance tendencies increase more quickly than approach tendencies as the "feared goal" is neared, because fear is a "learned drive". Thus avoidance is effected both by general fear and by the specific learned response of avoidance. Miller systematically tested alternative postulates, and eliminated all except the latter. His work "is an example of precise systematic theory building" (Hinde, 1970). Because the gradients of approach and avoidance cross, the rat will flee when near the goal box, but approach when distant from it. This conflict situation is therefore a stable one.

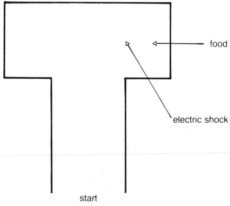

**Figure 5.6**  T-maze in which laboratory rats were both fed and subjected to electric shock.

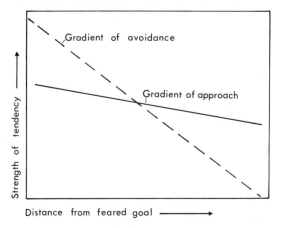

**Figure 5.7** Experimentally induced approach/avoidance conflict (after Miller, 1959).

Figure 5.7 is, of course, an oversimplification of the situation. First, straight lines or even smooth curves are an unwarranted assumption. Second, if the behaviour of the rat did conform precisely to the model, oscillation up and down the starting arm of the maze should not occur: the rat should freeze at the cross-over point. All that we can say with confidence about the rat's behaviour is that the tendencies to approach and withdraw are both present and, since these tendencies are largely incompatible, some form of "conflict" must be assumed.

More recently, several attempts have been made to apply catastrophe theory to behaviour in conflict situations, e.g. Zeeman (1976) attempts to describe aggression in dogs in terms of one of the elementary catastrophies, the cusp catastrophe. While the model is successful in predicting sudden changes in behaviour (i.e. catastrophies), it relies on an oversimplified account of aggressive behaviour and hence is, at present, of little real value in aiding interpretation.

Despite the shortcomings of present models, the phenomenon of "stable conflict" is nevertheless a real one, and animals engaging in social interactions can also be said to be in stable conflict. In social interactions, the other animal, be it mate or opponent, is the "feared goal". Evidence in support of this contention includes the following.

(i) Animals holding territories almost always attack intruders into their own territorial space, but flee when intruding into other animals' territory.

The same two individuals may oscillate back and forth over their neutral territorial boundary in what has been referred to as a "pendulum fight". It therefore seems reasonable to suggest that on the territorial boundary itself, the tendencies to attack and retreat are more or less in balance. It is on the territorial boundary that a variety of postures and actions, normally lumped into the category of "threat behaviour", tend to occur. Many of these threat behaviours are not identifiable with attack and retreat behaviour patterns as such, but resemble activities shown in other contexts.

(ii) The courtship of many passerines has been interpreted in terms of changing strengths of the three tendencies to attack, flee and mate. Hinde's work on courtship in greenfinches (1954), goldfinches (1955/56) and chaffinches (1953) is particularly successful in this respect. As an example, we have paraphrased his summary of courtship in the chaffinch (Hinde, 1970).

At the start of the breeding season male birds are highly aggressive and tend to threaten any adjacent individuals. However, unlike threatened males, females that are threatened do not fly off but adopt a fluffed posture, and are then gradually responded to with courtship behaviour rather than threat. The change in mood of the male is inferred from his lateral rather than head-on orientation to the female. The female gradually assumes dominance over the male, as shown for example, by her ability to drive him away from food. In the later stages of courtship the male approaches the female only with hesitation, his body upright, orientation lateral and using small pattering steps and a zig-zag walk. Finally, after perhaps several unsuccessful attempts, the male mounts the female, but as soon as copulation is over he flees, giving the same call as that which is given in the presence of a flying predator.

The most parsimonious explanation of the events in terms of underlying tendencies is that the balance between attack, retreat and mating gradually changes during the breeding period. Initially aggression is ascendant; then sexual approach and retreat are in balance; sexual approach finally dominates briefly but, after copulation, sexual tendencies presumably drop sharply and the male is left with "naked fear"—hence the alarm call.

(iii) Morris (1956) interpreted courtship in the 3-spined stickleback in much the same way. Of particular interest is his quantification of behaviour following the zig-zag dance: early in courtship zig-zagging was followed on 70·4% of occasions by attack on the female and on 24·1% of occasions by leading to the nest. Later on, however, the corresponding figures were 5·3% and 93·7%.

Wiepkema (1961) applied factor analysis to data gathered on courtship and other behaviour of the bitterling. Three factors, which Wiepkema labelled "fighting", "mating", and "other behaviours" (including fleeing) accounted for 90% of the variance. A number of threat behaviours had high loadings on more than one factor, again indicating the "bi-" or "trivalent" nature of their causation.

(iv) External coloration in a variety of fish and cephalopods is often highly correlated with the tendency to be aggressive, to flee, or to mate. In situations where one would predict these tendencies to be in conflict, external coloration, too, is sometimes a mixture of the main patterns.

Coloration of *Tilapia mariniae* was shown by Baldaccini (1973) to conform to three main patterns:

(a) The barred pattern typical of schooling non-aggressive individuals.
(b) The spotted pattern typical of fish showing territorial aggression.
(c) The dark pattern indicating escape/stay-put tendencies.

Fish engaged in territorial disputes often show gradual replacement of the spotted aggression pattern by the dark and/or barred pattern. The extents of barred/dark patterns shown in these situations were correlated with the probabilities that the fish would stay or leave (i.e. lose the dispute). The ambivalent nature of the coloration of these fish is indicative of internal conflict.

(v) A few authors have succeeded in manipulating the external situation to achieve simultaneous "activation" of opposing tendencies. For example, Blurton-Jones (1968) manipulated the tendencies to attack, feed (stay put) and escape in great tits, and found that, when stimuli eliciting attack or fleeing were simultaneously presented, there was an increase in the occurrence of threat displays. This kind of evidence is encouraging because here the hypothesis that conflicting tendencies promote the appearance of display behaviour is actually being explicitly tested.

Thus there are several cases where conflict between opposing tendencies does seem to occur. Furthermore, this conflict is relatively long-lived, and animals tend to remain at what appears to be the point of effective equality of those tendencies. In certain cases, the type of behaviour shown as the result of this conflict may also have a stabilizing effect. Chance

(1962) proposed that certain displays may have been selected for because they "cut off" arousing input (sight of "feared goal"). Preening movements of ducks and "facing away" in gulls involve the performer in movements where the head is turned away from the mate or opponent. This reduces visual input from the partner and may therefore reduce fleeing tendencies in the performer. This is supposition, but there is no reason to suppose that the types of behaviour shown during conflict do not, by their own performance, and irrespective of their effects on the recipient, affect the nature of the conflict (see also p. 163). In the case of "cut off" displays we would expect either a stabilization of the conflict or a move towards more positive "approach" behaviours.

Because of the number and nature of the variables involved, it is difficult to generate testable hypotheses regarding the causation of behaviour in social situations, but if we accept the conflict hypothesis, despite the problems of detailed interpretation, then we can start to explain the origins of many vertebrate displays. Displacement activities and other kinds of behavioural phenomena occur predominantly in what appear to be "conflict situations" and, if some means of "stabilizing" the behavioural phenomena exists, then we have a host of "nascent" displays at "our" disposal.

(i) *Intention movements*. This is probably a heterogeneous category but includes preparatory or incompletely suppressed actions resulting in behaviour that is less intense or incomplete, e.g. in the Carnivores the start of a biting attack involves opening of the mouth, lifting of the lips away from the teeth, and adjustment of the body position preparatory to moving forward. These movements have become emphasized to form threat display: the lip retraction is intensified to expose the teeth, dramatic crouched positions are adopted, and vocalizations are added (growling in dogs, hissing in cats). The whole performance is emphasized and prolonged. Many species of birds have displays that have derived from flight intention movements, e.g. the "full forward" display of the green heron seems to have developed from the pre-flight crouch preparatory to taking off (figure 5.8). Flight preparatory movements such as crouching, bobbing and "take-off leaps" have provided the sources for displays in a wide variety of birds.

(ii) *Alternation*. Alternate employment of acts representative of two competing tendencies. The rats in Miller's (1959) maze showed alternate approach and retreat from the feared goal. Male chaffinches show alter-

**Figure 5.8** Full forward threat display of the green heron (after Meyerrieks (1960) *Publ. Nuttall Orn. Club* **2**, 1–158).

nate movements towards and away from the female. The orientation to the female is lateral, and the steps are short and rapid; the whole performance is predictable and may well be communicative. The zig-zag dance of the male 3-spined stickleback is also alternation, in this case between the tendency to aggressive approach and leading away towards the nest (see also Morris (1954) for zebra finches).

(iii) *Ambivalent behaviour*. Displays may have been derived by combining various elements of competing tendencies, e.g. the upright threat posture of the herring gull combines elements of attack from above (where the aggressor pecks and beats his wings against the opponent) and elements of fleeing (such as lateral orientation to the opponent and sleeked feathers) (figure 5.9). The skuas also exhibit upright threat postures but, unlike the herring gull, do not incorporate raised wing carpals as part of the display. The skuas do not use wing beating in fights.

These are classic examples but some degree of ambivalence can be discerned in most threat displays where the animal is stationary. In many ways ambivalence can be regarded as a continuum with alternation behaviour.

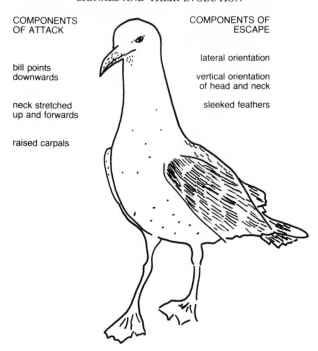

COMPONENTS
OF ATTACK

bill points
downwards

neck stretched
up and forwards

raised carpals

COMPONENTS OF
ESCAPE

lateral orientation

vertical orientation
of head and neck

sleeked feathers

**Figure 5.9** "Aggressive" upright threat display of the herring gull—
an example of ambivalence.

(iv) *Displacement activities* were originally described as activities irrelevant to the situation in hand, and explained in terms of a "spark-over"
of specific action energy into an inappropriate channel. Hence irrelevant
behaviours would be activated and provide an outlet for the energy. This
seemed to explain the rather abnormal form of some displacement
activities which appear jerky and more dramatic than the behaviour as it
would normally be shown. Thinking on this matter has changed, and
displacement activities are no longer regarded as entirely irrelevant
actions. Andrew (1956) proposed that displacement activities occurred as
the result of *disinhibition*; this depends on the major conflicting tendencies
"cancelling" each other out, allowing a lower-priority tendency to be
exposed in the ongoing behaviour. Van Iersel and Bol (1958) came to a
similar conclusion from their studies of preening in terns. They showed
that displacement activities were most likely to occur when the conflicting tendencies of approach to the nest and retreat (from the observers)

were both very strong, both intermediate in strength, or both weak, i.e. when the conflicting tendencies were "effectively equal". Furthermore, one of the displacement activities, preening, was more likely to be shown if the birds' plumage was wet. The *disinhibition hypothesis* implies that displacement activities represent the expression of tendencies that are appropriate but that are expressed only when more strongly activated tendencies cancel each other. The grooming shown by the rats in Miller's (1959) T-maze can now be explained: unable to feed, the animals perform the next most relevant activity; they groom the fur that was ruffled during the handling that preceded the testing.

At first sight it would seem rather a tall order that displacement activities occur only when conflicting tendencies are effectively equal. However the most likely point for an interacting individual to end up at is precisely the point where the conflicting tendencies *are* effectively equal. Hence, sticklebacks contesting territorial boundaries and any male courting a female he is "afraid of" will, almost inevitably, end up stationary, where approach and retreat tendencies are equal. The very nature of the stable conflict predisposes to effective equality of underlying tendencies and the consequent disinhibition of tertiary-level tendencies. Displacement is therefore a misnomer, but is still a useful term.

(v) *Autonomic activities.* The prolonging of "fear states" by stable conflict situations should also make a variety of autonomic activities available for use as displays. Sympathetic system arousal induces widespread changes in the vascular supply of the skin and muscle tonus, and therefore perhaps stance and hair and feather profiles, and can also cause initiation of defaecation and urination. Prolonged sympathetic activation may also result in compensatory parasympathetic activity, such as dermal vasodilation. Hence, fur and feather erection, defaecation and urination, for example, have become available for display material. The widespread development of odour glands associated with urinary and defaecatory tracts in mammals is an example of the opportunism of selective processes. In the territorial species, the most likely places for autonomic responses to occur are near the boundaries —precisely where the odour signals will have most value. Of course body cooling responses, defaecation and urination could equally well be termed "displacement activities". The important point is that they are likely to appear in stable conflict situations, and hence provide material from which signals can be developed. The thermoregulatory activities of birds and mammals are among the most clear-cut precursors of ritualized displays. In birds, the thickness of the insulating layer of air trapped in the feathers can be increased by "fluffing"; the feathers are raised only to the extent where the tips still make contact with the feathers behind. Further raising of the feathers results in loss of warm air, with consequent cooling. Feather fluffing can be seen in many submissive postures in birds, e.g. during food begging in juvenile gulls. Feather raising beyond this point (i.e. ruffling) can be seen in aggressive displays (e.g. the green heron) and in courtship (e.g. Gouldian finches).

(vi) *Redirection.* This is the direction of behaviour (in most cases aggressive acts) at substitute objects, supposedly as a result of thwarting. The intense grass pulling of gulls involved in territorial disputes is believed to be a substitute for a form of fighting where the opponent is grasped with the bill and pulled. Tule elk bulls often engage in mock sparring, where the antlers, instead of being used to interlock with and push against those of the opponent, are waved in the air or even used to engage shrubbery. Thwarting has also been suggested as a possible cause of some displacement activities.

It would thus appear that social interactions predispose animals to produce a variety of movements and postures that may then come to serve communicative function. Because social interactions bring about relatively long-term conflict between incompatible tendencies, and because the behaviour that results is to some extent irrelevant, it is likely to be "reliable" from the start, i.e. the same displacement activity, or whatever, is likely to occur at the same point in the interaction. If this is so, then such activities will have a head start as displays in their own right, and we should expect them to evolve into fully-fledged members of the species' display repertoire very rapidly. However, before looking at this latter process, it is important to bear in mind that there are many other sources from which displays can develop. Many signals have probably developed from already established signals in other modalities, e.g. courtship in newts involves much tail waving by the male (p. 187)—the original functions of tail waving were probably stimulation of the female's mechanoreceptors and wafting of scent towards her. Tail waving in newts now operates, additionally, as a visual signal; this is indicated by the white markings and certain of the tail movements employed. Long calling in gulls is terminated by a throwing back of the head in what seems to be a strong visual signal. It is a good bet that the acoustic elements of the display preceded the visual elements. Presentation of the ano-genital area by female primates is homologous to the lordosis posture of other mammals (p. 70). This posture facilitates olfactory investigation, followed by mounting by the male. Many Primates have developed a striking visual display from this posture by the addition of swollen and coloured skin around the genital opening.

Since these latter examples of signal development all originate in highly reliable, already existing, signals employing other modalities, their own "reliability" is far greater than any signal developing *de novo* from a stable conflict situation.

One of the problems with the conflict hypothesis is that we do not know how widespread the phenomenon is. We are reduced to arguing by example, always a dangerous practice, because examples can be chosen to fit the theory. Furthermore, the arguments tend to become rather circular, particularly if the concept of emancipation (p. 161) is brought into play.

Some authors (e.g. Andrew, 1972) have expressed discomfort over the conflict hypothesis. It is a very attractive explanatory principle but, because of its very attractiveness, tempts one to disregard other, possibly simpler, explanations of the phylogeny of displays. Andrew (1963) put forward convincing explanations of the derivation of primate facial expressions, not from conflict but from simple protective and attack preparation behaviours. Displays such as the "bared teeth scream face" and other displays where the teeth are exposed, involve a "screwing-up" of the face similar to certain facial expressions shown by humans when anticipating injury to the face. The eyes are protected by semiclosure of the lids, helped by the tensing of the cheek muscles; the upper lip is raised as a result and the upper teeth may be exposed. The lifting of the upper lip may also close off the nostrils, and explosive vocalizations may clear the mouth of noxious substances. Bared teeth displays *are* shown most frequently by primates that are threatened or attacked. Conversely, facial expressions shown by animals making, or about to make, an attack are characterized by a direct stare, tension in the jaw muscles (with resultant tightening of the lips) and silence! All these are anticipatory features of the behaviour about to be engaged in. The conflict hypothesis is not the most parsimonious explanation of the derivation of these displays (figure 5.10).

However, let us not "throw the baby out with the bathwater"; the sensible approach, at present, is to accept that signals can derive from a variety of sources, whether they result from conflict situations or not. Whatever the source, when a behaviour or an emission of any kind does start to acquire signalling function, selection will inevitably operate to

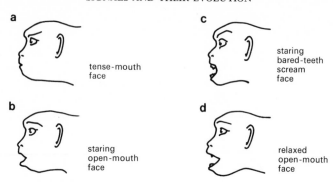

**Figure 5.10** Extreme facial expressions in a Macaca type primate (after van Hooff (1967) in Morris (Ed.) *Primate Ethology,* Weidenfeld and Nicolson).

improve its effectiveness as a signal. Such improvements are often referred to under the term "ritualization".

*Ritualization*

Tinbergen (1952) defined ritualization as "adaptive evolutionary change in the direction of increased efficiency as a signal". The word *ritualization* came into common usage as a result of Huxley's description of the ritual-like behaviour of courting birds such as the great crested grebe but, as can be deduced from Tinbergen's definition, the term has now come to be used in a wider sense. The ritual-like or stereotyped nature of display behaviour is one of the main results of the process of ritualization, but a variety of other changes can also occur.

(*a*) *Stereotypy.* Compared with behaviour patterns that apparently have no signal function, behaviour patterns that are employed as signals tend to be less variable in form and extent, i.e. they tend to be stereotyped. This assertion is the result of many ethologists' subjective impressions gained from extensive observations of display behaviour. There are several ways of measuring stereotypy, e.g. a coefficient of variation (C.V.) can be obtained by dividing the standard deviation (S.D.) of a selected parameter by the mean ($\bar{x}$) and multiplying by 100 to express it as a percentage of the mean.

The number 1 is added to the denominator to avoid the awkward situ-

Thus,

$$C.V. = \frac{100 \text{ S.D.}}{\bar{x}}$$

This can be converted to a measure of stereotypy (S.T.) by:

$$S.T. = \frac{100}{\dfrac{100 \text{ S.D.}}{\bar{x}} + 1} = \frac{\bar{x}}{\text{S.D.} + 0.01\bar{x}}$$

ation of "stereotypy" being infinite when C.V. is zero (Barlow, 1977). Stereotypy and C.V. are thus approximately the inverse of one another: when C.V. is zero, stereotypy is 100 and when C.V. is 100%, stereotypy is 0.99.

The easiest, and therefore most frequently used, parameter of a display is its duration, but this may not be the most suitable parameter for analysis. For one thing, we might expect lengthy displays to be more variable in duration than quick displays. Thus the more rapid displays of the goldeneye duck (e.g. bowsprit, simple-head-throw and head flick) have S.Ts. of 36.8, 13.9 and 6.25 respectively, whereas a longer display (the masthead) has an S.T. of 1.88. However, an intermediate length display (e.g. display drinking) has in this case the highest S.T. of all, 94.8, so that duration is not the only cause of variability by any means (Dane et al., 1959).

Relatively few authors have used parameters other than duration of display, but one example (unfortunately not from the vertebrates) is the work of Hazlett (1972a) on the behaviour of the spider crab (*Microphrys bicornutus*). He noted the angle between the body and chelipeds, and the angle between first walking legs and body. The chelipeds and first walking legs were held higher when displaying than when feeding. Further, the final angle was less variable when the spider crabs were displaying. Thus, in this case, in one particular parameter, display behaviour can be said to be stereotyped.

Most studies on behavioural stereotypy fail to distinguish between intra- and inter-individual variation (p. 126) and in fact the ideas about the phenomenon are still rather vague. But, as far as we can tell, displays do appear to be *relatively* stereotyped (and it must always be a matter of *comparison* with non-display behaviour). Not all signals are stereotyped, and not all behaviour patterns that are stereotyped have signalling functions. Thus, many static displays of birds appear to be extremely variable in form and duration, whereas egg retrieval in geese, egg fanning in sticklebacks and many preening movements in birds (all behaviours lacking signal function) appear to be stereotyped.

Stereotypy is presumably selected for because of the advantages conferred by a "common code". Thus we gain a strong impression that when "noise levels" are high (e.g. when animals not individually acquainted with each other, or when animals separated by relatively great distances, are attempting to communicate), stereotypy also tends to be high. When interactions are rapid, as in the courtship of polygamous birds such as the sage grouse (p. 191), or when there is a high risk of injury, as in territorial disputes, stereotypy and ritualization again tend to be at a high level.

Morris (1957) pointed out that once a display is elicited it tends to be performed with "typical intensity". The timing and amplitude of the display tend to remain the same despite variation in the eliciting stimuli. At first sight this just seems to be another way of describing stereotypy, but it is an important point because non-signalling behaviour tends to vary with the strength of the eliciting stimuli, whereas display behaviour does not. There are, of course, exceptions to this rule, e.g. Barlow (1968) asserts that the size of the mate of the orange chromid (*Etroplus maculatus*, Cichlidae) influences the coupling between head quivering and flickering of the pelvic fins. Further, Hazlett (1972*b*) found that the height at which the hermit crab *Pagurus longicarpus* holds its chelipeds varies with the distance away of the opponent. Nevertheless, typical intensity is generally a concomitant of stereotypy and is probably a contributing feature to the ritualistic nature of communicative interactions.

So far, we have concentrated on inherited contributions to performance of displays, but it is worth bearing in mind that individuals can learn to "polish" their performances. Any regular performance tends to show a decrease in its variability. A useful term to describe this process is "stylization" and it is a feature of many caged animals. Carnivores can develop automaton-like movements about their cages which are far more rigid in form than most naturally-occurring behaviour.

There may therefore be a variety of factors promoting the development of stereotypy. We are probably not aware of all the factors involved, and we have not discussed considerations such as the effects of competition and the advantages of individual distinctiveness. Further, when sympatric species employ similar distance signals, there appears to be strong selection pressure towards signal distinctiveness. One effect of this is to increase the stereotypy of the distance signals. However, distinctiveness and stereotypy are rather different issues and should not be confused.

(b) *Change of function.* Any behaviour that comes to be employed as a signal can be thought of as changing its function, but some examples deserve special attention. In particular, cases are known where already elaborated signals serving one function have been further "derived" to serve another function, e.g. the domestic fowl *Gallus domesticus* sometimes employs "food calling" associated with the discovery of a source of food. Other chickens in the vicinity are attracted and benefit from the new food source. *G. domesticus* cocks are known to employ food calling during courtship: the cock ground scratches, steps back, and pecks at the ground while uttering the food calls. In fact, the cock may pick up pebbles instead of food, and is often successful in enticing females to his side. He then switches to more overt forms of courtship such as waltzing. A number of phasianids show elaboration of the "food enticement" ploy (figure 5.11). The Impeyan pheasant *Lophophorus impejanus* bows rhythmically before the hen with tail and wings outspread; the peacock pheasant *Polyplectron bicalcaratum* ground scratches and then bows with outspread wings and tail. If food is made available to him at this time, he will offer it to the female, a good indication of the origin of the display. The most elaborated form of food enticing is shown by the peacock *Pavo pavo*. The erected tail feathers are shaken at length in front of nearby females, followed by several backward steps and bowing. Juvenile male peacocks have been observed to food entice in the original form with ground scratching and pecking. This last example is also a good illustration of the development of adornments; the tail feathers of the male become more and more bizarre as the display becomes more central to courtship.

Presentation of the ano-genital area is a signal inviting copulation in female mammals and has been the subject of careful study in primates. In a number of primates the signal now fulfills the dual role of invitation and appeasement. Even males, when faced with aggression from an animal dominant over them, will present and may consequently be briefly mounted.

Food begging displays in juvenile gulls have been incorporated into courtship, although here the display has changed very little. The female not only establishes non-aggressive contact with the male in this way but also causes him to regurgitate food which she then consumes. Ritualized food begging is widespread among birds and is employed not only in courtship but as an appeasement signal. It is used to appease dominant flock mates by subordinate Canada jays *Perisoreus canadensis* (Smith, 1977).

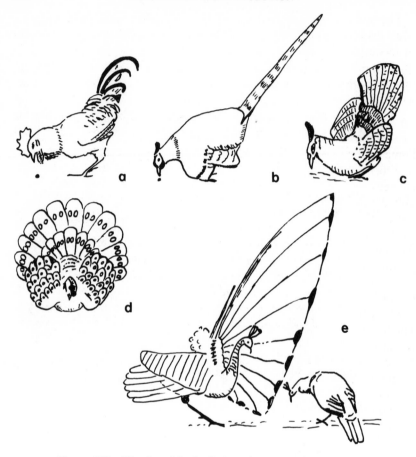

**Figure 5.11** "Food enticing" displays in some phasianids. (*a*) domestic cock; (*b*) ring-necked pheasant; (*c*) Impeyan pheasant; (*d*) peacock pheasant; (*e*) peacock (after Schenkel (1956) *Ornithol. Beobacht.* **53,** 182).

(*c*)  *Change of form*. With change in function comes change in form. Thus, movements may be:

(i) simplified, as in display preening in ducks;
(ii) speeded up, as in head shaking displays of Gouldian finches which appear to have been developed from bill wiping;
(iii) slowed down or even frozen into postures, as in the baring of the teeth in threatening dogs and the static displays of peacocks;
(iv) rhythmically repeated, as in the bobbing movements of birds, lizards, etc.
(v) exaggerated, as in a variety of head shaking, drinking, etc., in water birds.

The extent to which behaviour will change in form is of course limited. Most display behaviours appear to have been derived from basic patterns of locomotion, feeding, respiration, elimination and protective reflexes (p. 150). These basic patterns will generally take primacy, and display behaviour will be developed only to the extent that it does not interfere with the efficient performance of these basic patterns.

(d) *Morphological changes.* Changes in structure and colouring have clearly developed to enhance signalling behaviours in the visual modality. Some of the most dramatic changes are shown in birds. It is also clear that behavioural changes proceed hand-in-hand with morphological changes, e.g. in the tit genus *Parus*, the "head-up" threat posture (probably developed from flight intention movements) is used most by those species that have conspicuous throat and breast coloration (figure 5.12). In the blue tit *Parus caeruleus*, where breast coloration is less intense, the "head-up" posture is less often used than the "head-forward" threat posture. The blue tit is also one of the few tits which can erect the feathers of the facial disc in such a way as to enhance the size of the face (Hinde, 1970).

Many birds have crests, and all these are capable of raising the crests. The habit of erecting feathers seems to have come first, morphological enhancement second. Of course, the situation is not always so clear cut. The development of combs and wattles in the game birds, and manes in mammals, are more difficult to associate with specific signals, and we cannot be dogmatic about whether behavioural change always precedes morphological change.

(e) *Emancipation.* It has been suggested that the process of ritualization also involves freeing or "emancipation" of displays from their original causal factors, as in the peacock food enticement behaviour. Similarly, the "nose kissing" of courting grasshopper mice *Onychomys leuogaster* is derived from a fighting posture known as the boxing stance, where the combatants rear up on their hind legs and paw and bite each other. Biting is completely inhibited during nose kissing, and the whole performance may be interpreted anthropomorphically as a "mutual non-aggression pact".

The courtship of many ducks involves sequences in which displays derived from "displacement preening" and "displacement drinking" follow each other in a fixed order. If the displays still depended on their original causations, this should not be so. Emancipation seems to be the most parsimonious explanation.

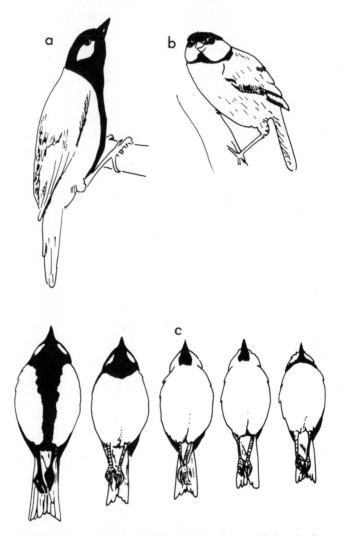

**Figure 5.12**   Morphological enhancements of threat displays in tit-mice. (*a*) head-up threat posture of great tit; (*b*) head forward threat posture of blue tit; (*c*) ventral markings of, from left to right, great tit, coal tit, willow tit, marsh tit, blue tit. The extent to which the head-up display is employed by species within the genus *Parus* tends to be positively correlated with the extent of the dark ventral markings (after Hinde (1970, 1974) *Biological Bases of Human Social Behaviour*, McGraw-Hill, London).

The understanding of emancipation at the physiological level is still beyond our reach, but the phenomenon does not pose any serious contradictions to known central nervous system operation. Motor patterns above the reflex level are not inexorably linked to one patterning mechanism. Such an arrangement would be most impractical. Animals use the same pattern of leg movements whether they are walking to food, water, shelter, etc. Chickens use the same sharp blows of the bills on food and foe alike. The difference between fixed action patterns and display behaviours can only be one of degree. There is an increase in the specificity of response for displays, but the majority of them should not be regarded as being completely fixed to one specific "social releaser" from the start. Just as with pecking, walking, etc., the animal will "try out" the displays in a number of contexts. It is in this kind of flexibility that the process of emancipation must originate.

Since the origin of this concept, authors have been well aware of the danger of overgeneralization, but the original proposals concerning emancipation came in a climate of opinion that nascent displays arose in situations where *motivational* conflicts abounded. As pointed out earlier, we cannot be certain what the nature of the conflict is, and we certainly cannot ignore the role of external factors. It is all very well to hypothesize about the freeing of a display from its original motivational causation, as long as motivation is regarded as an isolated internal variable. However, since we now suspect that external events do influence internal state (chapter 3), the whole argument starts to crumble. External events will not be so susceptible to change; the same basic situation of the presence of the feared goal *re* mate or opponent will always obtain. Hence Baerends (1975) asserts that no display is probably fully emancipated from its original *causal* factors.

Any discussion of emancipation results in a walk along an interpretational tightrope, and it is not surprising that many authors avoid the topic altogether. However, despite all the circular arguments and lack of concrete evidence, the firm impression remains that displays do originate as a result of stable conflict, and that they then tend (in some as yet unknown way) to become autonomous from *some* of the original causes. A strong candidate for a display that originates as a result of internal conflict is facing away in gulls. Beer (1975) found two distinct forms of facing away in the laughing gull:

(i) "Black upright facing away", where the back of the black hood and prominent white feathers above and below the eyes remain visible to the partner;
(ii) "White upright facing away", where the hood was hidden because the bill tended to point downwards, the neck was not so stretched, and white feathers at the base of the hood were erected (figure 5.13).

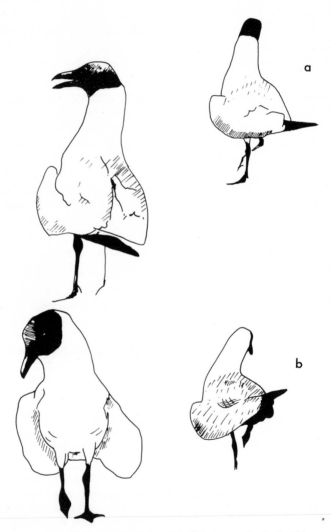

**Figure 5.13**   The two forms of upright facing away in the laughing gull: (*a*) black; (*b*) white (after Beer, 1975).

Both types of facing away incorporate lifting of the carpal joints from the side of the body, a characteristic element of threat in gulls. Beer suggests that the two forms of facing away serve different functions: "white upright" appears to evoke less aggression from the partner and is shown when aggressive interactions "wish" to be avoided. Furthermore, each of the two forms can be shown in a variety of circumstances. "White upright facing away", for example, can be shown in courtship inter-actions, when it seems to reflect lack of fear coupled with sexual attraction, and in hostile interactions, when it seems to reflect lack of hostile intention coupled with fear. The external events bringing about the display appear to differ slightly and the underlying causations of the display are quite variable; emancipation is a reasonable explanation of these observations. The fact that one display, "upright facing away", can give rise to two distinct forms serving different functions and often being shown in a variety of different circumstances, is further support for some degree of autonomy from the original causations of the behaviour.

## Numbers of displays

Surveys of the numbers of displays in species repertoires have been con-ducted by Moynihan (1970) and Smith (1969). Both authors arrived independently at an upper limit of about 40 displays per repertoire. Problems arose in conducting the survey in that differing procedures and definitions were adopted by the numerous behaviourists whose obser-vations were included in the survey. Further, less obvious displays may have been overlooked. But even taking these factors into account, Smith (1977) guesses that the upper limit to most species repertoires is no more than 60 to 80 displays. Even this seems a remarkably low number con-sidering that the main form of communication for the majority of species is by means of genetically-programmed stereotyped behaviour. A possible explanation for this low number is that for a display to be effective it must be distinguishable from all other displays in the repertoire. An animal such as the peacock, with extreme morphological enhancement of one courtship display, would find difficulty in performing a large number in the visual modality without high probability of engendering confusion in the recipient. There are limits on the extent to which displays can be elaborated and hence made distinct from one another. Costs in time spent displaying and attending to a display is one problem.

The problem of specificity of response in terms of costs to central nervous flexibility also arises. Preprogramming sensory input, central nervous filtration processes and motor patterns is expensive in terms of the information that is lost. Every species has concerns with inputs other than those emanating from conspecifics. There is competition between social success and recognition of food, predators, etc.; in other words, survival.

Darwin's (1872) *principle of antithesis*, where displays of opposite function tend to be opposite in form, is shown in dogs where aggression is accompanied by piloerection, raised head and tail, and where in the submissive posture the hair is depressed and the head and tail are down. This may, in part, be accounted for by the problem of confusion between displays in a large repertoire. In fact, Darwin's rule of opposites is somewhat arbitrary; distinctiveness is the key to the issue.

Moynihan (1970) argues that, since new displays are constantly being developed, and because there appears to be an upper limit on the number of displays in a repertoire, other displays must fall into disuse and eventually disappear from the repertoire. He sees this being accomplished by changes in threshold of release of the display. Alternatively, displays might become "deritualized", gradually reverting to less stereotyped states. Smith (1977) believes that he has identified some examples of nearly "extinct" displays in the vocal repertoire of the eastern phoebe (an "Andean" flycatcher *Sayornis phoebe*), e.g. the doubled vocalization consists of a pair of rapid double up-and-down frequency sweeps, and is so rare in occurrence that it was only heard in very extensively studied individuals, and not even in all of them. However, this vocalization is among the more common calls of two western species of phoebes. Dilger (1962) found that in species of the parrot genus *Agapornis* that he studied, displays commonly performed by some species were not present in other species. Occasionally, however, individual parrots did perform what he had considered "extinct" displays for that species. Moynihan's (1962) observations on the displays of gulls and terns also revealed a similar evolutionary replacement of displays within species' repertoires, and the phenomenon must now be accepted as established, at least for birds.

Whatever the causes of relatively fixed numbers of displays per species, there are a number of ploys whereby information flow can be increased.

## Context

The same display can be used in different situations. Such displays would, in Smith's (1977) terminology, be broad message displays, where the intentions of the signaller can only be assessed in detail by reference to the context in which the display is performed. The multiple functions of laughing gull displays (Beer, 1975) such as "upright facing away" and the long-call are examples of the use of context by a species.

*Graded signals*

Information can be increased by producing graded forms of one signal. Thus the intensity of alarm calls, aggressive actions, etc., can all be informative. Also, the number of times a signal is repeated, and the number of individuals giving the signal (as in the alarm calls of gulls, p. 5) can also be informative. Although certain signal "constellations" can be recognized in primates, a complete intergrading range of signals is produced by combining eye, mouth and body movements with vocalizations. Estimates for human nonverbal signals put the total at around 150 recognizable displays, a large proportion of which are composites of facial expressions and nonverbal vocalizations. Relaxation of stereotypy is, of course, a necessary concomitant of the use of graded signals, and the opportunities available for learning about communication systems must also, undoubtedly, play a role.

## Conclusions

The signals employed in the animal kingdom originate from a wide variety of sources: from metabolic secretions, chance acoustic output, from other signals or from behaviour shown in conflict situations. What is also clear is that the modality used for signalling exerts its own peculiar constraints upon the form and content of the signal. In other words the evolution of signals occurs within the environmental constraints appropriate to that modality; whatever the origin of the signals, once signal function has been acquired, the appropriate shaping forces of natural selection take over. The trends towards stereotypy and increase in signal strength are discernible in all the sensory modalities, but are at their most obvious in the visual modality.

Display repertoires are often strictly limited, hence it is surprising that many signals often appear to mean the same thing. This is particularly true in courtship. It is easy to see that, for example, particular distance signals need to be repeated over and over again as a means of overcoming environmental noise and hence attracting a partner. The redundancy here is only apparent. However, this does not explain the use of more than one signal for the same function. One possibility is that employment of different signals meaning the same thing sustains the attention of the intended recipient and hence perhaps maintains a state of high arousal. It is, of course, quite possible that we are missing subtle differences in meaning between such signals, but this seems unlikely. The same signal can also have different meanings in different contexts, and hence a limited repertoire may be expanded by the use of contextual information.

It has, in the past, been conventional to consider signals and responses almost as isolated units, and this has been the method of approach adopted here. But what if displays are part of a higher level of communicative organization, just as words are parts of sentences? The mosaic approach we have adopted so far hardly touches upon this question. So in chapter 6 we take a more holistic line and examine sequences of behaviour.

# CHAPTER SIX

# THE SHAPING OF COMMUNICATION SEQUENCES, COURTSHIP

SO FAR WE HAVE DEALT WITH SIGNALS LARGELY AS ISOLATED UNITS OF communication. Many interactions are organized by one or just a few signals, but there are also interactions which are comprised of a series of signals and responses. The best examples are found in courtship, and Tinbergen (1951) described such sequences as "reaction chains" because each response acts as a signal to the partner which then releases the next step in the chain. Furthermore, the release of various responses in the chain can depend on whether or not other actions have been made prior to the reception of the relevant releasing signal. This establishes the interaction as a chain with identifiable "links" and seems to be the result of successive "gating of responses". Reaction chains are never fixed, of course; they are probabilistic in both a positive and a negative sense, i.e. some behaviours are highly likely to occur in response to a particular signal, some are highly unlikely. The degree of "determination" of a reaction chain varies with individuals and with species. We shall discuss the extent of this variation and the order in which the behaviour occurs. In courtship the latter is related to the reproductive requirements of the particular species, and we shall illustrate these themes with examples chosen from a few selected groups. Methods of analysing some of the sequences described in this chapter are presented in chapter 7.

## Butterfly courtship

Butterfly courtship occurs in relatively stereotyped sequences, and the several studies in this area provide interesting comparisons. One of the simplest and most rapid examples is that of the small sulphur butterfly *Eurema lisa* (Rutowski, 1978). *E. lisa* is a small pierid butterfly with a wing span of about 3 cm occurring in sandy waste places from Central N. America to Costa Rica. The wings of the male are strongly ultravioletreflectant whereas the female's are not. Rutowski (1977*a*) showed that the males decide whether or not to court a sitting butterfly on the basis of ultraviolet reflectance and the "flutter response". Although other morphological features also confer recognition of sex and species (on the part of both male and female), if the perched butterfly is not strongly ultraviolet or does not give the flutter response (a stereotyped and repetitive opening and closing of the wings) the male will court. Courtship can start in the air or when the female is perched, but Rutowski (1978) showed that relatively few aerial interactions end in successful copulation. Only when the female lands more-or-less immediately is there any likelihood of successful mating. Once the female has perched, the male repeatedly buffets her, making contact with wings and/or legs. Most females and also perched males wing flutter in response to the approach of another butterfly, and maintain the fluttering until the unwanted attention ceases. Receptive females stop fluttering after about 3 to 5 seconds, then spread the antennae and extend the abdomen sideways. The abdominal extension of the female is elicited within 5 seconds in response to a chemical signal emitted from the base of the forewings of the male (Rutowski, 1977*b*). The male then alights on the female, usually on her wing tips, and walks, flapping his wings until he is holding on to her thorax. With claspers open, the male probes with curled abdomen down towards the anal margins of the female's hindwings. Genital contact is effected when the male's claspers grab the tip of the female's abdomen; both animals then become quiescent. During copulation, the pair only take to the air if disturbed; it is always the male who flies, carrying the motionless female. Copulation lasts for 30 to 60 minutes. In approximately one third of successful pairings the female did not perform the flutter response but responded to the male with wing closure almost immediately (figure 6.1).

Courtship in *E. lisa* is comparatively rapid and simple, lacking the complex and often repetitive aerial and ground manoeuvres seen, for example, in the nymphaline, danaine and satyrine butterflies. This may in part be due to the strong sexual dimorphism in ultraviolet reflectance that confers rapid discrimination between sexes. Other visual cues may occur, but this has yet to be tested.

---

**Figure 6.1** Sequences of behaviour in the courtship of *Eurema lisa* (*a*) with and (*b*) without a female flutter response. The number to the right is the number of courtships on which the data for a given step are based. Mean duration is given to the right (from Rutowski, 1978).

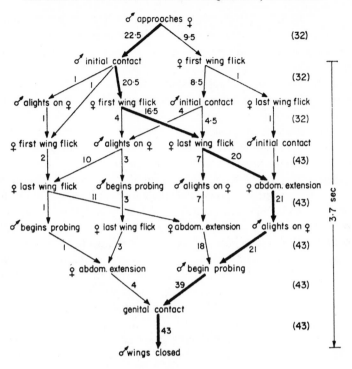

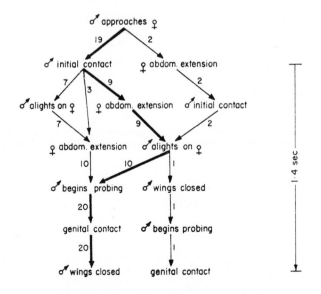

An example of a longer and more involved courtship is found in *Argynnis paphia* (Nymphalinae), the silver winged fritillary. This is a European species inhabiting clearings and the edges of woods. The adults fly during July and August, the females mainly in the mornings and the males in the afternoons. Mating therefore occurs in the period around midday. The males respond to fluttering yellow objects by approach, and then fly in tight circles around the object. Leaves and other smaller yellow butterflies are approached, but are soon abandoned. A responsive female *Argynnis* responds to the male's attention by fluttering on the spot with a peculiar whirring movement. The female then flies slowly away on an exceptionally-straight course, very unlike her normal erratic flight pattern. The male pursues the female and, starting from a position above and behind, glides beneath her to rise suddenly and almost vertically in front of her (figure 6.2). This upward dart brakes the female temporarily in her flight. The male repeats his performance until the female alights to initiate the *ground courtship* phase. Ground courtship may be the only form of courtship if a male happens to encounter a settled female. At first the male flies in a semicircle around the female, she in turn fluttering and raising her abdomen, probably to release scent. The male alights beside the female, whereupon she stops her wing fluttering and beats her wings slowly up and down. This allows the male to approach and clasp the wings of the female with his own in a typical bowing movement. By this means he probably funnels scent from glands on his hindwings onto the female, his wings being opened and closed sharply to facilitate this "scenting" of

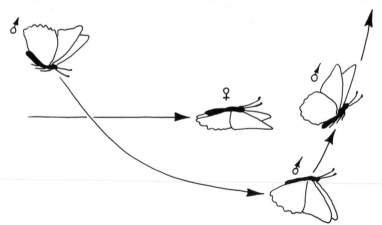

**Figure 6.2** The pursuit flight of the male fritillary *Argynnis paphia* (after Magnus, 1950).

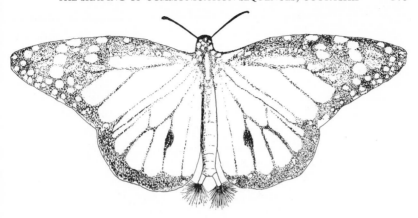

**Figure 6.3**    Male Queen butterfly with fully extruded hair pencils.

the female. The male also employs tactile signalling, by vibrating his antennae and middle legs against her hind wings. Copulation occurs with the pair side by side: a receptive female extends her abdomen sideways and this is clasped by that of the probing male (Magnus, 1950).

The Queen butterfly *Danaus gilippus berenica* also shows elaboration and stereotypy of the aerial stage, but differences from the nymphaline species occur. *Danaus* males use hair pencils, consisting of a pair of bundles of hollow hairs, which are protrusible from the tip of the abdomen (figure 6.3). They arise from invagination of the intersegmental membrane between the eighth and ninth sternites and are used to disseminate phero-mone over the female's antennae. After sighting a female, the male Queen pursues and overtakes her from above and flutters in front of her with hair pencils everted. By rapid downward sweeps of the abdomen the male brings his hair pencils into contact with the female's antennae. Receptive females are induced to alight in this manner, but the male continues his hair pencilling and bobbing flight around the settled female until she stops fluttering her wings. The male then alights and palpates the female's head and antennae alternately with his own. Again, copulation occurs with the pair parallel to each other. Once the male has achieved a clasp on the female he flaps his wings once or twice, the female releases her hold on the herbage and the pair take to the air, the female passive, the male actively flying. They eventually settle in foliage some distance from the original site of pairing. The copulation flight may serve to remove the mated pair to a location less exposed to predators (figure 6.4).

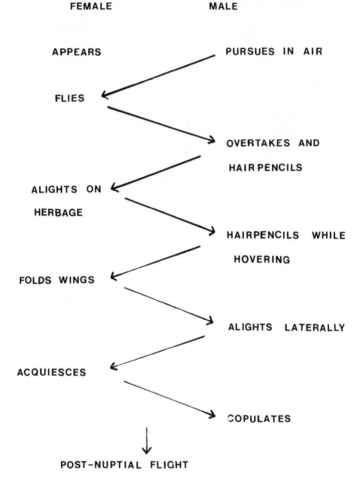

**Figure 6.4**   Courtship sequence of the Queen butterfly (after Brower *et al.*, 1965).

Courtship of *D. chrysippus* is essentially identical to that of the Queen (Seibt *et al*, 1972) but the courtship of a closely-related species, the Monarch butterfly *Danaus plexippus*, reveals some interesting differences which are apparently due to differences in their chemical communication systems (Pliske, 1975). Male Monarchs perch in suitable sunny positions on herbage and fly towards any fluttering objects of the right size and colour as conspecifics. All except female Monarchs are abandoned after

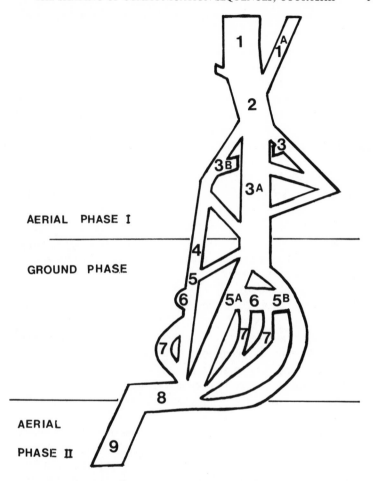

AERIAL  PHASE  I

GROUND  PHASE

AERIAL

PHASE  II

**Figure 6.5**  Possible sequences in monarch butterfly courtship behaviour. 1. male nudging; 1A, female nudging; 2, aerial pursuant; 3, aerial pounce; 3A, aerial takedown; 3B, aerial hairpencilling; 4, pair alight; 5, lateral copulation attempt; 5A, dorsal copulation attempt; 5B, ventral copulation attempt; 6, antennal palpation (concurrent with all copulation attempts); 7, female proboscis extension; 8, copulation; 9, post-nuptial flight (after Pliske, 1975).

one or two darting passes. Females are usually "nudged", the male flying rapidly towards her and making several slow bobbing movements towards her posterior. The female flight is characteristically slow at this stage, "sailing" alternating with bursts of flapping. Females occasionally nudge males in exactly the same manner. After nudging, an *aerial pursuit* phase occurs in which the male chases the female in fast erratic flight. This may last from 5 seconds to 1 minute and is very similar to the flight used when escaping from predators. All successful Monarch courtships include this phase. *Aerial takedown* then occurs, the male dropping onto the dorsum of the female, clutching her head, thorax and abdomen with his legs and impeding her flight. The male ceases flying but keeps his wings open so that the pair slowly float down to earth. Aerial takedown may be preceded by one or more aerial pounces which are probably unsuccessful takedown attempts. Also the aerial takedown may be preceded by aerial hair pencilling which is more-or-less identical to that of Queen males. The ground phase of courtship is also very similar to that of the Queen butterfly, antennal palpation and lateral copulation being the rule. During copulation the male snaps his wings several times and then takes to the air carrying the passive female on a *post-nuptial flight*. The pair remains secluded for 2–14 hours, usually in dense shrubbery while a spermatophore is exchanged (figure 6.5).

The courtship of the Monarch is, in outline, essentially similar to that of other *Danaus* species. All the members of this genus studied so far engage in "nudging", aerial pursuit, aerial hair pencilling, lateral copulation, antennal palpation and post-nuptial flights. All species also show common mechanisms for terminating courtship, such as aerial and foliage evasion, abdominal evasion and "apathy" on the part of the females, and aerial dismissal, desertion and homocourtship by the males.

However, in the Monarch butterfly, the new development of aerial takedown is the dominant means of entering the ground phase of courtship. In fact, males with their hair pencils experimentally removed are apparently not at a disadvantage in courtship, whereas male Queen butterflies are (Pliske and Eisner, 1969). Further, the Monarch male does not employ hair pencilling in the ground phase of courtship. The hair pencils of males are probably the smallest in the danaine subfamily, being approximately one third the length of those of the male Queens. The males of many species of Danainae and Ithomiinae ingest dihydropyrolizine alkaloids from the dead shoots of plants (Bull *et al.*, 1968; Edgar *et al.*, 1974; Edgar and Culvenor, 1974). The ingested alkaloids are then modified to produce the dihydropyrolizine sex pheromone secreted by the large trichogen cells at the bases of the hair pencils. Hair pencil dihydropyrolizines are critically important in the mating success of *D. gillipus* and *D. chrysippus*. Removal of the hair pencils or rearing the males in isolation from plant alkaloids causes lack of pheromone production and reduction of success in getting female conspecifics to "co-operate". In both species, liquid hair pencil secretion is transferred to the female's antennae on hair pencil dust, minute particles derived from hair pencil cuticle. Viscous terpinoid compounds act as solvents for the di-hydropyrolizidines and as adhesives for the dust particles (Pliske, 1975; Pliske and Eisner, 1969). Meinwald *et al.* (1968, 1969) failed to isolate any dihydropyrolizidines from Monarch hair pencils, even though Monarch males do visit alkaloid-containing plants (but less often than other danaines) and Monarch males do extrude their hair pencils in at least some courtship flights. Schneider and Seibt (1969) showed that isolated Monarch antennae respond to male Queen dihydropyrolizidines as strongly as antennae of Queens themselves. Why then has aerial take-down superseded hair pencilling in the Monarch? Pliske (1975) suggests that female passivity during the ground phase of courtship may be en-hanced by the takedown, and that this behaviour may have developed from the aerial phase of hair pencilling. An alternative possibility is that aerial takedown may have developed from aerial attempts at copulation by the male.

Wing glands are developed in a wide variety of lepidopteran males and are the main secretors of pheromone in species such as *Argynnis paphia*, the silver washed fritillary. Wing glands are also present in the danaines, but their role is not clear. Much interest has centred on the relationship between the hair pencils and the hindwing glands in the danaines. A number of species have been seen to insert their hair pencils into the glands, but early suggestions that the hair pencils acted as disseminators of pheromone produced in the wing glands are incorrect. The main sexual attractant is produced at the bases of the hair pencils. There may be synergism of some kind between wing gland and hair pencil secretions as Brower *et al.* (1965) suggest, or the wing gland secretions may serve as a preening substance for the hair pencils.

Male butterflies are catholic in their choice of mate, at least in the initial approach phases. One's impression is that the final decision lies with the female, and that it is the detection of pheromonal secretions from conspecific males that is the main factor inducing cooperation. The Monarch is highly unusual among the danaines, and indeed among other lepidopteran groups, in that olfactory cues are apparently not a dominant feature of their courtship.

In conclusion, butterfly courtship shows three distinct stages: aerial, ground, and post-nuptial. The aerial phase has been elaborated in a variety of groups within the Papilionoidea and seems to be based on visual attraction by males and "escape" responses by the females. The "whirring" and straight flight of the fritillary *Argynnis paphia* may not be developed directly from escape flight. Some form of "buffeting" of the female by the male is ubiquitous and, although scenting of the female seems to be the main purpose of this behaviour, tactile and visual signals cannot be ruled out. The overall effect of this "buffeting" is to arrest the flight of the female and bring the pair into a position where copulation is possible. The Monarch male shortcuts this phase by employing aerial takedown. Males that encounter perched females enter into the ground phase of courtship immediately. Presumably the aerial phase of courtship has been developed in order to increase the chances of opposite sexes encountering each other. The fact that pierids such as *E. lisa* largely dispense with an aerial phase may be linked with their comparative vulnerability to predation and/or with much more effective visual signalling. Pierids are quite palatable to birds and other predators, relying on rapid erratic flight as their primary defence. *Danaus gilippus* and *D. plexippus* on the other hand are chemically well-protected, obtaining cardiac glycosides from the milkweed plants on which they feed. The orange-brown coloration of the wings is probably aposematic, and selection for rapid courtship will not have been so strong. Furthermore, visual discrimination between *Danaus* species is not easy. A number of species are sympatric and there are also mimics, such as the Viceroy *Limenitis archippus*. Aerial olfactory signals and the development of special scent disseminators, the hair pencils, may be associated with the problem of visual discrimination.

The ground phase of courtship in *E. lisa* is far more rapid than in the danaine species we have been considering. The mean duration for *E. lisa* courtship, including a female flutter response, is 3 to 5 seconds, whereas the ground components average 32 seconds for the Queen and 37 seconds for the Monarch (Rutowski, 1978). The sexual dimorphism in ultraviolet reflectance in *E. lisa* confers rapid visual recognition and may well account for this ten-fold difference in duration. The transmission and reception of olfactory information is a much slower process and may account for the differences in duration of the ground phase.

Wing flapping and/or holding the wings horizontally seems to be a universal indicator of non-receptivity in butterflies. However, the flutter response also serves as a visual signal indicating the sex of the butterfly, for it is the presence or absence of wing glands that is the main visual difference between the sexes. The *duration* of the flutter response must therefore be regarded as informative of the state of receptivity. Closure of the wings seems to act as a signal of readiness to mate, but distance away of the male is also important. If he is some distance removed from the female he is *less* likely to continue courting, probably because he can no longer locate her (Rutowski, 1978).

Lateral copulation and concomitant tactile signals are also the rule, but differences again arise in the final stages of mating, the post-nuptial flight. Only certain species engage in post-nuptial flight, but estimates of durations of copulation are too few to suggest any reason for the presence or absence of such flights. In most species it is the male that carries the female. In species showing sex-limited mimicry (and it is always the female that is mimetic), the female carries the male. This ploy presumably serves to decrease the possibility of attack by a predator—the flapping, apparently aposematic, wings of the female being a far more obvious signal than the closed and immobile wings of the male. In species where the male carries the female during the post-nuptial flight, she has her wings closed throughout the final stages of courtship, whereas the male's wings are held open until clasping is completed. This is particularly obvious in *Argynnis paphia*. This situation ensures that mechanical damage produced as a result of the hind wings of the male hitting those of the female is minimized when the male takes flight. In *Hypolimnas misippus*, where the female carries, copulation is carried out with the male's wings closed and the female's open.

Butterfly courtship provides some interesting behavioural comparisons. Male Euploeini such as *Euploea lore* patrol with hair pencils fully extended in the absence of females, who are attracted from some distance, presumably in response to olfactory cues. Courtship then proceeds in the normal danaine manner. Thus the male pheromone seems to be acting first as an attractant and then as an arrestant.

It has been suggested that distance chemical signals are more frequently employed at night because air flow is more uniform and not subject to the extreme daytime thermals from local solar-induced temperature variations. Hence the more common use of distance chemical attractants by the nocturnal Lepidoptera. *Euploea* is an exception to this rule.

## Fish courtship

Of the 20 000 or so species of fish, the breeding habits of only about 300 species have been described in detail (Breder and Rosen, 1966) and a disproportionate number of these are freshwater species. However, even described species show a wide range of mating habits which vary with regard to the method of fertilization and the amount of parental care. The possession of territory may also affect the type of courtship shown. Since most fish are polygamous, and fertilization is external, we start with a consideration of this type.

The whitefish *Coregonus lavaretus* is marine but migrates into brackish or fresh water to mate. It is a shoaling species, but the shoals break up at the onset of the breeding migrations. They are not territorial and show no distinctive coloration or aggressive behaviour. However, at the onset of courtship, individuals do show "attachment" to a particular area of stream bottom for a short time. Although the type of bottom patrolled by individuals varies, it is thought that the types of substrate selected (usually a mixture of sand and stone) are those most suitable for the fertilized eggs to settle in and be relatively well protected. Individuals start courtship by adopting a characteristic posture, involving full fin spreading followed by a slow display of swimming termed "sailing". Sailing may continue for several hours (even after dark), but it gradually intensifies into a more rapid sailing to the surface, accompanied by rapid turning movements which cause splashing (Fabricius and Lindroth, 1954).

Approaches, mainly by males, are made to fish sailing near the bottom. Mutual sailing then occurs, the fish oriented in parallel, their flanks often touching. The movements are rapid and accompanied by undulations of the bodies. The displaying pair head into the water current, the undulations increasing in intensity and becoming synchronized. As soon as synchrony is achieved, the pair release eggs and sperm simultaneously. Because the pair have swum upstream, the eggs often settle on the substrate originally patrolled. The eggs are not placed, but fall into crevices. After mating, the pair separate and may repeat the process many times with other individuals. Thus, mating in the whitefish is rapid, *symmetrical* and both sexes are polygamous. The only orientation is to each other and to the water current. There is no aggression to overcome in this type of fish, and no nest to build or direct the partner to.

Courtship in the bitterling *Rhodius amarus* has been studied by Wiepkema, and the details of his analysis are discussed in chapter 7 (Wiepkema, 1961). This species is aggressive, and shedding of the eggs is more accurate than in the whitefish. Bitterlings of both sexes start to show interest in freshwater mussels of the genera *Unis* and *Anodonta* in early spring, swimming around the mussels and performing reactions to them which are typical of the reproductive period. The males gradually start to defend a particular area around a mussel, displaying to and butting and chasing other fish. Ripe females, however, are led to the mussels, where they deposit eggs within the gills of the mussel where they are quickly fertilized by the males. The acceptance of the female by the male depends primarily on the length of the female's ovipositor. When a female is ready to spawn, the papilla or ovipositor becomes many times longer than the anal fin. Initially a male rushes at a female when she intrudes into his territory. Sometimes he butts her but usually ends the rush with a "quivering", which is a rapid lateral undulating movement of the entire body, of high frequency and small amplitude. Fin spreading, a signal employed in male–male encounters, is not shown. After the initial quivering, the male turns and "leads" the female to the mussel. Leading is characterized by movement away from the female and is accompanied by quivering and "tail bending" where the male's tail is bent to the side away from the female and the dorsal and anal fins bent towards her (figure 6.6).

Leading will be repeated until the female arrives at the mussel. The male then adopts a head-down posture and, if the female is close behind, he begins "skimming". The head-down posture is usually performed with the fish's snout just above the exhalent siphon of the mussel. Skimming is a rapid swimming from the head-down posture such that the male's ventral surface skims over the siphon area of the mussel. Very often, the skimming movements of the male are accompanied by sperm ejection, visible as a small grey cloud. After performing a skimming movement,

**Figure 6.6**    Male bitterling leading a female towards a mussel (redrawn from Wiepkema, 1961).

the male quivers beside the mussel continuously. The female now performs a head-down posture similar to, but often steeper than, that of the male. If the siphons of the mussel are fully open, the female swims down and forward and touches the siphon area with her ventral surface, when the ovipositor is placed inside the exhalent siphon. At this time only the thick proximal part of the ovipositor is erected. Immediately after insertion, 1 to 4 eggs are pressed rapidly through the ovipositor which becomes stiffened by a fluid (probably urine) which is used to eject the eggs. This stiffening causes the hitherto slack distal portion of the ovipositor to penetrate deeply into the gill cavity of the mussel. Oviposition is completed within one second and the ovipositor becomes slack again and is pulled out as the female rises away from the mussel. The male, probably in response to chemical cues from the act of oviposition, now becomes very aggressive towards the female and chases her away. He then performs more skimming and ejects large quantities of sperm over the mussel (figure 6.7).

This is a very differently-organized courtship from that of the whitefish. It is *asymmetrical*, the male being the more active in displaying and leading. The biology of the bitterling is, of course, rather unusual in that the young hatch and spend their early days in the mantle cavity of the

**Figure 6.7** Skimming with sperm ejection in the male bitterling (redrawn from Wiepkema, 1961).

mussel. It might therefore be argued that the details of courtship are unusual because of this. In fact, this is not the case. Freshwater fish, where the male defends a territory in which he builds a nest, commonly employ leading behaviour and head-down postures to "show the nest entrance". The three-spined stickleback *Gasterosteus aculeatus* is a case in point. Like the bitterling, the male stickleback's initial approach to the female is usually aggressive, but is converted into a zig-zag display as a result of the visual appearance of the globular female in a head-up orientation. Zig-zagging is followed by leading, where the male swims directly to the nest, the female close behind. He then "shows" the nest in a head-down posture, his snout placed at the entrance. The female enters the nest, he trembles against her flank, and she spawns. Possibly in response to chemical cues emanating from the eggs, the male chases the female out of the nest. He finally enters the nest himself and fertilizes the eggs. Hence, the overall form of courtship in the bitterling is similar to that of the stickleback. The main differences are in the initial display, quivering *v.* zig-zagging, and in the details of gamete release.

As a final example, the guppy *Lebistes reticulatus* is a schooling species with internal fertilization (Baerends *et al.*, 1955). The guppy is a native of Trinidad and the north-east coast of S. America. There is no territory or parental care, but the female is viviparous. Although not territorial, the male guppy is very aggressive towards other males. This pugnacity may help to limit interference in mating which takes place within the overall home range of the school. Guppies are sexually dimorphic, the male having a comparatively larger tail and a series of black markings on the flank which come and go with the "mood" of the individual. The male also tends to be smaller than the female (figure 6.8).

Baerends *et al.* (1955) showed that of the black markings on courting

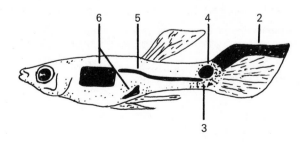

**Figure 6.8**  Dark markings that appear during courtship in male guppies. See text for explanation (from Baerends *et al.*, 1955).

male guppies, patterns 1 (an overall darkening of the body), 4 and 6 were associated with various stages of courtship, 6 always being present at copulation. Pattern 2 was associated with aggression, often accompanying pattern 1. Patterns 5 and 3 came and went in conjunction with various stages of courtship.

Guppy courtship begins with a male orienting to and following a female. He concentrates in particular on the genital pore, often biting at it. He then alternates following with "posturing" beside or ahead of the female. This posturing is characterized by jerky swimming, rapid opening and closing of the fins, and holding the body in an S or sigmoid shape. If the female responds by not swimming away or by orienting to the male, the posturing develops into a more obvious series of little jumps away and then back towards the female. This is termed "luring" and has been equated by various authors to the leading shown in other species. If the female continues to follow, the male adopts a sigmoid posture ahead of the female, but unlike earlier posturing the fins are spread. From briefly-held sigmoid postures the male may occasionally "jump", a startling display performed with fins spread and often involving the male almost turning head-over-tail (figure 6.9). Jumps may cover 10 cm or more, and seem to be an intensified form of luring. More commonly, the sigmoid posture is held and movements of the male become slow and smooth, movement of the rays of the caudal fin often being the only sign of activity. The strange contrast of body stillness with the flickering caudal fin rays has often lead observers to call this behaviour "shimmering". A responsive female at this time becomes completely motionless in the water, and the male then moves slowly round her in a smooth curve to approach from behind, gonopodium swung forward, and attempt copulation. If the female inclines her body towards the male, successful copulation is likely. Because the later stages of courtship involve the male displaying in front of a motionless female, they have been termed the "checking stage".

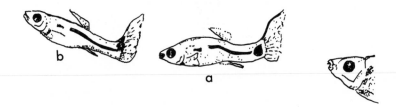

**Figure 6.9**  Intense sigmoid display (*a*) followed by a display jump (*b*) in the male guppy (after Baerends *et al.*, 1955).

The sequence of guppy courtship is in fact highly variable and, although a chain of events can be discerned, Baerends *et al.* (1955) represented it as a flow diagram of *intramale transitions* (figure 6.10). In species such as the guppy, where the female apparently does very little apart from move towards or away from the male, there is little point in representing the courtship as a "reaction chain".

Figure 6.10 shows that the main sequence of events is from approach to following, to posturing, to luring, to the sigmoid display, and finally to a copulation attempt. However, it is *usual* for the sequence to be repeated (at least in part) several times before a copulation attempt is made. Furthermore, early activities such as approach may be immediately followed by the sigmoid display. Only in the last stage of courtship can the sequence be regarded as in any way fixed or rigid, and even here the sigmoid display itself tends to be rather variable in duration.

Fish courtship is clearly divisible into symmetrical forms, as shown by the whitefish, and asymmetrical forms as shown by species where specific orientations to a chosen spawning place occurs. This place is

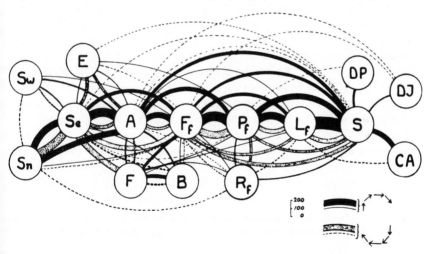

**Figure 6.10**  Male guppy courtship behaviour. Black bands and continuous lines should be read from left to right. Hatched bands and dotted lines from right to left. The thickness of the bands represents the number of times an act was seen to follow another. A, approach; B, biting; CA, copulation attempt; DP, display posturing; DJ, display jumping; E, evading; F, following; L, luring; P, posturing; R, retreating; S, sigmoid; Se, searching; Sn, snapping; Sw, swimming about. The index f, means with fins folded (from Baerends *et al.*, 1955).

chosen by one partner, usually the male. Even within the symmetrical courtships, extensive differences in timing and types of display occur, e.g. in the jewel fish *Hemichromis bimaculatus*, courtship is a far more leisurely affair than in the whitefish, the partners selecting a spawning site, clearing it and finally spawning during skimming (Baerends and Baerends, 1950). The jewel fish show joint parental care, the young being taken to small pits after the eggs hatch, and the parents sharing the guarding and patrolling duties. Here there is less pressure on rapid matings than in the polygamous whitefish. Furthermore, it may be advantageous that the pairing jewel fish spend time in mutual display in order to promote individual recognition.

In the asymmetrical courtships, the behaviour of the female seems to be of less importance. Very often she displays only upon entering the male's territory, and thereafter remains passive until she spawns or copulates. In species such as the bitterling and stickleback, this may be because the male is sufficiently stimulated by the egg-laying alone. Most asymmetrical of all are the displays of the guppy, where fertilization is internal. Here the female is totally passive, and male display seems to proceed as long as she remains so. The checking phase of guppy courtship is clearly a means of bringing about complete lack of motion in the female, so that the male's gonopodium can be precisely positioned into the female; but why the complex luring stage of courtship? Baerends suggests that luring is necessary to get the pair away from the school, and from interference from other individuals. As previously stated, male guppies are highly aggressive, and interference with a mating pair is a likely event. The swordtail *Xiphophorus helleri* is also a schooling species employing internal fertilization. However, *Xiphophorus* males are not so continuously aggressive, and a long luring phase is absent from their courtship. Male swordfish follow females, but then quickly dart in front of them to display spread fins and tails; they then shimmer slowly around into a copulation attempt. Thus the whole courtship, apart from the initial following, is remarkably similar to the later stages of guppy courtship.

The type of courtship employed by fish depends more on the particular needs of the species than on taxonomic position. Because of this diversity of needs, it is not possible to construct taxonomic groupings of fish based on their courtship behaviour, as it is for example with ducks (p. 125). Fish displays seem to have been derived from swimming movements in the main, but some of the quivering displays, undulations and skimming may have developed from movements involving the shedding of ectoparasites.

**Courtship in the newt, the problem of the spermatophore**

A variety of invertebrate and lower vertebrate males use spermatophores as a means of transferring sperm to the female. The advantage of this method is that large amounts of sperm can be introduced into the female without recourse to the development of special intromittent devices and copulatory behaviour. However, problems arise in transferring the spermatophore. An example of a courtship sequence involving spermatophore transference is that of the smooth newt *Triturus vulgaris* (Halliday, 1975).

Courtship starts with a prolonged "orientation phase", in which a male approaches a female and closely investigates her cloaca. The male then attempts to overtake the female and to take up a display position in front of the female. If she becomes stationary, the male is increasingly likely to display. This is the next stage of courtship and is termed the "static phase". Three types of display are shown by the male in this phase (figure 6.11) and the sequence is highly variable:

(i) *Waving*. The male holds his tail at an obtuse angle to his flank and waves his tail slowly with high amplitude.

(ii) *Whipping*. This develops from waving. The tail is brought back violently against his flank, which directs strong jets of water at the snout of the female.

(iii) *Fanning*. Holding the same orientation to the female as for the other two displays, the tip of his tail is waved. The movements are of higher frequency and smaller amplitude than in (i) and (ii).

Throughout the static phase, the body of the male is held rigidly concave ahead of the female. If she approaches, the male shows an increased likelihood of entering the next phase, the "retreat phase". Here the male backs slowly away from the female, maintaining the same posture and displays, but predominantly whipping. If the female still follows, the male shows an increased probability of turning away from the female and slowly "creeping" forward about 5 to 10 cm. He then stops and quivers the tail from side to side. A cooperating female will touch the male's tail at this time. The male then folds and lifts his tail and extrudes a spermatophore. He then creeps forward through exactly one body length, stops and swings into a position perpendicular to his previous path and to the long axis of the female. This stops the female so that her cloaca is positioned over the extruded spermatophore; this phase is termed "braking". In successful matings, the female sucks the spermatophore into the cloaca. Finally the male pushes back on the female almost as if to provide the female with a second chance of picking up a missed spermatophore. However,

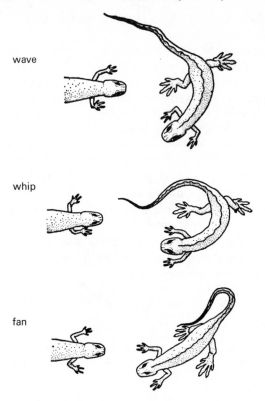

wave

whip

fan

**Figure 6.11**   Three displays of the male smooth newt (from Halliday, 1975).

Halliday never saw this manoeuvre to be successful; once a spermatophore had been missed, pushing back never remedied the situation. The sequence of courtship can be repeated in part or in whole several times. Interactions were usually brought to an end by the need of one or both participants to go to the surface for air (figure 6.12).

Throughout the courtship, the behaviour of the female smooth newt is quite simple: she either moves towards or away from the male, or she remains static. Halliday was able to show that these actions were monitored by the male, and that they did affect his ongoing behaviour. The methods he employed for analysing his data are considered in chapter 7.

The courtship behaviour of the male newt seems to function firstly as a stimulant to the female, and secondly as a means of positioning the

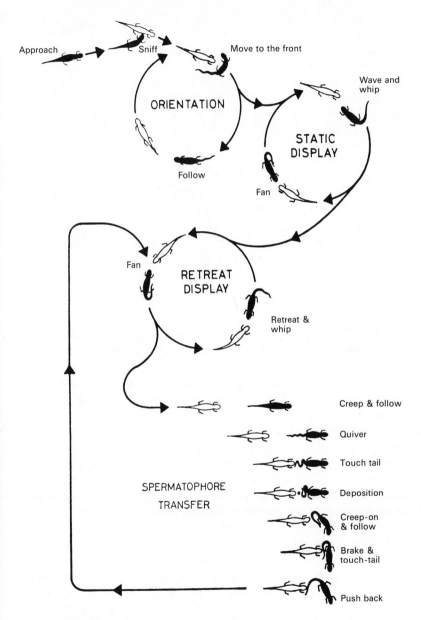

**Figure 6.12**   The sexual behaviour sequence of the smooth newt. The male is in black (from Halliday, 1975).

female precisely over his extruded spermatophore. Sex and species identification are probably effected through visual and chemical information. Both sexes possess hedonic scent glands distributed over the cheeks, body, cloaca and tail, and initial identification of species and sex may well depend on the secretions of these glands. Tail movements of the male have probably developed, in part, as a means of mechanically stimulating and wafting his scent to the female. However, the tail movements also act as a visual signal to the female, and the tail has a white stripe in the mid-lateral area.

Spermatophore transfer occurs in a variety of arthropods, in particular arachnids. A very dramatic form of female manoeuvring occurs in scorpions. The male effects a grip on the female's mandibles with his own and is able to push and pull her onto his extruded spermatophore. Before this, the locked pair engage in a "promenade à deux" which seems to select and perhaps further flatten and clear a suitable area for spermatophore transfer.


**Courtship in birds**


Ornithological interests have provided a wealth of data on the courtship of birds. Most species, particularly among the passerines, are territorial, form relatively stable and long-lasting pair bonds, and share joint responsibility in rearing the young. All birds employ internal insemination, and the vast majority show some kind of nest-building and parental care. Hence we should not expect as great a diversity in courtship displays as is shown, for example, in the fish. Nothing could be more wrong, for birds occupy a greater range of habitats and have a greater variety of signals at their disposal. Displays may be performed on the ground, on water, or in the air—communally or singly. Displays given on the water tend to incorporate drinking and preening components, as in ducks, whereas terrestrial displays can include feeding movements, such as ground scratching (Galliformes) and walking and running movements (many finches). Differences between fish and birds arise in the sensory modalities employed during courtship. Both classes concentrate on visual displays, but thereafter the two diverge. Fish still employ chemical signals, whereas the birds use structured acoustic signals. Bird song is one of the most conspicuous features of early display, serving both as a territorial signal and as an advertisement to prospective mates. Relatively few fish use acoustic signals, though the list is growing.

Within the birds the length of courtship can differ considerably; thus, polygamous species tend to mate more rapidly than those which form stable pairs. As an example of the former, the polygamous sage grouse *Centrocercus urophasianus* is outstanding, rivalling species such as the black grouse *Lyrurus tetrix* in its polygyny—relatively few cocks mating with most of the hens in any one mating ground.

Sage grouse reach their greatest abundance on the high basins of the mid and western United States. The main foodplant is the big sage brush *Artemisia tridentata*, an evergreen shrub. Males begin to aggregate on the communal display grounds (leks) during February and March, the largest leks having over 400 birds. Males usually attend their leks in the morning and late in the evening, often staying there all night. Visits by females peak in the last days of March, and most copulations have been reported (Wiley, 1973) as occurring in the three-week period around these days. The territories of the males within the lek range from 13 to 100 square metres, the central territories being smaller than the more peripheral ones. The females tend to aggregate in one or two of the central territories. The male (or males) whose territory includes the aggregation centre performs most of the copulations occurring at that lek.

While on the lek, each male "struts" every 7 to 10 seconds (figure 6.13). This is an elaborate visual and auditory display of which the main feature

**Figure 6.13**  The strutting posture of the male sage grouse (drawn from a photograph in Wiley, 1973).

is the expansion of the "chest sac". This is an enlarged diverticulum of the oesophagus overlaid with oedematous and vascularized skin. The strut starts from a "strutting posture" where the head is held high, tail and neck plumes erect and spread, and the yellowish combs over his eyes expanded. He then raises and drops the chest sac twice. Each time before lifting the sac he extends his wings forwards and then, as the sac rises, he pulls the wings backwards across specialized stiff feathers on the sides of his chest, producing a swishing sound. As the sac is raised and dropped, it fills with air causing two yellow/olive patches of skin on the chest to expand. On the second fall of the chest sac special muscles force air into these two skin patches which balloon out and then suddenly collapse. This produces two sharp snaps approximately 0·1 second apart. A peculiar resonant quality accompanies the snaps, and several brief soft coos precede them. The whole display sounds like "swish-swish-coo-oo-poink" and lasts for just over 2 seconds.

The female responds to male display by "solicitation", a posture in which she crouches close to the ground with her wings arched and the primaries fanned to the ground. The male mounts the soliciting female, treading her back with his feet, spreading his wings to the ground on either side to retain his balance and then lowering his tail with a rotary motion to effect cloacal contact. This lasts for only 1 to 2 seconds. The female then dashes out from under the male and indulges in a characteristic bout of post-copulatory preening. The male resumes strutting within 5 to 10 seconds. The female sage grouse mates only once per season and the whole affair is very brief for her. After mating she may fly several miles from the lek before alighting to build her nest on the ground and lay her clutch of 6 to 8 eggs.

The polygamy shown by such birds depends on uniparental care of the young. In turn, this is often associated with precocious nidifugous young, where the main onus for obtaining food rests on the chicks themselves from an early stage.

One of the classics of the ornithological literature is Huxley's (1914) description of courtship and mating in the great crested grebe *Podiceps cristatus*. This species provides a strong contrast with the sage grouse in that the sexes form long-term pairs and the species is aquatic. The courtship is complex, intermittent and lasts for weeks, rather than minutes. The most frequent displays are head-shaking and "preening" movements directed at the feathers of the wings and back. Erection of the long black feathers of the crest and ruff emphasize these movements. Individual displays are often grouped into distinct "ceremonies", e.g. in the weed ceremony, the birds dive (and the erect ruff indicates that the dive itself is a display), obtain a small quantity of weed, surface, approach each other rapidly and rise out of the water, chest to chest, body and neck extended vertically. They continue to tread water and perform distinctive side-to-side head movements while holding the weed in the bill. The "weed ceremony" seems to be preparatory to nest building. Another ceremony is the "discovery ceremony", which is usually shown when the pair have been separated for some time. In contrast to the behaviour during the weed ceremony, the partners behave asymmetrically, one bird diving and surfacing in front of the partner, and then twisting through 180°. Although the actions of one partner induce predictable responses in the other partner, "reaction chains" are not a feature of this stage of courtship. The same displays and ceremonies are performed many times by each pair, and there is no rigid ordering of the sequence in which the displays appear. It is generally held that lengthy courtships such as those shown in species like the great crested grebe serve not only the normal functions of courtship, but also establish the pair bond. Partners cooperate in a variety of activities such as nest building and care of the young; multiple mutual displays may serve to reduce aggression and fleeing tendencies, as well as conferring mutual individual recognition.

## Conclusions

In many ways, courtship can be viewed as a signalling system between prospective mates, and the examples reviewed in this chapter serve to illustrate some of the principles which operate. Courtship signalling evolves when there is some barrier to immediate mating. These barriers include:

(a) *Spatial separation*. Distance signals, noted for their species specificity, unambiguity, attention-getting ability and directional properties, are developed in a variety of modalities. They have been dealt with in earlier chapters.

(b) *Female coyness*. Hybrids almost always show reduced "fitness" in some respect, and individuals that tend to engage in cross mating are therefore disadvantaged in the evolutionary sense. Many females tend to mate once or only a few times, whereas males can potentially mate far more often. It is to the advantage of such females that, before mating, they receive clear signals informing of the species and perhaps other aspects of the fitness of the courting male. Female "coyness" may therefore be an adaptive advantage in certain species. Conversely, many males are rather catholic in their choice of mates. Selection pressures for speed of mating probably result from inter-male competition and these, in turn, may have contributed to the development of female coyness.

(c) *Partner aggression*. Charging in on a partner who is as likely to kill you as mate with you is undoubtedly maladaptive. Hence the elaboration of distance signals in spiders and empid flies, for example. The preying mantis male seems to have evolved an alternative strategy. He keeps his head well down during copulation but, even if the female does decapitate him, the copulation still proceeds to completion. In fact, decapitation of male preying mantids disinhibits the "fixed action patterns" of copulation, the control of which resides in the ganglia of the thorax and abdomen. Male territorial aggression may also be a problem, and female signals develop accordingly. "Food begging" by the female gulls is an example of such a signal.

(d) *Physiological state*. Many species delay bringing the gametes and accessory structures into fertilizable condition until a suitable male presents himself. This is particularly true of female birds where the large ovum has a limited life after shedding from the ovary. Hence, courtship in birds functions partly as a means of bringing the female into a state where she is prepared to ovulate. Animals that employ external fertilization are advantaged by the simultaneous release of sperm and ova. Hence the synchronized courtship of whitefish and the massive aggregations of the palolo worm in response to the lunar cycle.

(e) *Interference by other males*. A courting couple often attracts a great deal of attention from conspecific males. This attention may prevent successful mating and hence, for example, the development of "luring" in guppies. Territorial singing in male birds and crickets serves both as a deterrent to other males and an attractant to conspecific females.

(f) *Incorrect location*. The meeting place of a male and female may not be a suitable place for mating. Butterflies that encounter potential mates in the air have developed signals that serve to bring the pair to a perch where mating can occur. The elaborate aerial mating displays of the Nymphalidae are entirely lacking in species such as the small sulphur butterfly, where the male usually encounters females already perched. The "reaction chain" shown in stickleback courtship is, in the early stages, a means of bringing the pair to the nest. The early stages of newt courtship are very variable; only when the male has succeeded in releasing female approach does a recognizable "reaction chain" occur. Accurate positioning of the female over the spermatophore is the cause of this increased predictability of response. Bird courtship, in general, lacks this kind of predictability. Only in the behaviour associated with copulation itself, where the male must accurately position himself on the female does the degree of predictability approximate that shown in the classical "reaction chains" of certain other species. Thus "reaction chains" are largely the result of the need for accurate location of a courting pair.

A "reaction chain" is a series of signals and responses which are highly predictable and where the response of one partner acts as a signal for the other partner. The noteworthy feature of such chains as described in the early ethological literature was the *length* of the chain. Predictable signal-response relationships abound, but it is usually not necessary that long chains of such relationships be evolved as preliminaries to copulation. Only when a particular location is required for successful pairings do predictable signal-response relationships of any length develop.

Apart from this last point, courtship undoubtedly serves many different functions. The details will depend very much on the needs of the different species, and no two species will have precisely the same needs. This is shown clearly in fish, where details of courtship differ not according to "relatedness" but according to social factors, methods of insemination, and rearing of the young.

# CHAPTER SEVEN

# SOME METHODS OF ANALYSING SEQUENCES OF BEHAVIOUR

## Introduction

A variety of statistical methods is now available to the behaviourist. We propose to concentrate only on techniques suitable for dealing with the kinds of data that accrue from the study of animal communication. In the main, such studies have to deal with sequences of behaviour. The analysis of naturally-occurring sequences is a more complex task than the analysis of experimental results where only one, or a few, variables are present (assuming that the experiment is competently designed). When large numbers of variables are present in the data we must apply some form of *multivariate analysis*. A variety of multivariate treatments is available, but the first step is common to almost all of them: the data must be represented in *matrix* form. The most common form of matrix used in behavioural studies is the two-dimensional *transition matrix*. Behaviour must first be categorized into units (usually "FAPs") and the sequence in which the animal performs the units is recorded. The chosen units of behaviour are then paired. Hence a series $A \rightarrow B \rightarrow C \rightarrow D$ consists of the pairs of *transitions* AB, BC, CD. The matrix is then constructed, usually with the preceding acts or units listed in the horizontal rows and the following acts in the vertical columns, as shown in figure 7.1. Here the matrix has been made to represent only the three transitions. In practice, data from many repeated observations of sequences must be aggregated. This itself leads to certain problems, which are dealt with later in the chapter.

## Intra-individual transition matrices

The simplest kind of transition matrix is the intra-individual one. The usual aim of this type of analysis is to pinpoint activities which tend to arise in temporal groups or clusters. Hence Wiepkema's (1961) first stage

Following acts

|  |  | A | B | C | D | Tot |
|---|---|---|---|---|---|---|
| Preceding acts | A |  | 1 |  |  | 1 |
|  | B |  |  | 1 |  | 1 |
|  | C |  |  |  | 1 | 1 |
|  | D |  |  |  |  | 0 |
|  | Tot | 0 | 1 | 1 | 1 | 3 |

**Figure 7.1**    A simple transition matrix.

of analysis of the reproductive behaviour of the bitterling was to construct an intra-individual transition matrix of male behaviour (see p. 180). Note that in Wiepkema's matrix, the preceding acts are listed in the *vertical* column margin and the following acts in the *horizontal* row margin (figure 7.2).

The first figure in each *cell* is the observed number of transitions. Hence, in the first cell of row 1, there were 654 jerkings followed by jerking, and in the 2nd cell along, 101 turning beats followed by jerking. The second figure in each cell is the expected frequency calculated on the hypothesis that the relations of the 12 acts to each other are random. For this kind of matrix, expected frequencies can be calculated by:

$$\frac{\text{relevant column total} \times \text{relevant row total}}{\text{overall total}}$$

Thus, the expected frequency in the first cell is

$$\frac{1169 \times 1157}{6967} = 194{\cdot}1$$

When observed frequencies are substantially higher than expected frequencies for a particular cell in the matrix, then the transition is often termed *directive*; when the observed frequencies are lower than expected, *inhibitive*. Thus in cell one of figure 7.2, jerking is clearly directive towards more jerking. In fact, close examination of the matrix will reveal that most acts are strongly directive towards themselves (the descending *preceding component*

| | jk | tu | hb | chs | fl | qu | le | hdp | sk | sn | chf | ffl | marginal total |
|---|---|---|---|---|---|---|---|---|---|---|---|---|---|
| jk | 654<br>195·2<br>3·35 | 101<br>60·2<br>1·67 | 171<br>115·2<br>1·48 | 60<br>77·6<br>0·77 | 19<br>82·1<br>0·23 | 36<br>230·8<br>0·15 | 4<br>51·3<br>0·07 | 22<br>145·3<br>0·15 | 3<br>60·3<br>0·05 | 42<br>83·6<br>0·50 | 18<br>32·0<br>0·56 | 27<br>21·4<br>1·26 | 115 |
| tu | 128<br>61·7<br>2·07 | 132<br>19·0<br>6·94 | 62<br>36·4<br>1·70 | 22<br>24·5<br>0·89 | 2<br>25·9<br>0·07 | 1<br>69·5<br>0·01 | 0<br>16·2<br>0·00 | 9<br>45·9<br>0·19 | 2<br>19·0<br>0·10 | 2<br>26·4<br>0·07 | 3<br>10·1<br>0·29 | 6<br>6·7<br>0·44 | 36 |
| hb | 172<br>114·9<br>1·49 | 62<br>35·4<br>1·75 | 197<br>67·8<br>2·90 | 152<br>45·7<br>3·32 | 0<br>48·3<br>0·00 | 18<br>135·8<br>0·13 | 0<br>30·2<br>0·00 | 40<br>85·5<br>0·46 | 7<br>35·5<br>0·19 | 17<br>49·2<br>0·34 | 10<br>18·8<br>0·53 | 6<br>12·6<br>0·47 | 68 |
| chs | 56<br>77·9<br>0·71 | 27<br>24·0<br>1·12 | 130<br>46·0<br>2·82 | 135<br>31·0<br>4·35 | 0<br>32·8<br>0·00 | 5<br>92·1<br>0·05 | 0<br>20·5<br>0·00 | 37<br>58·0<br>0·63 | 38<br>24·1<br>1·57 | 16<br>33·4<br>0·47 | 13<br>12·8<br>1·01 | 5<br>8·5<br>0·58 | 46 |
| fl | 27<br>85·0<br>0·31 | 5<br>26·2<br>0·19 | 0<br>50·2<br>0·00 | 0<br>33·8<br>0·00 | 419<br>35·7<br>11·73 | 12<br>100·5<br>0·11 | 0<br>22·3<br>0·00 | 9<br>63·3<br>0·08 | 0<br>26·2<br>0·00 | 20<br>36·4<br>0·54 | 6<br>13·9<br>0·43 | 10<br>9·3<br>1·07 | 50 |
| qu | 25<br>232·2<br>0·10 | 1<br>71·5<br>0·01 | 25<br>137·0<br>0·18 | 8<br>92·3<br>0·09 | 19<br>97·7<br>0·19 | 789<br>274·5<br>2·87 | 57<br>61·1<br>0·93 | 245<br>172·8<br>1·41 | 120<br>71·7<br>1·67 | 70<br>99·4<br>0·70 | 5<br>38·1<br>0·13 | 13<br>25·5<br>0·50 | 137 |
| le | 1<br>52·6<br>0·02 | 1<br>16·2<br>0·06 | 0<br>31·0<br>0·00 | 0<br>20·9<br>0·00 | 0<br>22·1<br>0·00 | 119<br>62·2<br>1·91 | 167<br>13·8<br>12·10 | 7<br>39·1<br>0·17 | 8<br>16·2<br>0·49 | 11<br>22·5<br>0·48 | 0<br>8·6<br>0·00 | 0<br>5·7<br>0·00 | 31 |
| hdp | 28<br>151·8<br>0·18 | 11<br>46·8<br>0·23 | 50<br>89·6<br>0·55 | 43<br>60·4<br>0·71 | 2<br>63·9<br>0·03 | 295<br>179·5<br>1·64 | 73<br>39·9<br>1·82 | 171<br>113·0<br>1·51 | 134<br>46·9<br>2·85 | 67<br>65·0<br>1·03 | 8<br>24·9<br>0·32 | 18<br>16·6<br>1·08 | 90 |
| sk | 0<br>62·6<br>0·00 | 0<br>19·3<br>0·00 | 14<br>36·9<br>0·37 | 16<br>24·9<br>0·64 | 0<br>26·3<br>0·00 | 26<br>74·0<br>0·35 | 0<br>16·4<br>0·00 | 287<br>46·6<br>6·15 | 19<br>19·3<br>1·00 | 9<br>26·8<br>0·33 | 0<br>10·2<br>0·00 | 0<br>6·8<br>0·00 | 37 |
| sn | 46<br>88·0<br>0·52 | 8<br>27·1<br>0·29 | 18<br>51·9<br>0·34 | 15<br>35·0<br>0·42 | 17<br>37·0<br>0·45 | 70<br>104·1<br>0·67 | 8<br>23·1<br>0·34 | 53<br>65·5<br>0·80 | 28<br>27·2<br>1·02 | 225<br>37·7<br>5·96 | 24<br>14·4<br>1·66 | 10<br>9·6<br>1·04 | 52 |
| chf | 14<br>30·7<br>0·45 | 5<br>9·4<br>0·53 | 14<br>18·1<br>0·77 | 12<br>12·2<br>1·00 | 5<br>12·9<br>0·38 | 1<br>36·3<br>0·03 | 0<br>8·0<br>0·00 | 8<br>22·8<br>0·35 | 4<br>9·4<br>0·42 | 12<br>13·1<br>0·91 | 97<br>5·0<br>19·40 | 8<br>3·3<br>2·42 | 18 |
| ffl | 18<br>22·1<br>0·81 | 9<br>6·8<br>1·32 | 12<br>13·0<br>0·92 | 4<br>8·7<br>0·45 | 11<br>9·3<br>1·18 | 14<br>26·1<br>0·53 | 0<br>5·8<br>0·00 | 13<br>16·4<br>0·79 | 0<br>6·8<br>0·00 | 12<br>9·4<br>1·27 | 9<br>3·6<br>2·50 | 29<br>2·4<br>12·08 | 13 |
| marginal totals | 1169 | 362 | 693 | 467 | 494 | 1388 | 309 | 897 | 363 | 503 | 193 | 129 | 696 |

sum t

**Figure 7.2**    An intra-individual transition matrix of the behaviour of the male bitterling.

The first number in each cell is the observed number of transitions; the second number is the expected number of transitions determined by Column total × Row total divided by Sum total; the third number is the ratio of observed to expected. jk, jerking; tu, turning beat; hb, head butting; chs, chasing; fl, fleeing; qu, quivering; le, leading; hdp, head down posture; sk, skimming; sn, snapping; chf, chafing; ffl, fin flickering (from Wiepkema, 1961).

diagonal). Furthermore, aggressive acts such as jerking, turning beats, head butting and chasing, tend to be clustered together in time, as do sexual acts such as head down posture, skimming, quivering and leading.

Although most acts tend to be strongly directive towards themselves the "strength" of the relationship often depends on the particular author's criterion of what an "act" is. A common solution to this problem is to score an act (or unit) as having been completed only when another act (or unit) takes over (and we must include the category "does nothing" if necessary). Thus, in Dawkins and Dawkins' (1976) study of grooming in the blowfly, "head grooming" could include one or several wipes of the head with the forelegs; the "act" was thus highly variable in duration and only finished when a different kind of behaviour was shown. Hence the transition "head grooming" → "head grooming" could not occur in the matrix. Dawkins and Dawkins applied a similar approach to all their behavioural units, and the descending diagonals of their matrices were therefore empty. Matrix cells may also be unoccupiable for other reasons, e.g. if food and water are separated, then "feeding" and "drinking" will always have the unit "walking" interposed between them. When cells are unoccupiable, such matrices are termed *incomplete*, and the calculations of expected frequencies becomes more difficult. But, as a general approach, it is safer to admit that certain cells in a matrix are not occupiable. This allows more reliable comparisons between authors working on the same subjects. It also avoids having high scoring and highly directive cells—which tells us little and seems only to generate misleading estimates of expected frequencies in other cells.

Goodman (1968) has described a method for calculating expected frequencies in incomplete matrices, but a quicker method (although admittedly a more approximate one) has been proposed by Lemon and Chatfield (1971). They suggest using the formula

$$e_{ij} \simeq \frac{n_{i.}\,n_{.j}}{n - n_{j.}}$$

where   $e_{ij}$ is the expected number of transitions between acts
      $n_{i.}$ is the number of pairs in which the *first* act is type $i$
      $n_{.j}$ is the number of pairs in which the *second* act is type $j$
      $n$  is the total number of pairs of acts
      $n_{j.}$ is the number of pairs in which the *first* act is type $j$.

Note the use of the full stop here to denote the presence of any act either preceding or following the named act (in this case $i$ and $j$). It should be stressed that this formula is an approximation and becomes less accurate with increasing discrepancies in column and row totals.

Having obtained an expected value for a particular transition $\chi^2$ can then be calculated by the usual formula:

$$\chi^2_{ij} = \sum_{\substack{ij \\ i \neq j}} \frac{(n_{ij} - e_{ij})^2}{e_{ij}}$$

with $c^2 - 3c + 1$ degrees of freedom, where $c$ is the number of different acts. Because $e_{ij}$ is only an approximation of expected frequency, Lemon and Chatfield suggested that the null hypothesis only be rejected if $P < 0.01$.

The raw data of frequencies of transitions can be represented in terms of a flow diagram (figure 7.3), where the width of lines is proportional to number of transitions and where, conventionally, lines above the mid-horizontal read from left to right, those below from right to left. The circles represent the behavioural units themselves, and the size of the circles can be made proportional to the actual frequency of occurrence of the unit they represent. An alternative type of flow diagram is possible, where the flow lines are proportional, not to actual frequency, but to the ratio $\left[\dfrac{\text{observed}}{\text{expected}}\right]$ frequency. This guards against very common acts apparently dominating the flow diagram, but it is more difficult to interpret, and is not commonly used.

In representing data in matrix form and then estimating expected values, we should have a relatively simple method of assessing behaviour in an objective manner. There are, however, a number of pitfalls in this type of treatment.

(1) In constructing the matrix the data are paired. The estimation of expected frequencies of pairs makes the assumption that pairs are independent. This may not be the case; higher-order effects such as triplets, quadruplets, etc., may be present and, if this is so, estimated frequencies will be inaccurate and $\chi^2$ values misleading. In other words, in a sequence A → B → C, the frequency B → C may change with presence or absence of A. Sequences where the probabilities of occurrence of different events depend only on the immediately preceding event and not on any earlier ones are termed *first-order Markov chains*. When the probability of C depends on A as well as B we have a *second-order* Markov chain. With four linked events we have a *third-order* Markov

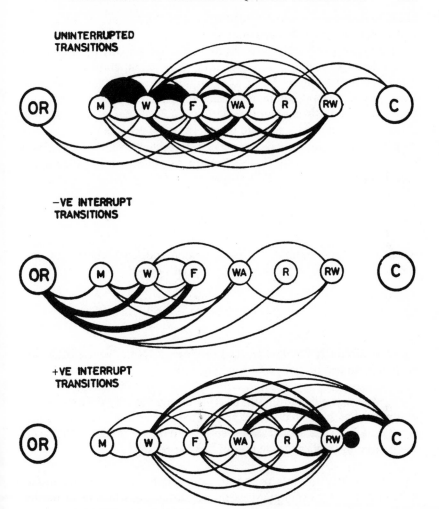

**Figure 7.3** Male courtship-act transitions in the smooth newt. Width of lines is proportional to the frequency of transition. Lines above the mid-horizontal read from left to right; those below from right to left. Frequency of transition to the same act, e.g. W to W, is proportional to the width of the dot to the right of each act. C, creep; F, fan; M, move to the front; OR, orientation; R, retract; RW, retreat and whip; W, whip; WA, wave (from Halliday, 1975).

chain and so on. Cane (1978) discusses some techniques of fitting low-order Markov chains to behaviour sequences.

In practice it is rarely possible to check for second- or third-order effects, because extensive data are required to obtain enough triplets or quadruplets for analysis. What most authors have done is to check the frequency of the most commonly-occurring triplets. If a suspiciously high frequency of a particular pair then occurs in a particular triplet, a second-order effect is likely. Lemon and Chatfield (1971) provide a more precise method of assessing second-order effects. Expected frequencies of triplets (on the null hypothesis that there are no higher-order effects) are calculated from:

$$e_{ijk} = \frac{N_3 n_{ij} n_{jk}}{n_{j.}}$$

where $N_3$ = total number of triplets. Lemon and Chatfield suggest that the null hypothesis only be rejected if $n_{ijk}$ falls outside the range:

$$e_{ijk} \pm 1 \cdot 96 \sqrt{e_{ijk}\left(1 - \frac{n_{jk}}{n_{j.}}\right)}$$

which is effectively the 95% level of confidence. (Note the use of the full stop in $n_{j.}$ to denote any pair beginning with $j$.)

(2) In scanning a large number of cells for significantly different values of observed as compared with expected frequencies, the chances are that some cells will yield significance even if the data are random. The larger the matrix, the higher the chances of this happening!

(3) "Stationarity" of data is also an assumption we have made. In fact behaviour tends to occur in cycles, the best known of which is the diurnal cycle. Furthermore, changing "mood", changing environment, etc., may all contribute to "drifts" of one kind or another. Observing animals at the same time of day, under as standardized conditions as possible, may get around some of these effects. In practice, one attempts to keep "drift" within acceptable limits. In checking for stationarity it is usual to divide data into broad-based time periods and check for discrepancies. Thus, in observation periods of one hour, data recorded from the first $\frac{1}{2}$ hour can be compared with data from the second $\frac{1}{2}$ hour. Dingle (1969) divided his data, from his one-hour observation periods, into 10-minute blocks,

and did indeed find significant differences in the frequencies of certain transitions, particularly when comparing the first 10 minutes with later blocks. He lumped later parts of the tests, but decided to treat the first 10 minutes separately.

(4) Even if pitfalls 1–3 have been successfully avoided, the problem of interpretation remains. Most analyses aim at some understanding of the causation of behaviour but, as we have discussed, causation is the result of both internal and external factors. We are thus dealing with confounding variables and, in general, no matter how sophisticated the methods of analysis, purely observational work will not isolate the effects of each of these factors. Some attempts at tackling this problem are dealt with later in this chapter.

(5) It should be pointed out that not all complex behaviour is suitable for analysis of the kind we have been discussing. The construction of a matrix (or chains, flow diagrams, etc.) depends on *regularly occurring "units"* of behaviour which, ideally, should be identical from performance to performance. In practice there is always some variation, but such behaviour as that shown in stereotyped displays is generally sufficiently invariant to allow of this type of analysis. Outside communicative contexts, behaviour tends to be less stereotyped. Furthermore, with increasing complexity of the central nervous system, more individual variation tends to be "built in" to behaviour. Hence primate behaviour, even in communicative contexts, becomes extremely difficult to analyse. It is therefore essential that the extent of variation in the categories to be analysed is assessed before matrix analysis is attempted. Recording behaviour with film, video-tape or audio-tape is the best way of doing this. Despite these cautionary points, a number of extensive analyses of quite variable and complex behaviours have been attempted (e.g. Altmann, 1967, on rhesus monkeys; van Hoof, 1970, on chimpanzees). Examples of these are dealt with in the last section of this chapter.

### Inter-individual matrices

Collecting data for inter-individual matrices is, generally speaking, more difficult than for intra-individual matrices. In the latter, the animal under study can only do one thing at a time, and it is clear which activity follows which. In the case of an interaction between two animals, transitions become much more a matter of arbitrary assessment on the part of the observer. Even if the techniques of high-speed film or video-recording are used, the decisions can still be arbitrary, because paired animals will often perform activities simultaneously. At the other extreme, one member of a pair may be relatively inactive; several successive acts by the more active partner may coincide with only one activity of the other partner. Many females tend to stand and watch their males perform. Problems such as these severely limit the use of inter-individual matrices in behaviour.

On the other hand, all cells in the matrix are usually occupiable, and estimation of expected frequencies is simpler. Matrices may be *symmetrical* (as they usually are in intra-individual transitions) or *asymmetrical*. Examples of asymmetrical interactions are the courtships of a wide variety of species where behaviour of the male and female are not identical. Interspecific interactions such as those between symbionts will also be asymmetrical. The basic treatment of an asymmetrical matrix is the same as that for a symmetrical one. However, *two matrices* must be used to fully represent asymmetrical data.

Most inter-individual matrices are suitable for information analysis, but let us first consider some alternative methods of dealing with communicative interactions.

(1) If the behaviour of the participating animals is markedly asymmetrical, as is often the case between courting males and females, it is often possible to examine intra-individual transitions in the more-active partner for each different type of behaviour of the less-active partner. Thus Halliday (1975) in a study of courtship in the smooth newt (chapter 6, p. 187) constructed three intra-individual matrices for male behaviour. The three matrices represented male behaviour when the female was:

(a) static (i.e. did not interrupt ongoing male behaviour in any obvious way);
(b) moving away from the male (− ve interrupt);
(c) moving towards the male (+ ve interrupt).

The three flow diagrams of male behaviour are shown in figure 7.3. There are clear cut differences between the three diagrams, indicating that the male does monitor female behaviour.

(2) In an extensive investigation of agonistic behaviour in the siamese fighting fish *Betta splendens*, Simpson (1968) examined the main displays without recourse to matrices. Frequencies of particular displays of one partner were monitored after the other partner had started a particular

display. The results were represented graphically with time after the start of the partner's display.

(3) Correlation techniques can tell us much about the temporal grouping of behaviour, but they give no information about the actual sequence of events. Cross correlation procedures, where units occurring in different time blocks are correlated, can give information about sequence effects, however. Delius (1969) and Heiligenberg (1973) show examples of this kind of procedure; in a graphical way, so does Simpson (1968).

## Information analysis

In addition to assessment of "directive" and "inhibitive" effects in interactions between individuals, methods now exist for assessment of overall "effects" in the matrices. One of the most powerful of these methods is *information analysis*.

The relevant information analysis techniques were devised by Shannon and his colleagues for the Post Office. Communication is said to occur when the conditional probability that an act following a "display" is *not* equal to the conditional probability of that act occurring in the absence of that "display". The basic unit of information is the *binary digit* or *bit*. The number of bits is the power to which the number 2 must be raised to give the number of equiprobable messages in a signal or system. Hence, if a sender by using 1 of 2 signals can control in a yes/no (or binary) fashion which of two equiprobable responses is made by a recipient, then one bit of information is being transmitted. If $N$ = number of equiprobable responses (i.e. messages) and $H$ is the number of bits, then

$$N = 2^H$$

For the control of two equiprobable messages, $N = 2$ and $2 = 2^1$, therefore $H = 1$ bit.
If $N = 4$, then $4 = 2^2$ and $H = 2$ bits.
If $N = 8$, then $8 = 2^3$ and $H = 3$ bits.
In general, if $N = 2^H$ then $H = \log_2 N$.

Use of the binary code is simply a matter of convenience. $\log_{10}$ could be used equally well. However, $\log_2$ is now accepted as the measure of information in a variety of fields, and there is little point in changing at this late stage. A $\log_2$ table is provided in the Appendix (p. 218).

So far, we have been dealing with the simple case of equiprobable messages. When messages are of unequal probability, then the amount of information being conveyed is less. If we think of information in terms of reduction of uncertainty, then this will be greatest when there is a 50/50 chance of a particular unit (of behaviour) being performed. If one unit occurs frequently and the other rarely, then we have a better bet on our hands as to which unit will "appear"; the reduction of uncertainty is less. To deal with unequally probable units we simply extend the basic formula

$$H = \log_2 N \quad \text{to} \quad H(X_i) = -\Sigma p(i) \log_2 p(i)$$

Where $p(i)$ is the probability of each signal $X_i$. The logarithms of all $p(i)$ values greater than 0 are negative; the $-ve$ sign in the equation is a counter to this. An example of a 2-unit system is given in figure 7.4.

We thus have a measure of the amount of information available in an $N$-unit system where the units are not equiprobable. However, this takes only one side of the communication system into account and is hence only a measure of potential information or *signal entropy*. No natural systems of communication realize their full potential. This is because of "noise". Noise can be divided into:

(1) *ambiguity*, a given signal evoking more than one response;
(2) *equivocation*, when a given response may be evoked by more than one signal.

This is diagrammatically represented in figure 7.5. It is clear from this figure that actual information transmitted can be calculated either by signal entropy minus equivocation, or by receiver entropy minus ambiguity.

If we now return to an example of an inter-individual matrix, but this time with the transitions represented in terms of their frequencies or probabilities (figure 7.6) then we can see in detail how these calculations are carried out. Actions $(X_i)$ are in the rows and responses $(Y_j)$ are in the columns. Equivocation $H_Y(X)$ is calculated by taking each response $(Y_j)$ in turn and noting the conditional probabilities for each $X_i$ that evokes it. Thus when $Y_1$ is evoked $X_2$ is responsible $0.001 \div 0.010 = 0.1$ (10 percent) of the time; $Y_1$ is evoked by $X_3$ $0.5$ of the time and by

| Message $X_i$ | Frequency of message $p(i)$ | $p(i) \log_2 p(i)$ |
|---|---|---|
| $X_1$ | 0·80 | −0·2575 |
| $X_2$ | 0·20 | −0·4644 |
| | $\sum_i = 1\cdot00$ | $-H(X) = \sum_i = 0\cdot7219$ |

**Figure 7.4** "Potential information" available in a two-signal system.

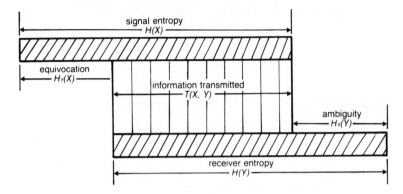

**Figure 7.5** The relationship between noise (ambiguity and equivocation) and information flow (redrawn from Quastler, 1958).

$X_4$ 0·4 of the time. The potential information or entropy of these 3 transitions is given by the usual formula:

$$H_j(i) = -\sum_i p_j(i) \log_2 p_j(i), \quad \text{(where } p_j \text{ is probability of } Y\text{)}$$
$$= -\left[ 0\cdot1 \log_2 0\cdot1 + 0\cdot5 \log_2 0\cdot5 + 0\cdot4 \log_2 0\cdot4 \right]$$

Note that the symbolism conventionally employed here, e.g. $p_j(i)$ refers to the probability of $j$, $i$ having been the preceding signal.

Having obtained the entropies for all $p_j(i)$, each entropy value must be weighted according to the frequency with which each response $p_j$ occurs. In the case of response $Y_1$ this is

$$(0\cdot001 + 0\cdot005 + 0\cdot004) = 0\cdot010.$$

The formal expression of this procedure is

$$H_Y X = -\sum_j p.(j) . H_j(i)$$

$p(j)$ is the probability of occurrence of the response (= the weighting factor) and, as previously stated,

$$H_j(i) = -\sum_i p_j(i) \log_2 p_j(i)$$

The expanded equation therefore becomes

$$H_Y X = -\sum p.(j) \left[ -\sum_i p_j(i) \log_2 p_j(i) \right]$$

The information transmitted can now be calculated by

$$H_t = H(X) - H_Y X$$

$$= -\sum_j p(i) \log_2 p(i) - \left[ -\sum_j p \cdot (j) \cdot H_j(i) \right]$$

$H(X)$ is readily calculated from the sums of individual signal entropies as shown in figure 7.6.

| Action (signal) | Response | | | | | | $p(i)$ | $-p(i)\log_2 p(i)$ |
| | $Y_j = Y_1$ | $Y_2$ | $Y_3$ | $Y_4$ | $Y_5$ | $Y_6$ | | |
|---|---|---|---|---|---|---|---|---|
| $X_i = X_1$ | — | 0·001 | — | — | — | — | 0·001 | 0·01 |
| $X_2$ | 0·001 | 0·007 | 0·006 | 0·001 | — | — | 0·015 | 0·09 |
| $X_3$ | 0·005 | 0·022 | 0·060 | 0·027 | 0·005 | — | 0·119 | 0·37 |
| $X_4$ | 0·004 | 0·042 | 0·156 | 0·152 | 0·039 | 0·001 | 0·394 | 0·53 |
| $X_5$ | | 0·009 | 0·075 | 0·175 | 0·095 | 0·010 | 0·364 | 0·53 |
| $X_6$ | — | 0·001 | 0·011 | 0·035 | 0·039 | 0·010 | 0·096 | 0·32 |
| $X_7$ | — | — | — | 0·003 | 0·006 | 0·002 | 0·011 | 0·07 |
| $p(j)$ | 0·010 | 0·082 | 0·308 | 0·393 | 0·184 | 0·023 | 1·000 | $\sum = 1·92$ |
| $-p(j)\log_2 p(j)$ | 0·07 | 0·30 | 0·52 | 0·53 | 0·45 | 0·13 | $\sum = 2·00$ | |

$H(X) = -\sum_i p(i) \log_2 p(i) = 1·92$ bits      Source entropy

$H(Y) = -\sum_j p(j) \log_2 p(j) = 2·00$ bits      Receiver entropy

$H_Y(X) = -\sum_j p(j) \cdot H_j(i)  = 1·70$ bits      Equivocation (of source)

$H_X(Y) = -\sum p(i) \cdot H_i(j)  = 1·78$ bits      Ambiguity (of receiver)

$T(X_j Y) = H(X) - H_Y(X)$      Information transmitted
$\quad\quad\quad = H(Y) - H_X(Y)$
$\quad\quad\quad = 0·22$ bits

$H_j(i) = -\sum_i p_j(i) \log_2 p_j(i)$

$H_i(j) = -\sum_j p_i(j) \log_2 p_t(j)$

**Figure 7.6** Computation of signal entropy, receiver entropy, equivocation and ambiguity in an imaginary communication system (modified from Quastler, 1958, after Wilson, 1975).

Thus information transmitted:

$$H_t = H(X) - H_Y X = 1{\cdot}92 \text{ bits } - 1{\cdot}70 \text{ bits } = 0{\cdot}22 \text{ bits}$$

The calculation can also be made by

$$H_t = H(Y) - H_X Y = 2{\cdot}00 \text{ bits } - 1{\cdot}78 \text{ bits } = 0{\cdot}22 \text{ bits}$$

Information transmission as calculated here is what Quastler (1958) defines as the mutual reduction in uncertainty. As such, it represents the restriction of the receiver's behaviour by that of the signaller. It can be considered to be the amount of information that the receiver indicates by his actions that he has received from the signaller. It is thus a *minimum* estimate of the information transmitted.

In practice, having obtained values for $H_t$ it is possible to calculate:

(i) The average amount of information transmitted *per individual*: the number of acts taking place during the average interaction between two individuals multiplied by $H_t$. Dingle (1969) found that in aggressive interactions in the mantis shrimp, the average amount of information transmitted per individual ranged from 1·57 to 2·09 bits per individual.

(ii) Steinberg and Conant (1974) suggest that the information conveyed by a particular signal $x$ can be measured by $p(x)J(x;Y)$ which gives the contribution of $x$ to the overall transmission $T(X;Y)$ and where

$$J(x;Y) = \sum_y p\left(\frac{x}{y}\right) \log_2 \frac{p(y/x)}{p(y)}$$

where

$p\left(\dfrac{x}{y}\right)$ is the conditional probability of $x$, $y$ having been performed;

$p\left(\dfrac{y}{x}\right)$ is the conditional probability of $y$, $x$ having been performed;

and    $p(y)$    is the overall frequency of acts $y$.

Steinberg and Conant (1974) assessed the relative contributions of individual signals to the overall $H_t$. One of their more surprising findings was that categories such as "does nothing" and "continues to do nothing" had quite high transmission. This may, in part, be artifactual because those actions accounted for 44 per cent of the data. Nevertheless, Steinberg and Conant stressed the importance of "remaining quiet" as a strong aggressive signal.

These findings stress the importance of careful choice of behavioural units. The overall number of units chosen will strongly affect estimates of $H_t$. In, for example, a 12-unit interaction, the maximum $H_X$ (signal entropy) is $\log_2 12 = 3.58$ bits. This assumes that all units are equiprobable and thus maximizes uncertainty. Lumping or splitting of units will lower or raise $H_{X\max}$ respectively, and thus affect estimates of $H_t$. If two workers are independently observing the same animals, the problem is exacerbated. Steinberg and Conant (1974) therefore proposed the use of the normalized transmission $t(X;Y)$ calculated from the ratio:

$$t(X;Y) = \frac{T(X;Y)}{H(Y)};$$

$$T(X;Y) = H(Y) - H\left(\frac{Y}{X}\right) \text{ (receiver entropy } - \text{ ambiguity)}$$

Therefore:     $$t(X;Y) = \frac{H(Y) - H\left(\dfrac{Y}{X}\right)}{H(Y)}$$

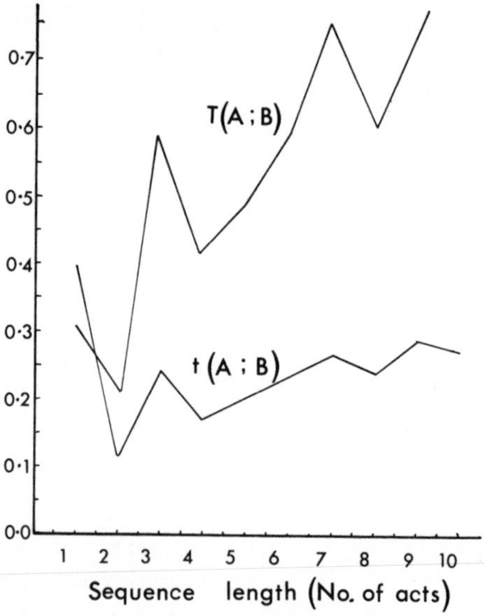

**Figure 7.7** Comparisons between information transmitted ($T$) and normalized transmission ($t$) between male *Chortophaga viridifasciata* (Acrididae). A, signals of initiator; B, signals of responder (data from Steinberg and Conant, 1974).

As $H(Y/X)$ (or $H_X Y$) approaches 0 (or as its predictability increases), $t(X:Y)$ approaches its upper limit of 1. As ambiguity $H(Y/X)$ rises, it approaches 0. $t(X;Y)$ is largely unaffected by choice of categories and is hence a better comparative measure between authors, and between species. Figure 7.7 is a comparison of $T(X;Y)$ and $t(x;y)$ as interactions proceed in acridid encounters.

Steinberg and Conant estimated overall $T(A;B) = 0.44$ bits compared with overall $t(A;B)$ of $0.22$.

Preston (1978) was the first worker to apply communication theory to an interspecific interaction; her estimates are given in figure 7.8.

There are a number of clear-cut advantages in using information techniques to assess interactions:

(1) Measuring information in bits means that systems using different forms of measurement are comparable. This is particularly so if normalized transmission is used.

(2) It can be computed for continuous as well as discrete variables.

(3) Rare messages contribute very little to $H_X$. Hence, it is possible to miss out rare units and still arrive at estimates of $H_t$ which are reasonably accurate (underestimates).

(4) The total information in separate signalling systems can be arrived at simply by summing the values of $H_X$ for the two systems.

To take a simple example: if $m$ equiprobable signals exist in $X$ and $n$ in $Y$, there are $mn$ equiprobable combinations of two signals;

$$H(X + Y) = \log_2 mn = \log_2 m + \log_2 n = H(X) + H(Y)$$

Information analysis was designed initially for artificial systems and it does suffer from a number of limitations when applied to animal behaviour. Many of these limitations are shared with the other methods of analysis discussed in this chapter, and most of them are caused by the way

| Category | $H_B$ | $H_t$ | NT | Acts | Encounters |
|---|---|---|---|---|---|
| Goby communicating to shrimp | | | | | |
| A. rapax | 2·35 | 0·32 | 0·14 | 2·2 | 1059 |
| A. rapacida | 2·34 | 0·35 | 0·15 | 2·0 | 1005 |
| Shrimp communicating to goby | | | | | |
| A. rapax | 2·40 | 0·31 | 0·13 | 3·2 | 1059 |
| A. rapacida | 2·21 | 0·31 | 0·14 | 3·5 | 1005 |

**Figure 7.8**  Information values for communication between gobies and shrimps. $H_B$, information present (bits per act); $H_t$, information transmitted (bits per act); NT, normalized transmission; Acts, acts/signaller/encounter (from Preston, 1978).

in which the data are collected, problems of stationarity, context and so on. However, information analysis is particularly vulnerable to the number of categories decided upon, and use of *normalized transmission* is therefore to be recommended. The end point of information analysis is the arrival at a number of estimates of "information flow", "rate of flow", etc., which tell us little about the reliability of the effects being examined. It is not a statistical technique and we are not justified in saying that communication has occurred simply because we have arrived at some estimate of "information flow". Information analysis is a means of comparing *different systems*.

## Multivariate analysis

Most of the techniques we have looked at so far are relatively straightforward and do not necessarily require the use of a computer, although a computer is to be recommended for any except the simplest information analyses. Multivariate techniques such as principal components analysis and cluster analysis almost always necessitate the use of a computer.

### Principal components analysis

Principal components analysis has been applied in ethological studies by a number of authors, e.g. by Huntingford (1976) in a study of territorial behaviour of the three-spined stickleback *Gasterosteus aculeatus*. In principal components analysis the variance in a matrix is accounted for by a succession of components. If there are $p$ acts, the data can be represented as vectors in $p$-dimensional space. The first component is defined by the axis along which maximum variance exists. The variance accounted for by the first component is removed, and the second component is found. This accounts for as much as possible of the variance remaining and lies along an axis perpendicular to that of the first component, so that the two components are uncorrelated. This process is repeated, each successive component accounting for a smaller proportion of the total variance and being uncorrelated with previous components. The total variance is completely accounted for by $p$ components. If, say, only the first two components account for an appreciable proportion of the total variance, we may decide to ignore the remaining components. Then the $p$-dimensional system will be described in only two dimensions, a considerable saving in complexity. Each component is defined as a weighted sum of the $p$ original acts. The magnitude and sign of the weights (or loadings) help to give a name to the component.

The loadings of, and the variance accounted for, by each component are usually found from matrices of correlations or of covariances by iterative methods, for which a computer is essential.

The correlations or covariances can be based on several types of data, e.g. transition frequencies, ranked ratios of observed to expected frequencies (Wiepkema), or standard sources (Huntingford).

*Factor analysis*

Factor analysis has aims similar to those of principal components analysis in that an attempt is made to reduce the $p$ dimensions of the data to a smaller number to facilitate interpretation. In this case the system is reduced to a small number of factors, but the number of factors is specified as part of the model of the system. This has the effect of replacing the 1's of the diagonal elements of the correlation matrix (i.e. correlation of an act with itself) by numbers smaller than 1 called *communalities*, which represent the proportion of the variance of an act which it shares with the other acts.

The components or factors emerging from one of these analyses (called the *direct solution*) have to be interpreted on the basis of their pattern of loadings over the $p$ acts. Sometimes they are rotated to alter the loadings according to various criteria. The results form a derived solution. The danger exists that rotation can be arranged so that the loadings can conform to preconceived theories about the structure of correlations between the acts.

Wiepkema's factor analysis of reproductive behaviour in the bitterling is thought to be a classic in the field. He was able to account for 90% of the total variance with 3 factors. The behaviour of the bitterling is described in chapter 6 and figure 7.9 is a representation in three dimensions of the factor analysis. It can be seen that aggressive acts such as chasing and head butting cluster about factor 1; skimming and head-up about factor 3; and fleeing, fin flickering and chafing about factor 2. The vectors representing turning beats, jerking, quivering and leading are, on the other hand, not so closely associated with any one factor. Thus the 3 factors were thought of as representing the underlying

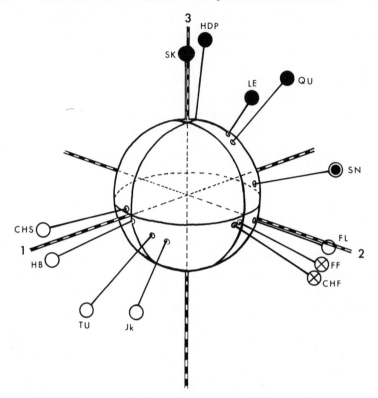

**Figure 7.9** Vector model of the behaviour of the male bitterling. Positive sides of aggressive factor, 1; sexual factor, 3; non-reproductive factor. 2. The vectors of the twelve variables are determined by the projections (i.e. factor loadings) of these variables on the three main axes. Abbreviations as in figure 7.2 (after Wiepkema, 1961).

tendencies of fighting, other behaviours (in particular fleeing), and mating —behaviour such as turning beats, jerking, leading and quivering being the result of bivalent and perhaps trivalent "internal factors". This interpretation is, of course, in keeping with some of the viewpoints discussed in chapter 5. However, the three factors can also be accounted for, at least in part, by external events. As a method of elucidating internal causations of behaviour, factor analysis is only of value if external conditions are held constant. This would suggest the study of smaller groupings of behaviour as perhaps being more suitable. However, even small movements by an animal can drastically change sensory input, and therefore interpretation in terms of causation is still confounded. Furthermore, rotation of the axes can take us further and further from the original data, until we are not clear just what the factors represent.

Despite these criticisms, the above techniques of analysis do afford us with an objective evaluation of complex sequences, and a way of summarizing data that can often pinpoint temporal clusters that less-sensitive methods miss. Thus Huntingford (1976), in a re-analysis of Cullen's (1960) data on territorial behaviour in three-spined sticklebacks raised under different "social isolation" conditions, confirmed Cullen's main findings that rearing conditions did not significantly affect "general sexual activity" or the fish's differentiation between the sexes. But she also unearthed a hitherto unnoticed effect: isolates showed significantly higher "aggressive levels" than normally reared fish. Van Hoof (1970) in a massive analysis of social behaviour in a semi-captive group of chimpanzees accounted for 83% of the total variance with 7 components.

Component I (26% of variance) included significant loadings on smooth approach, mating and various "affinitive behaviours";
component II (20%)—play behaviours;
component III (13%) "aggressive" displays;
component IV (10%)—submissive elements;
component V (6%)—displays which apparently signified "excitement";
component VI (5%) a number of displays associated with "male mating", in particular "vertical head nodding";
component VII (3%) allo- and auto-grooming.

Van Hoof's analysis was based on the mutual replaceability correlations of behaviour units:

The more causal factors two behaviour elements $a$ and $b$ have in common, the more $b$ will tend to pass over into each of the 52 elements to the extent that $a$'s tendency is itself great.

Thus the *patterns* of transition frequencies will be positively correlated. The correlations provided the basic matrix for components analysis. Further analysis of within-component relationships was carried out by lumping cells in the matrix which were held to be more closely associated with other components. This lumping procedure increased the differentiation among the remaining elements. An example of the results of this process is given in figure 7.10.

Hence with the large number of categories used by van Hoof, principal components analysis has proved an invaluable aid in indicating which behaviours form temporal clusters. As stated earlier, further interpretation is problematical, and to ascribe such temporal patterning to particular causations is really to indulge in guesswork.

| Component | SI | SII | SIII | SIV | SV |
|---|---|---|---|---|---|
| Bared-teeth scream [42] | **93** | −04 | 06 | 08 | 15 |
| Crouch [20] | **92** | −04 | 25 | 05 | −01 |
| Flight [7] | **90** | 17 | 06 | 17 | 33 |
| Bared-teeth yelp [43] | **80** | −35 | 25 | −19 | 13 |
| Stretched pout whimper [44] | 56 | −63 | −09 | −45 | 07 |
| "Play" | −03 | **88** | −29 | 04 | −02 |
| Parry [16] | **66** | **67** | −04 | −04 | −16 |
| "Excitement" | 03 | −07 | **96** | 05 | −01 |
| Hesitant approach [2] | **40** | −30 | **81** | 00 | −10 |
| Shrink-flinch [9] | 10 | −68 | **61** | −14 | 16 |
| Shrill bark [46] | 20 | −25 | 21 | **88** | −05 |
| "Aggressive + Bluff" | −16 | **56** | −07 | **76** | 08 |
| Avoid [8] | **44** | −12 | −07 | −18 | **83** |
| "Affinity" | −08 | −31 | 32 | −78 | 31 |
| Portion of the variance explained | 31% | 20% | 17% | 16% | 7·2% |

**Figure 7.10** Component analysis of "submissive behaviour" in a semi-captive group of chimpanzees. Behaviour categories having high loadings on other components (i.e. "play", "excitement", "aggression and bluff" and "affinity") have been "lumped". Positive sign values in bold print and negative sign values in italics correspond with a $p$ of about 1% for a Pearsons $r$ correlation coefficient (from van Hoof, 1970).

## Cluster analysis

Cluster analysis is proving an increasingly popular multivariate technique. Hence van Hoof (1970) used it in conjunction with principal components analysis in his study of chimpanzee interactions (figure 7.10), Davies (1978) used it to analyse flamingo postures, and Dawkins and Dawkins (1976) to analyze their blowfly grooming data. A wide variety of types of cluster analysis exists but, essentially, units (of behaviour) are grouped according to their temporal association, mutual replaceability (as in Dawkins and Dawkins, 1976) or some other parameter of "similarity". The first cluster found is the pair of units sharing most of the chosen feature in common. They are then treated as one unit, or lumped, the next most "similar" unit is identified, and so on. As the parameter chosen and, indeed, certain details of the computer program will determine the overall pattern of clustering, caution should be exercised in interpreting such patterns. An example of a cluster analysis result is shown in figure 7.11. A more detailed account of cluster analysis is given by Everitt (1974).

In conclusion, we should point out that, in the main, modern methods

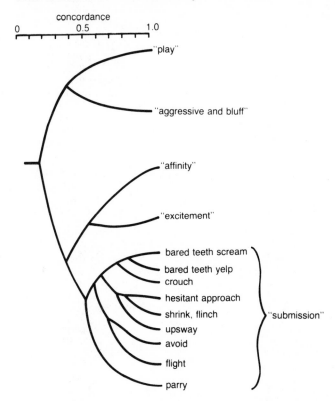

**Figure 7.11** Results of cluster analysis of behaviour of semi-captive chimpanzees. "Play", "aggression and bluff", "affinity" and "excitement" represent "lumped" categories (modified from van Hoof, 1970).

of analyzing complex data are really only sophisticated techniques for describing and summarizing results! They are not magical methods of unravelling the causation of behaviour, but merely an objective back-up to what is usually intuitively understood by the behaviourist. Sad to say, some recent publications are more impressive in terms of their methods of analysis than in terms of their data. Critical observation is still the most important first step in understanding behaviour, and experimentation comes second. Analysis, no matter how complex, should be regarded as a supplement to these.

Other analytical techniques are available which are not discussed in this chapter. Slater (1973) gives an overview of the area. Finally, the reader is recommended to consult a competent mathematician.

# APPENDIX

## $\log_2$ table, 0 to 1.

| | | | |
|---|---|---|---|
| 0·01 | $-6\cdot64386$ | 0·51 | $-0\cdot971431$ |
| 0·02 | $-5\cdot64386$ | 0·52 | $-0\cdot943416$ |
| 0·03 | $-5\cdot05889$ | 0·53 | $-0\cdot915936$ |
| 0·04 | $-4\cdot64386$ | 0·54 | $-0\cdot888969$ |
| 0·05 | $-4\cdot32193$ | 0·55 | $-0\cdot862496$ |
| 0·06 | $-4\cdot05889$ | 0·56 | $-0\cdot836501$ |
| 0·07 | $-3\cdot8365$ | 0·57 | $-0\cdot810966$ |
| 0·08 | $-3\cdot64386$ | 0·58 | $-0\cdot785875$ |
| 0·09 | $-3\cdot47393$ | 0·59 | $-0\cdot761213$ |
| 0·1 | $-3\cdot32193$ | 0·6 | $-0\cdot736966$ |
| 0·11 | $-3\cdot18442$ | 0·61 | $-0\cdot713119$ |
| 0·12 | $-3\cdot05889$ | 0·62 | $-0\cdot68966$ |
| 0·13 | $-2\cdot94342$ | 0·63 | $-0\cdot666576$ |
| 0·14 | $-2\cdot8365$ | 0·64 | $-0\cdot643856$ |
| 0·15 | $-2\cdot73697$ | 0·65 | $-0\cdot621488$ |
| 0·16 | $-2\cdot64386$ | 0·66 | $-0\cdot599462$ |
| 0·17 | $-2\cdot55639$ | 0·67 | $-0\cdot577767$ |
| 0·18 | $-2\cdot47393$ | 0·68 | $-0\cdot556393$ |
| 0·19 | $-2\cdot39593$ | 0·69 | $-0\cdot535332$ |
| 0·2 | $-2\cdot32193$ | 0·7 | $-0\cdot514573$ |
| 0·21 | $-2\cdot25154$ | 0·71 | $-0\cdot494109$ |
| 0·22 | $-2\cdot18442$ | 0·72 | $-0\cdot473931$ |
| 0·23 | $-2\cdot12029$ | 0·73 | $-0\cdot454032$ |
| 0·24 | $-2\cdot05889$ | 0·74 | $-0\cdot434403$ |
| 0·25 | $-2\cdot$ | 0·75 | $-0\cdot415038$ |
| 0·26 | $-1\cdot94342$ | 0·76 | $-0\cdot395929$ |
| 0·27 | $-1\cdot88897$ | 0·77 | $-0\cdot37707$ |
| 0·28 | $-1\cdot8365$ | 0·78 | $-0\cdot358454$ |
| 0·29 | $-1\cdot78588$ | 0·79 | $-0\cdot340075$ |
| 0·3 | $-1\cdot73697$ | 0·8 | $-0\cdot321928$ |
| 0·31 | $-1\cdot68966$ | 0·81 | $-0\cdot304006$ |
| 0·32 | $-1\cdot64386$ | 0·82 | $-0\cdot286304$ |
| 0·33 | $-1\cdot59946$ | 0·83 | $-0\cdot268817$ |
| 0·34 | $-1\cdot55639$ | 0·84 | $-0\cdot251539$ |
| 0·35 | $-1\cdot51457$ | 0·85 | $-0\cdot234465$ |
| 0·36 | $-1\cdot47393$ | 0·86 | $-0\cdot217592$ |
| 0·37 | $-1\cdot4344$ | 0·87 | $-0\cdot200913$ |
| 0·38 | $-1\cdot39593$ | 0·88 | $-0\cdot184425$ |
| 0·39 | $-1\cdot35845$ | 0·89 | $-0\cdot168123$ |
| 0·4 | $-1\cdot32193$ | 0·9 | $-0\cdot152003$ |
| 0·41 | $-1\cdot2863$ | 0·91 | $-0\cdot136062$ |
| 0·42 | $-1\cdot25154$ | 0·92 | $-0\cdot120294$ |
| 0·43 | $-1\cdot21759$ | 0·93 | $-0\cdot104697$ |
| 0·44 | $-1\cdot18442$ | 0·94 | $-0\cdot08927$ |
| 0·45 | $-1\cdot152$ | 0·95 | $-0\cdot07400$ |
| 0·46 | $-1\cdot12029$ | 0·96 | $-0\cdot05889$ |
| 0·47 | $-1\cdot08927$ | 0·97 | $-0\cdot04394$ |
| 0·48 | $-1\cdot05889$ | 0·98 | $-0\cdot02915$ |
| 0·49 | $-1\cdot02915$ | 0·99 | $-0\cdot01450$ |
| 0·5 | $-1\cdot$ | 1· | $-0\cdot00000$ |

# BIBLIOGRAPHY

Ades, H. W. (1959) "Central Auditory Mechanisms", in *Handbook of Physiology*, Section I: Neurophysiology, American Physiological Society, Washington D.C.

Altmann, S. A. (1965) "Sociobiology of rhesus monkeys. II. Stochastics of social communication", *J. Theoret. Biol.* **8**, 490–522.

Altmann, S. A. (1967) *Social Communication Among Primates*, University of Chicago Press, Chicago.

Amouriq, L. (1965) "L'activité et le phénomène social chez *Lebistes reticulatus* (Poeciliidae —Cyprinoidontiformes)", *Ann. Sci. Nat. Zool. Anim.* (12), **7**, 151–172.

Andrew, R. J. (1956) "Some remarks on behaviour in conflict situations, with special reference to *Emberiza* species", *Brit. J. Anim. Behav.* **4**, 41–45.

Andrew, R. (1963) "The origin and evolution of the calls and facial expressions of the Primates", *Behav.* **20**, 1–109.

Andrew, R. (1972) "The information potentially available in mammal displays", in R. A. Hinde (Ed.), *Non-verbal Communication*, C.U.P., Cambridge, England.

Ashby, W. R. (1958) *Introduction to Cybernetics*, 3rd. Imp., Chapman and Hall, London.

Ashby, W. R. (1960) *Design for a Brain*, Science Paperbacks, Chapman and Hall, London.

Autrum, H. J. (1958) "Electrophysiological analysis of the visual systems in insects", *Expl. Cell. Res. Suppl.* **5**, 426–439.

Autrum, H., Gallwitz, U. (1951) "Zur Analyse der Belichtungspotentiale des Insektenauges", *Z. vergl. Physiol.* **33**, 407–435.

Bacon, J., Tyrer, M. (1978) "The tritocerebral commissure giant (TCG): A bimodal interneurone in the locust, *Schistocerca gregaria*", *J. comp. Physiol.* **126**, 317–325.

Baerends, G. P. (1975) "An Evaluation of the Conflict Hypothesis as an Explanatory Principle for the Evolution of Displays", in G. Baerends, C. Beer and A. Manning (Eds.), *Function and Evolution in Behaviour*, Clarendon Press, Oxford.

Baerends, G. P., Baerends-van Roon, J. M. (1950) "An introduction to the study of cichlid fishes", *Behav. Suppl.* **1**.

Baerends, G. P., Brouwer, R., Waterbolk, H. Tj. (1955) "Ethological studies on *Lebistes reticulatus* (Peters). I: An analysis of the male courtship pattern", *Behav.* **8**, 249–334.

Bailey, W. J. (1976) "Species isolation and song types of the genus *Ruspolia* Schulthess (Orthoptera, Tettigonioidea) in Uganda", *J. Nat. Hist.* **10**, 511–528.

Baldaccini, N. E. (1973) "An ethological study of reproductive behaviour including the colour patterns of the cichlid fish *Tilapia mariae* (Boulanger)", *Monitore zool. ital.* (*N-S*), **7**, 247–290.

Barlow, G. W. (1968) "Ethological units of behaviour", in *The Central Nervous System and Behaviour*, D. Ingle, (Ed.), Chicago; U.C.P., 217–232.

Barlow, G. W. (1977) "Modal Action Patterns", in T. A. Sebeok (Ed.), *How Animals Communicate*, Indiana University Press, Bloomington and London.

Barlow, H. B. (1953) "Summation and inhibition in the frog's retina", *J. Physiol.* **119**, 68–88.

Barlow, H. B. (1961) "The Coding of Sensory Messages", in W. H. Thorpe and O. L. Zangwill (Eds.), *Current Problems in Animal Behaviour*, C.U.P., Cambridge, England.

Bastock, M., Manning, A. (1955) "The courtship of *Drosophila melanogaster*", *Behav.* **8**, 85–111.

Beer, C. G. (1973) "A View of Birds", *Minnesota Symposium on Child Psychology*, **7**, 47–86.

Beer, C. G. (1975) "Multiple Functions and Gull Displays", in G. Baerends, C. G. Beer and A. Manning (Eds.), *Function and Evolution in Behaviour*, Clarendon Press, Oxford.

Bekesy, G. von. (1960) *Experiments in Hearing*, McGraw-Hill, New York.

Bekesy, G. von. (1970) "Travelling waves as frequency analysis in the cochlea", *Nature*, London, **225**, 1207–1209.

Bennet-Clark, H. C. (1971) "Acoustics of Insect Song", *Nature*, London, **243**, 255–259.

Bennet-Clark, H. C. (1975) "Sound production in insects", *Sci. Prog. Oxf.* **62** (246), 263–284.

Bentley, D. R. (1969) "Intracellular activity in cricket neurons during the generation of song patterns", *Z. vergl. Physiol.* **62**, 267–283.

Bentley, D. R. (1977) "Control of cricket song patterns by descending interneurons", *J. comp. Physiol.* **116**, 19–38.

Beranek, L. L. (1954) *Acoustics*, McGraw-Hill, New York.

Blakemore, C. (1974) "Development of functional connections in the mammalian visual system", *Brit. Med. Bull.* **30**, 152–157.

Blurton-Jones, N. (1968) "Observations and experiments on causation of threat displays of the Great Tit (*Parus major*)", *Anim. Behav. Monographs*, **1**, 75–158.

Bredberg, G. (1977) "Innervation of the Organ of Corti as Revealed in the Scanning Electron Microscope", in E. F. Evans and J. P. Wilson (Eds.), *Psychophysics and Physiology of Hearing*, Academic Press, London, New York and San Francisco.

Breder, C. M. Jr., Rosen, D. E. (1966) *Modes of Reproduction in Fishes*, Natural History Press, New York.

Broadbent, D. E. (1971) *Decision and Stress*, Academic Press, London and New York.

Broughton, W. B. (1965) "Song learning among grasshoppers?" *New Scientist*, **27**, 338–341.

Brower, L. P., Brower, J. V. Z., Cranston, F. P. (1965) "Courtship behaviour in the queen butterfly *Danaus gillipus berenica* (Cramer)", *Zoologica*, New York, **50**, 1–39.

Buck, J., Buck, E. (1976) "Synchronous fireflies", *Sci. Am.*, May, 74–85.

Buddenbrock, W. von. (1952) *Vergleichende Physiologie, Vol. I, Sinnesphysiologie*, Verlag Birkhäuser und Cie. A. G., Basel.

Bull, L. B., Culvenor, C. C. J., Dick, A. T. (1968) *The Pyrrolizidine Alkaloids*, North Holland Publ. Co., Amsterdam.

Bullock, T. H. (1973) "Seeing the world through a new sense: electroreception in fish", *Amer. Sci.* **61**, 316–325.

Burrows, M. (1975) "Integration by Motoneurones in the Central Nervous System of Insects", in P. N. R. Usherwood and D. R. Newth (Eds.), *'Simple' Nervous Systems*, Arnold. London.

Busnel, R.-G., Dumortier, B. (1959) "Vérification par des méthodes d'analyse acoustique des hypothèses sur l'origine du cri du Sphinx *Acherontia atropos* (Linné)", *Bull. Soc. entomol. France* **64**, 44–58.

Cane, V. R. (1978) "On fitting low-order Markov chains to behaviour sequences", *Anim. Behav.* **26**, 332–338.

Casida, J. E., Coppel, H. C., Watanabe, T. (1963) "Purification and potency of the sex attractant from the introduced pine sawfly, *Diprion similis*", *J. Econ. Entomol.* **56**, 18–24.

Chance, M. R. A. (1962) "An interpretation of some agonistic postures: the role of 'cut-off' acts and postures", *Symp. Zoo. Soc. Lond.* **8**, 71–89.

Coles, R., Lewis, B., Hill, K., Hutchings, M., Gower, M. (1979) "Auditory directional sensitivity in the quail (*Coturnix coturnix japonica*). II. Cochlear microphonic responses", *J. exp. Biol.*, in Press.

Collett, T. (1974) "The Efferent Control of Sensory Pathways", in W. B. Broughton (Ed.), *The Biology of Brains*, Symp. Inst. Biol., London, **21**.

Comeau, A., Roelofs, W. L. (1973) "Sex attraction specificity in the Tortricidae", *Ent. Exp. Appl.* **16**, 191–200.

Cottrell, G. A., Usherwood, P. N. R. (1977) *Synapses*, Blackie, Glasgow and London.

Cullen, E. (1960) "Experiments on the effects of social isolation on reproductive behaviour of the three-spined stickleback", *Anim. Behav.* **8**, 235.

Dane, B., Walcott, C., Drury, W. H. (1959) "The form and duration of the display actions of the goldeneye (*Bucephala clangula*)", *Behaviour* **14**, 265–281.

Darwin, C. (1872) *The Expressions of the Emotions in Man and Animals*, Appleton, London.

Daumer, K. (1958) "Blumenfarben wie sie die Bienen Sehen", *Z. vergl. Physiol.* **41**, 49–110.

Davies, W. G. (1978) "Cluster analysis applied to the classification of postures in the Chilean flamingo (*Phoenicopterus chilensis*)", *Anim. Behav.* **26**, 381–388.

Davis, H. (1959) "Excitation of Auditory Receptors", in *Handbook of Physiology*, Section I: Neurophysiology, American Physiological Society, Washington D.C.

Dawkins, R. (1969) "A threshold model of choice behaviour", *Anim. Behav.* **17**, 120–133.

Dawkins, R. (1976) *The Selfish Gene*, O.U.P., Oxford.

Dawkins, R., Dawkins, M. (1976) "Hierarchical organisation and postural facilitation: rules for grooming in flies", *Anim. Behav.* **24**, 739–755.

Delius, J. D. (1969) "A stochastic analysis of the maintenance behaviour of skylarks", *Behav.* **33**, 137–178.

Dethier, V. G. (1963) *The Physiology of Insect Senses*, Methuen, London.

Dethier, V. G. (1964) "Microscopic brains", *Science*, New York, **143**, 1138–1145.

Dilger, W. C. (1962) "The behaviour of lovebirds", *Sci. Am.* **206**, 88–98.

Dingle, H. (1969) "A statistical and information analysis of aggressive communication in the mantis shrimp *Gonodactylus bredini* Manning", *Anim. Behav.* **17**, 561–575.

Doty, R. W. Sr. (1976) "The Concept of Neural Centres", in J. C. Fentress (Ed.), *Simpler Networks and Behaviour*, Sinauer, Sunderland, Mass.

Duke-Elder, S. (1958) *System of Ophthalmology*, Vol. I: The Eye in Evolution, Henry Kimpton, London.

Eccles, J. C. (1973) *The Understanding of the Brain*, McGraw-Hill, New York and London.

Edgar, J. A., Culvenor, C. C. J. (1974) "Pyrrolizidine ester alkaloid in danaid butterflies", *Nature*, London, **248**, 614–616.

Edgar, J. A., Culvenor, C. C. J., Pliske, T. E. (1974) "Co-evolution of Danaid butterflies with their host plants", *Nature*, London, **250**, 646–648.

Edmunds, M. (1976) *Defence in Animals: A Survey of Anti-predator defences*, Longman, Harlow.

Eibl-Eibsfeldt, I. (1959) "Der Fisch *Aspidontus taeniatus* als Nachamer des Putzers *Labroides dimidiatus*", *Z. Tierpsychol.* **16**, 19–25.

Eibl-Eibsfeldt, I. (1970), *Ethology. The Biology of Behaviour*, Holt, Reinhart and Winston, New York, London.

Elsner, N., Popov, A. V. (1978) "Neuroethology of Acoustic Communication", *Adv. Ins. Physiol.* **13**, 229–355.

Emlen, S. T. (1972) "An experimental analysis of the parameters of bird song eliciting species recognition", *Behav.* **41**, 130–171.

Etienne, A. S. (1968) "Die Beantwortung von Flimmerfrequenzen durch die Libellen larve *Aeschna cyanea*", *M. Z. vergl. Physiol.* **61**, 34–40.

Evans, E. F. (1977) "Frequency Selectivity at High Signal Levels of Single Units in Cochlear Nerve and Cochlear Nucleus", in E. F. Evans and J. P. Wilson (Eds.),

*Psychophysics and Physiology of Hearing*, Academic Press, London, New York and San Francisco.

Everitt, B. (1974) *Cluster Analysis*, Heinemann, London.

Ewert, J. P. (1974) "The neural basis of visually guided behaviour", *Sci. Am.* **230** (3), 34–42.

Ewing, A. W., Bennet-Clark, H. C. (1968) "The courtship songs of *Drosophila*", *Behav.* **31**, 288–301.

Eyzaguirre, C., Kuffler, S. W. (1955) "Processes of excitation in the dendrites and in the soma of single isolated sensory nerve cells of the lobster and the crayfish", *J. gen. Physiol.* **39**, 87–119.

Fabricius, E., Lindroth, A. (1954) "Experimental observations on the spawning of whitefish, *Coregonus lavaretus* L. in the stream aquarium of the Holle laboratory at River Indälsalven", Institute of Fresh-Water Research, Drottningholm, Report No. **35**, 105–112.

Fentress, J. C. (Ed.) (1976) *Simpler Networks and Behaviour*, Sinauer, Sunderland, Mass.

Flock, Å. (1971) "Sensory Transduction in Hair Cells", in *Handbook of Sensory Physiology*, Vol. I, Springer-Verlag. Berlin.

Flynn, J. P., Vanegas, H., Foote, W., Edwards, S. (1970) "Neural Mechanisms Involved in a Cat's Attack on a Rat", in R. Whalen (Ed.), *Neural Control of Behaviour*, Academic Press, London, New York and San Francisco.

Frisch, K. von. (1938) "The sense of hearing in fish", *Nature*, London, **141**, 8–11.

Frisch, K. von. (1941) "Uber einen Schreckstoff der Fischant und seine Biologische Bedeutung", *Z. vergl. Physiol.* **29**, 46–145.

Frisch, K. von. (1950) *Bees: Their Vision, Chemical Senses and Language*, Cornell University Press, Ithaca, New York.

Galambos, R. (1956) "Suppression of auditory nerve activity by stimulation of efferent fibres to cochlea", *J. Neurophysiol.* **19**, 424–437.

Gaze, R. M. (1974) "Neuronal specificity", *Br. Med. Bull.* **30**, 116–121.

Goldstein, S. S., Rall, W. (1974) "Changes of action potential shape and velocity for changing core conductor geometry", *Biophys. J.* **14**, 731–757.

Goodman, L. A. (1968) "The analysis of cross-classified data: Independence, quasi-independence and interactions in contingency tables with or without missing entries", *J. Am. Stat. Ass.* **63**, 1091–1131.

Gordon, G., Manson, J. R. (1967) "Cutaneous receptive fields of single nerve cells in the thalamus of the cat". *Nature*, London, **215**, 597–599.

Granit, R. (1955) "Centrifugal and antidromic effects on ganglion cells of the retina", *J. Neurophysiol.* **18**, 388–411.

Granit, R. (1975) "The functional role of muscle spindles—facts and hypotheses", *Brain*, **98**, 531–556.

Green, R., Carr, W. J., Green, M. (1968) "Authors' abstract", *J. Psychol.* **69**, 271–276.

Griffin, D. R. (1955) "Hearing and acoustical orientation in marine animals", *Deep Sea Research* **3** (Suppl.), 406–417.

Grunt, J. A., Young, W. C. (1952) "Psychological modification of fatigue following orgasm (ejaculation) in the male guinea pig", *J. comp. physiol. Psychol.* **45**, 508–510.

Hailman, J. P. (1967) "The ontogeny of an instinct", *Behav. Suppl.* **15**, 1–159.

Hailman, J. P. (1969) "How an instinct is learned", *Sci. Am.* **221** (6), 98–106.

Halliday, T. R. (1975) "An observational and experimental study of sexual behaviour in the smooth newt, *Triturus vulgaris* (Amphibia: Salamandridae)", *Anim. Behav.* **23**, 291–322.

Harris, G. W., Michael, R. P., Scott, P. P. (1958) "Neurological site of action of stilboestrol in eliciting sexual behaviour", Ciba Foundation Symposium, *The Neurological Basis of Behaviour*, Churchill, London.

Hartline, H. K. (1949) "Inhibition of activity of visual receptors by illuminating nearby retinal areas in *Limulus* eye", *Fed. Proc.* **8**, 69.

Hartline, H. K., Ratliff, F. (1956) "Inhibitory interaction of receptor units in the eye of *Limulus*", *J. gen. Physiol.* **40**, 357–376.

Hartline, H. K., Wagner, H. G., Ratliff, F. (1956) "Inhibition in the eye of *Limulus*", *J. gen. Physiol.* **39**, 651–673.

Hazlett, B. A. (1972*a*) "Stereotypy of agonistic movements in the spider crab *Microphrys bicornutus*", *Behav.* **42**, 270–278.

Hazlett, B. A. (1972*b*) "Ritualisation in Marine Crustacea", in H. E. Winn and B. L. Olla (Eds.), *Behaviour of Marine Animals*, Plenum, New York.

Heiligenberg, W. (1973) "Random processes describing the occurrence of behavioural patterns in a cichlid fish", *Anim. Behav.* **21**, 169–182.

Henson, O. W. (1965) "The activity and function of the middle ear muscles in echo-locating bats", *J. Physiol.* **180**, 871–887.

Hill, K. G., Boyan, G. S. (1977) "Sensitivity to frequency and direction of sound in the auditory system of crickets (Gryllidae)", *J. comp. Physiol.* **121**, 79–97.

Hill, K., Lewis, B., Hutchings, M., Coles, R. (1979) "Auditory directional hearing in the quail (*Coturnix coturnix japonica*). I. Biophysical mechanisms", *J. exp. Biol.*, in Press.

Hinde, R. A. (1953) "The conflict between drives in the courtship and copulation of the chaffinch", *Behav.* **5**, 1–31.

Hinde, R. A. (1954) "The courtship and copulation of the greenfinch (*Chloris chloris*)", *Behav.* **7**, 207–232.

Hinde, R. A. (1955) "A comparative study of the courtship of certain finches (Fringillidae)", *Ibis*, **97**, 706–745.

Hinde, R. A. (1956) "A comparative study of the courtship of certain finches (Fringillidae)", *Ibis*, **98**, 1–23.

Hinde, R. A. (1960) "Energy models of motivation", *Symp. Soc. exp. Biol.* **14**, 199–213.

Hinde, R. A. (1970) *Animal Behaviour, A Synthesis of Ethology and Comparative Psychology*, 2nd. Ed., McGraw-Hill Kogakusha Ltd., International Student Edition.

Hirsch, J., Lindley, R. H., Tolman, E. C. (1955) "An experimental test of an alleged innate sign stimulus", *J. comp. Physiol. Psychol.* **48**, 278–280.

Hodgson, E. S., Roeder, K. D. (1956) "Electrophysiological studies of arthropod chemo-reception. I. General properties of the labellar chemoreceptors of Diptera", *J. cell. comp. Physiol.* **48**, 51–76.

Holst, E. von. (1954) "Relations between the central nervous system and the peripheral organs", *Brit. J. Anim. Behav.* **2**, 89–94.

Holst, E. von, Mittelstaedt, H. (1950) "Das Reafferanzprinzip", *Naturwiss.* **37**, 464–476.

Hoof, J. A. R. A. M. van. (1970) "A component analysis of the structure of the social behaviour of a semi-captive chimpanzee group", *Experientia*, **26**, 549–550.

Horn, G., Hill, R. M. (1969) "Modification of sensory field occurring spontaneously and with body tilt", *Nature*, London, **221**, 186–188.

Horridge, G. A. (1964) "Multimodal interneurones of the locust optic lobe", *Nature*, London, **204**, 499–500.

Horridge, G. A. (1968) *Interneurones: Their Origins, Action, Specificity, Growth and Plasticity*, Freeman, London and San Francisco.

Horridge, G. A., Scholes, J. H., Shaw, S., Tunstall, J. (1965) "Extracellular recordings from single neurones in the optic lobe and brain of the locust", in J. E. Treherne and J. W. L, Beament (Eds.), *The Physiology of the Insect Central Nervous System*, Academic Press, London and New York.

Howse, P. E. (1974) "Design and Function in the Insect Brain", in L. Barton-Browne (Ed.), *Experimental Analysis of Insect Behaviour*, Springer-Verlag, Berlin, Heidelberg and New York.

Hoyle, G. (1964) "Exploration of Neuronal Mechanisms Underlying Behaviour in Insects", in R. F. Reiss (Ed.), *Neural Theory and Modelling*, Stanford University Press, Stanford, California.

Hoyle, G. (1976) "Approaches to Understanding the Neurophysiological Bases of Behaviour", in J. C. Fentress (Ed.), *Simpler Networks and Behaviour*, Sinauer, Sunderland, Mass.

Hubel, D. H., Wiesel, T. N. (1964) "Responses of monkey geniculate cells to monochromatic and white spots of light", *Physiologist* **7**, 162–163.

Hubel, D. H., Wiesel, T. N. (1965a) "Receptive fields and functional architecture in two nonstriate visual areas (18 and 19) of the cat", *J. Neurophysiol.* **28**, 229–289.

Hubel, D. H., Wiesel, T. N. (1965b) "Binocular interaction in the striate cortex of kittens reared with artificial squint", *J. Neurophysiol.* **28**, 1041–1059.

Huber, F. (1974) "Neuronal Background of Species-specific Acoustical Communication in Orthopteran Insects (Gryllidae)", in W. B. Broughton (Ed.), *Biology of Brains*, Symp. Inst. Biol. London, **21**.

Huber, F. (1975) "Principles of Motor Coordination in Cyclically Recurring Behaviour in Insects", in P. N. R. Usherwood and D. R. Newth (Eds.), *'Simple' Nervous Systems*, Arnold, London.

Huber, F. (1978) "The insect nervous system and insect behaviour", *Anim. Behav.* **26**, 969–981.

Hughes, P. R. (1974) "Myrcene: A precursor of pheromones in *Ips* beetles", *J. insect Physiol.* **20**, 1271–1275.

Huntingford, F. A. (1976) "The relationship between anti-predator behaviour and aggression among conspecifics in the three-spined stickleback, *Gasterosteus aculeatus*", *Anim. Behav.* **24**, 245–260.

Huntingford, F. A. (1976) "An investigation of the territorial behaviour of the three-spined stickleback (*Gasterosteus aculeatus*) using principal components analysis", *Anim. Behav.* **24**, 822–834.

Huxley, J. (1914) "The courtship habits of the great crested grebe (*Podiceps cristatus*) with an addition to the theory of sexual selection", *Proc. Roy. Soc. Lond.* **35**, 491–562.

Iersel, J. J. A. van, Bol, A. C. A. (1958) "Preening of two tern species. A study on displacement activities", *Behav.* **13–14**, 1–88.

Immelmann, K. (1969) "Song development in the zebra finch and other estrildid finches", in R. A. Hinde (Ed.), *Bird Vocalisations*, C.U.P., Cambridge and New York.

Jehl, J. R. Jnr. (1973) "Breeding biology and systematic relationships of the stilt sandpiper", *Wilson Bull.* **85**, 115–147.

Jenkins, P. F. (1978) "Cultural transmission of song patterns and dialect development in a free living bird population", *Anim. Behav.* **26**, 50–78.

Johnstone, J. R. (1977) "Properties of Ganglion Cells from the Extreme Basal Region of Guinea Pig Cochlea", in E. F. Evans and J. P. Wilson (Eds.), *Psychophysics and Physiology of Hearing*, Academic Press, London, New York and San Francisco.

Kaae, R. S., Shorey, H. H. (1972) "Sex pheromones of noctuid moths. XXVII. Influence of wind velocity on sex pheromone releasing behaviour of *Trichoplusia* $N_1$ females", *Ann. Entomol. Soc. Amer.* **65**, 436–440.

Kaae, R. S., Shorey, H. H., Gaston, L. K. (1973) Pheromone concentration as a mechanism for productive isolation between two lepidopterous species", *Science*, **179**, 487–488.

Kalmring, K. (1975) "The afferent auditory pathway in the ventral cord of *Locusta migratoria* (Acrididae), I and II", *J. comp. Physiol.* **104**, 103–159.

Kalmring, K., Kuhne, R., Moysich, F. (1978) "The auditory pathway in the ventral cord of the migratory locust (*Locusta migratoria*): response transmission in the axons", *J. comp. Physiol.* **126**, 25–33.

Kalmring, K., Lewis, B., Eichendorf, A. (1978) "The physiological characteristics of the primary sensory neurons of the complex tibial organ of *Decticus verrucivorus* L. (Orthoptera, Tettigonioidea)", *J. comp. Physiol.* **127**, 109–121.

Kennedy, J. S. (1974) "Changes of responsiveness in the patterning of behavioural sequences", in L. Barton-Browne (Ed.), *The Experimental Analysis of Insect Behaviour*, Springer, Berlin.

Kessel, E. L. (1955) "The mating activities of balloon flies", *System. Zool.* **4**, 97–104.

Klopfer, P. H., Hatch, J. J. (1968) "Experimental Considerations", in T. A. Sebeok (Ed.), *Animal Communication*, University of Indiana Press, Bloomington.

Knudsen, E. I., Konishi, M. (1978) "A neural map of auditory space in the owl", *Science*, **200**, 795–797.

Knudsen, E. I., Konishi, M. (1978) "Space and frequency are represented separately in auditory midbrain of the owl", *J. Neurophysiol.* **41**, 870–884.

Knudsen, E. I., Konishi, M., Pettigrew, J. D. (1977) "Receptive fields of auditory neurons in the owl", *Science*, **198**, 1278–1280.

Konijn, T. M., Barkley, D. S., Chang, Y. Y., Bonner, J. T. (1968) "Cyclic AMP. A naturally occurring acrasin in the cellular slime molds", *Amer. Nat.* **102**, 225–233.

Kuhne, R., Lewis, B., Kalmring, K. (1979) "The responses of ventral cord neurons in *Decticus verrucivorus* L. to sound and vibration stimuli", *Behav. Biol.*, in Press.

Kupfermann, I., Weiss, K. R. (1978) "The command neuron concept", *Behav. Brain Sci.* **1**, 3–39.

Larsen, O. N., Michelsen, A. (1978) "Biophysics of the ensiferan ear. III. The cricket ear as a four-input system", *J. comp. Physiol.* **123**, 217–227.

Lehrman, D. S. (1965) "Interaction between internal and external environments in the regulation of the reproductive cycle of the ring dove", in F. A. Beach (Ed.), *Sex and Behaviour*, Wiley, New York.

Lemon, R. E., Chatfield, C. (1971) "Organisation of song in cardinals", *Anim. Behav.* **19**, 1–17.

Leong, C. Y. (1969) "The quantitative effect of releasers on the attack readiness of the fish *Haplochromis burtoni* (Cichidae, Pisces)", *Z. vergl. Physiol.* **65**, 29–50.

Lettvin, J. Y., Maturana, H. R., McCulloch, W. S., Pitts, W. H. (1959) "What the frog's eye tells the frog's brain", *Proc. Instit. Radio Engrs.* **47**, 1940–1951.

Lewis, D. B. (1974) "The physiology of the tettigoniid ear I–IV", *J. exp. Biol.* **60**, 821–869.

Lewis, D. B., Broughton, W. B. (1980) *Insect Acoustics: An Analysis of Behaviour*, Hodder and Stoughton, London.

Lisk, R. D. (1962) "Diencephalic placement of estradiol and sexual receptivity in the female rat", *Amer. J. Physiol.* **203**, 493–496.

Lissmann, H. W. (1958) "On the function and evolution of electric organs in fish", *J. exp. Biol.* **34**, 156–191.

Lissmann, H. W., Machin, K. E. (1958) "The mechanism of object location in *Gymnarchus niloticus* and similar fish", *J. exp. Biol.* **35**, 451–486.

Lorenz, K. (1941) "Vergleichende Beiregungsstudien an Anatinea", *J. für Ornithologie*, **89**, Erganzungsband 19–29 and 194–293. Reprint (1951–1953 in parts). "Comparative studies on the behaviour of the Anatinae", *Aviculture Magazine* **57–59**.

Lorenz, K. Z. (1950) "The comparative method in studying innate behaviour patterns", *Symp. Soc. exp. Biol.* **4**, 221–268.

Lorenz, K. (1974) "Analogy as a source of knowledge", *Science*, **185**, 229–234.

Lorenz, K. Z., Tinbergen, N. (1938) "Taxis und Instinkthandlung in der Eirolbewegung der Graugans I", *Z. Tierpsychol.* **2**, 1–29.

McCullough, J. M., Quadagus, D. M., Goldman, B. D. (1974) "Neonatal gonadial hormones: Effect on maternal and sexual behaviour in the male rat", *Physiol. Behav.* **12**, 183–188.

McDougall, W. (1923) *An Outline of Psychology*, Methuen, London.

McFarland, D. J. (1971) *Feedback Mechanisms in Animal Behaviour*, Academic Press, London and New York.

McKay, J. M. (1969) "The auditory system of *Homorocoryphus* (Tettigonioidea, Orthoptera)", *J. exp. Biol.* **51,** 787–802.

Magnus, D. B. E. (1950) "Beobachtungen zur Balz und Eiablage des Kaisermantels *Argynnis paphia* L. (Lep. Nymphalidae)", *Z. Tierpsychol.* **7,** 435–449.

Manning, A. (1979) *An Introduction to Animal Behaviour* (3rd. Ed.), Arnold, London.

Markl, H. (1968) "Die Verständigung durch Stridulationssignale bei Blattschneiderameisen. II. Erzeugung und Eigenschaften der Signale", *Z. vergl. Physiol.* **60,** 103–150.

Markl, H. (1970) "Die Verständigung durch Stridulationssignale bei Blattschneiderameisen. III. Die Empfindlichkeit für Substratvibrationen", *Z. vergl. Physiol.* **69,** 6–37.

Marler, P. (1961) "The Filtering of External Stimuli During Instinctive Behaviour", in W. H. Thorpe and O. L. Zangwill (Eds.), *Current Problems in Animal Behaviour*, C.U.P., Cambridge, England.

Marler, P., Tamura, M. (1962) "Song 'dialects' in three populations of white-crowned sparrows", *Condor*, **64,** 368–377.

Marler, P., Tamura, M. (1964) "Culturally transmitted patterns of vocal behaviour in sparrows", *Science*, **146,** 1483–1486.

Meinwald, J., Chalmers, A. M., Pliske, T. E., Eisner, T. (1968) "Pheromones. III. Identification of trans, trans-10-hydroxy-3, 7-dimethyl-2, 6-decadienoic acid as a major component in 'hairpencil' secretion of the male monarch butterfly", *Tetrahedron Lett.* **47,** 4893–4896.

Meinwald, J., Chalmers, A. M., Pliske, T. E., Eisner, T. (1969) "Identification and synthesis of trans, trans-3, 7-dimethyl-2, 6-decadienol, 10-dioic acid, a component of the pheromonal secretion of the male monarch butterfly", *Chem. Commun.* **3,** 86–87.

Melzack, R., Penick, E., Beckett, A. (1959) "The problem of 'innate fear' of the hawk shape; an experimental study with mallard ducks", *J. comp. Physiol. Psychol.* **52,** 694–698.

Michelsen, A. (1971) "The physiology of the locust ear I–III", *J. comp. Physiol.* **71,** 49–128.

Michelsen, A., Larsen, O. N. (1978) "Biophysics of the ensiferan ear. I. Tympanal vibrations in the bushcrickets (Tettigoniidae) studied with laser vibrometry", *J. comp. Physiol.* **123,** 193–203.

Miles, F. A. (1972) "Centrifugal control of the avian retina I, II", *Brain Res.* **48,** 65–145.

Miller, L. A. (1977) "Directional hearing in the locust *Schistocerca gregaria* Forskål (Acrididae, Orthoptera)", *J. comp. Physiol.* **119,** 85–98.

Miller, N. E. (1959) "Liberalisation of Basic S-R Concepts", in S. Koch (Ed.), *Psychology: A Study of a Science*, Study I, Vol. 2, McGraw-Hill, New York.

Moody, M. F. (1962) "Evidence for the intraocular discrimination of vertically and horizontally polarised light by *Octopus*", *J. exp. Biol.* **39,** 21–30.

Morris, D. (1952) "Homosexuality in the ten-spined stickleback", *Behav.* **4,** 233–261.

Morris, D. (1954) "The reproductive behaviour of the Zebra finch (*Poephila guttata*) with special reference to pseudofemale behaviour and displacement activities," *Behaviour* **6,** 271–322.

Morris, D. (1956) "The feather postures of birds and the problem of the origin of social signals", *Behav.* **9,** 75–113.

Morris, D. (1957) "'Typical Intensity' and its relation to the problem of ritualisation", *Behav.* **11,** 1–12.

Moulton, J. M. (1956) "Influencing the calling of sea robins (*Prionotus* spp.) with sound", *Bio. Bull.* **111,** 393–398.

Moulton, J. M. (1963) "Acoustic Behaviour of Fishes", in R.-G. Busnel (Ed.), *Acoustic Behaviour of Animals*, Elsevier, Holland.

Moynihan, M. (1962) "Hostile and sexual behaviour patterns of South American and Pacific Laridae", *Behav. Suppl.* **VIII**, 1–365.

Moynihan, M. (1970) "The control, suppression, decay, disappearance and replacement of displays", *J. Theoret. Biol.* **29**, 85–112.

Moynihan, M. (1975) "Conservation of Displays and Comparable Stereotyped Patterns Among Cephalopods", in G. Baerends and A. Manning (Eds.), *Essays on Function and Evolution in Behaviour: A Festschrift for Professor Niko Tinbergen*, Clarendon Press, Oxford.

Muller-Schwartze, D. (1971) "Pheromones in black-tailed deer (*Odocoileus hemionus columbianus*)", *Anim. Behav.* **19**, 141–152.

Mustaparta, H. (1975) "Responses of single olfactory cells in the pine weevil *Hylobius obietis* L (Col.: Ciculionidae)", *J. comp. Physiol.* **97**, 271–290.

Nottebohm, F. (1970) "Ontogeny of bird song", *Science*, **167**, 950–956.

O'Shea, M. (1975) "Two sites of axonal spike initiation in a bimodal interneuron", *Brain Res.* **96**, 93–98.

Otte, D. (1974) "Effects and functions in the evolution of signalling systems", *Ann. Rev. Ecol. Syst.* **5**, 385–417.

Payne, R. S., McVay, S. (1971) "Songs of humpback whales", *Science*, **173**, 585–597.

Payne, R. S., Webb, D. (1971) "Orientation by means of long range acoustic signalling in baleen whales", *Ann. N.Y. Acad. Sci.* **188**, 110–142.

Pearson, K. G. (1976) "Nerve Cells Without Action Potentials", in J. C. Fentress (Ed.), *Simpler Networks and Behaviour*, Sinauer, Sunderland, Mass.

Pfaff, D. W., Diakow, C., Zigmond, R. E., Kow, L.-M. (1974) *Neural and Hormonal Determinants of Female Mating Behaviour in Rats*, Neurosciences Third Study Program, 621–644, M.I.T. Press.

Pfeiffer, W. (1974) "Fish and Pheromones", in M. C. Birch, (Ed.), *Pheromones*, Elsevier, Amsterdam.

Pliske, T. (1975) "Courtship behaviour in the monarch butterfly, *Danaus plexippus*", L. *Ann. ent. Soc. Am.* **69**, 143–151.

Pliske, T. E., Eisner, T. (1969) "Sex pheromones of the queen butterfly: biology", *Science*, **164**, 1170–1172.

Potts, G. W. (1973) "The ethology of *Labroides dimidiatus* (Cuv. and Val.) (Labridae, Pisces) on Aldabra", *Anim. Behav.* **21**, 250–291.

Preston, J. L. (1978) "Communication systems and social interactions in a goby-shrimp symbiosis", *Anim. Behav.* **26**, 791–802.

Pumphrey, R. J. (1940) "Hearing in Insects", *Biol. Rev.* **15**, 107–132.

Pumphrey, R. J. (1961) "Part I: Sensory Organs: Vision", in A. J. Marshall (Ed.), *Biology and Comparative Physiology of Birds*, Vol. II. Academic Press., London and New York.

Quastler, H. (1958) "A Primer on Information Theory", in H. P. Yockey, R. L. Platzman and H. Quastler (Eds.), *Symposium on Information Theory in Biology*, Pergamon Press, Oxford.

Ransom, T. W., Ransom, B. S. (1971) "Adult male-infant relations among baboons (*Papio anubis*)", *Folia Primatolog.* **16**, 179–195.

Rheinlaender, J. (1975) "Transmission of acoustic information at three neuronal levels in the auditory system of *Decticus verrucivorus* (Tettigoniidae, Orthoptera)", *J. comp. Physiol.* **97**, 1–54.

Risler, H., Schmidt, K. (1967) "Der Feinbau der Scolopidien im Johnstonschen Organ von *Aedes aegypti* L.", *Naturforsch.* **22b,** 705–762.

Robertson, A. (1974) "Information handling at the cellular level. Intercellular communication in slime-mould development", in W. B. Broughton (Ed.), *The Biology of Brains,* Symp. Inst. Biol. Lond. **21.**

Roeder, K. D. (1966) "Interneurons of the thoracic nerve cord activated by tympanic nerve fibres in noctuid moths", *J. insect Physiol.* **12,** 1227–1244.

Roeder, K. D. (1967) *Nerve Cells and Insect Behaviour* (Revised Ed.), Harvard University Press, Cambridge, Mass.

Rose, J. E., Mountcastle, V. B. (1959) "Touch and Kinesthesis", in *Handbook of Physiology,* Section I: Neurophysiology, American Physiological Society, Washington D.C.

Rothblum, L., Jenssen, T. A. (1978) "Display repertoire analysis of *Sceloporus undulatus hyacinthinus* (Sauria: Iguanidae) from south-western Virginia", *Anim. Behav.* **26,** 103–137.

Rowell, C. H. F. (1963) "A method for implanting chronic stimulating electrodes in the brains of locusts and some results of stimulation", *J. exp. Biol.* **40,** 271–284.

Rowell, C. H. F. (1970) "Incremental and Decremental Processes in the Insect Central Nervous System", in G. Horn and R. A. Hinde (Eds.), *Short-term Changes in Neural Activity and Behaviour,* C.U.P., Cambridge, England.

Rozenzweig, M. R., Bennett, E. L. (Eds.). (1976) *Neural Mechanisms of Learning and Memory,* M.I.T. Press, Cambridge, Mass. and London.

Russell, I. J. (1968) "Influence of efferent fibres on a receptor", *Nature,* London, **219,** 177–178.

Russell, I. J., Selick, P. M. (1977) "The Tuning Properties of Cochlear Hair Cells", in E. F. Evans and J. P. Wilson (Eds.), *Psychophysics and Physiology of Hearing,* Academic Press, London, New York and San Francisco.

Rutowski, R. L. (1977*a*) "The use of visual cues in sexual and species discrimination by males of the small sulphur butterfly *Eurema lisa* (Lepidoptera: Pieridae)", *J. comp. Physiol.* **115,** 61–74.

Rutowski, R. L. (1977*b*) "Chemical communication in the courtship of the small sulphur butterfly *Eurema lisa* (Lepidoptera, Pieridae)", *J. comp. Physiol.* **115,** 75–85.

Rutowski, R. L. (1978) "The courtship behaviour of the small sulphur butterfly, *Eurema lisa* (Lepidoptera: Pieridae)", *Anim. Behav.* **26,** 892–903.

Sales, G., Pye, D. (1974) *Ultrasonic Communication By Animals,* Chapman and Hall, London.

Samways, M. J. (1977) "Song modification in the Orthoptera. IV. The *Platycleis intermedia/P. affinis* interaction quantified", *Physiol. Entomol.* **2,** 301–315.

Schleidt, W. M. (1961) "Reaktionen von Truthühnern auf fliegende Raubvögel und Versuch zur Analyse ihrer AAM's", *Z. Tierpsychol.* **18,** 534–560.

Schneider, D., Seibt, V. (1969) "Sex pheromones of the queen butterfly: Electroantennogram responses", *Science,* **164,** 1173–1174.

Seibt, V., Schneider, D., Eisner, T. (1972) "Duftpinsel, Flugeltaschen und Balz des Tagfalters *Danaus chrysippus* (Lepidoptera: Danaidae)", *Z. Tierpsychol.* **31,** 513–530.

Selverston, A. (1976) "A model system for the study of rhythmic behaviour", in J. C. Fentress (Ed.), *Simpler Networks and Behaviour,* Sinauer, Sunderland, Mass.

Seymour, C., Lewis, B., Larsen, O. N., Michelsen, A. (1978) "Biophysics of the ensiferan ear. II. The steady-state gain of the hearing trumpet in bushcrickets", *J. comp. Physiol.* **123,** 205–216.

Shepherd, G. M. (1972) "Synaptic organisation of the mammalian olfactory bulb", *Physiol. Rev.* **52,** 864–917.

Shepherd, G. M. (1974) *The Synaptic Organisation of the Brain,* O.U.P., London, New York and Toronto.

Shepherd, G. M. (1978) "Microcircuits in the nervous system", *Sci. Am.*, Feb. 1978.

Sherrington, C. S. (1906) *The Intergative Action of the Nervous System*, Seribner, New York.

Sherrington, C. S. (1909) "On plastic tonus and proprioceptive reflexes", *Quart. J. exp. Physiol.* **2**, 109–156.

Sherrington, C. S. (1917) "Reflexes excitable in the cat from pinna, vibrissae and jaws", *J. Physiol.* **51**, 404–431.

Simpson, M. J. A. (1968) "The threat display of the Siamese fighting fish, (*Betta splendens*)", *Anim. Behav. Monogr.* **1**, 1–73.

Slater, P. J. B. (1973) "Describing Sequences of Behaviour", in P. P. G. Bateson and P. H. Klopfer (Eds.), *Perspectives in Ethology*, Plenum, New York and London.

Slater, P. J. B. (1978) *Sex Hormones and Behaviour*, Studies in Zoology, 103, Arnold, London.

Smith, W. J. (1969) "Displays and messages in intraspecific communication", *Semiotica*, **1**, 357–369.

Smith, W. J. (1977) *The Behaviour of Communicating*, Harvard University Press, Cambridge, Mass. and London.

Spira, M. E., Yarom, Y., Parnas, I. (1976) "Modulation of spike frequency by regions of special axonal geometry and by synaptic inputs", *J. Neurophysiol.* **39**, 882–899.

Steinberg, J. B., Conant, R. C. (1974) "An informational analysis of the inter-male behaviour of the grasshopper (*Chortophaga viridifasciata*)", *Anim. Behav.* **22**, 617–627.

Suga, N., Schlegel, P. (1972) "Neural attenuation of responses to emitted sounds in echolocating bats", *Science*, New York, **177**, 82–84.

Sulak, K. J. (1975) "Cleaning behaviour in the centrarchid fishes, *Lepomis macrochinis* and *Micropterus galmoides*", *Anim. Behav.* **23**, 331–334.

Tavolga, W. N., Wodinsky, J. (1963) "Auditory capacities in fishes", *Bull. Amer. Mus. Nat. Hist.* **126**, 177–240.

Thorpe, W. H. (1958) "The learning of song patterns by birds, with special reference to the song of the chaffinch, *Fringilla coelebs*", *Ibis*, **100**, 535–570.

Tinbergen, N. (1951) *The Study of Instinct*, Clarendon Press, Oxford.

Tinbergen, N. (1952) "Derived activities; their causation, biological significance, origin and emancipation during evolution", *Quart. Rev. Biol.* **27**, 1–32.

Tinbergen, N. (1953) *Social Behaviour in Animals*, Methuen, London.

Tinbergen, N., Perdeck, A. C. (1950) "On the stimulus situation releasing the begging response in the newly hatched herring gull chick (*Larus argentatus argentatus* Pont.)", *Behav.* **3**, 1–39.

Tischener, H. (1953) "Über den Gehörsinn von Steckmücken", *Acoustica*, **3**, 335–343.

Tolman, C. W. (1964) "Social facilitation of feeding behaviour in the domestic chick", *Anim. Behav.* **12**, 245–251.

Usherwood, P. N. R., Newth, D. R. (Eds.). (1975) '*Simple*' *Nervous Systems*, Arnold, London.

Valone, J. A. Jnr. (1970) "Electric emissions in *Gymnotus carapo* and their relation to social behaviour", *Behav.* **37**, 1–14.

Waterman, T. H. (1961) "Light Sensitivity and Vision", in T. H. Waterman (Ed.), *The Physiology of the Crustacea*, Vol. II, Academic Press, New York.

Whitfield, I. C. (1967) "Coding in the auditory nervous system", *Nature*, **213**, 756–760.

Wiepkema, P. R. (1961) "An ethological analysis of the reproductive behaviour of the bitterling", *Arch. néerl. Zool.* **14**, 103–199.

Wiersma, C. A. G., Bush, B. M. H., Waterman, T. H. (1964) "Efferent visual responses of contralateral origin in the optic nerve of the crab *Podophthalmus*", *J. cell. comp. Physiol.* **64,** 309–326.

Wiesel, T. N. (1960) "Receptive fields of ganglion cells in the cat's retina", *J. Physiol.* **153,** 583–594.

Wiley, R. H. (1973) "Territoriality and non-random mating in sage grouse, *Centrocercus urophasianus*", *Anim. Behav. Monog.* **6,** 87–169.

Wilson, D. M. (1961) "The central nervous control of flight in a locust", *J. exp. Biol.* **38,** 471–490.

Wilson, D. M. (1970) "Neuronal Operations in Arthropod Ganglia", in *The Neurosciences*: Second Study Program, The Rockefeller University Press, New York.

Wilson, E. O. (1975) *Sociobiology: The New Synthesis*, Belknap Press of Harvard University Press, Cambridge, Mass. and London.

Wilson, E. O., Bossert, W. H. (1963) "Chemical communication among animals", *Recent Progress in Hormone Research*, **19,** 673–716.

Wynne-Edwards, V. C. (1962) *Animal Dispersion in Relation to Social Behaviour*, Oliver and Boyd, Edinburgh.

Yau, K.-W. (1976) "Receptive fields, geometry and conduction block of sensory neurones in the central nervous system of the leech", *J. Physiol.* **263,** 513–538.

Young, D., Hill, K. G. (1977) "Structure and function of the auditory system of the cicada *Cystosoma saundersii*", *J. comp. Physiol.* **117,** 23–45.

Zeeman, E. C. (1976) "Catastrophe Theory", *Sci. Am.* **234** (4), 65–83.

# INDEX